AF519345

SAARC
RELEVANCE IN NEW WORLD ORDER

SAARC
RELEVANACE IN NEW WORLD ORDER

FARHAT EHSAS

Reference Press
4831/24, Ansari Road
Darya Ganj
New Delhi-110 002
Phone: 3260807
Fax: 3274173
E-mail: essess@del3.vsnl.net.in

SAARC: Relevance in New World Order

©Publishers

First Published, 2003

ISBN 81-88583-13-8

Price Rs.675/-

All rights reserved. No part of this publication may be reproduced, stored in a retrieval system or transmitted in any form or by any means, electronic, mechanical, photocopying, recording or otherwise, without the prior written permission of the copyright holder.

Published by:
Reference Press
4831/24, Ansari Road,
Darya Ganj,
New Delhi -110002.
Phone:3260807
Fax:3274173
E-mail: essess@del3.vsnl.net.in

Printed in India at:
Mehra Offset Press, Delhi.

Contents

PART II : SUMMITS

PART III: RECORD SHEET

Preface

The world has cultivated itself into a global village, in the real sense of the terms. The earth has shrunk and distances have, virtually ceased to be. In such a state of affairs, the meanig of nationality and polity are also changing day by day. Now geographical boundaries have no relevance. Hence, a tendency of unity beyond borders. Various nations have come into a fold, for creating a common forum or group, in order to secure their interests — commercial, cultural and political as well. European Union, Arab League and ASEAN are some examples of the same approach. SAARC is an experiment on the same line. SAARC is a small organisation, with only seven members, but this does not lessen its importance.

South Asian Association for Regional Cooperation (SAARC), includes as member states: India, Pakistan, Bangladesh, Sri Lanka, Nepal, Bhutan and Maldives. It's a regional entity, confined to South Asia only.

SAARC may not be as big as Arab League or African Union or as important as European Union, but its significance lies in the strategic location of the region, where its wings are spread.

All the seven member countries are separate nations, independent and sovereign and have their own identities. But, these nations have a common history. Five of these, viz. India, Pakistan, Bangladesh, Sri Lanka and Maldives have a shared colonial past. The rest two, viz., Nepal and Bhutan had managed to remain free of the shackles of direct slavery, though they were also under immense imperial pressure, bound by enforced treaties. Hence, a common past again.

Incidentally, all the SAARC nations have a common heritage and culture. By and large, it's a homogenous region, more or less like Central Asia or Western Europe.

Surprisingly, despite all factors for the creation of a common forum evident, it took almost four decades for the South Asian nations to conclude that they badly required a common platfarm for improving mutual relations and developing cooperation for their economic growth and development.

Flipping through, the pages of history, one learns that India and Pakistan became independent in 1947 and Sri Lanka in 1948, Bangladesh took birth by abandoning Pakistan in 1971. Nepal and Bhutan were already free of all influence. Only Maldives gained independence in 1966. At last, reason prevailed in early eighties and the South Asian nations agreed to have a regional association of their own. Then, in 1985, SAARC became a reality.

SAARC, basically, is a cultural, economic and commercial association, aimed at creating a free zone, which may ultimately turn into a geographical entity, like European Union. However, at the moment it's a distant dream, as the pace of advancement towards such goals have been very slow and not very much encouraging.

Now, the whole world looks forward to 12th SAARC Summit, slated to be held at Islamabad in 2003, where concrete results are awaited.

The aim of this study is to discuss SAARC, as a living and developing organisation. Efforts have been made to cover all the aspects—background, growth, problems, issues and prospects—in an elaborate manner, with objectivity and rationality in mind.

Hopefully, this work would be able to provide the scholars, researchers, students and the general readers, with an authentic, comprehensive and exhaustive book on the subject. The author should feel encouraged, if this volume serves the purpose in sight. It would naturally, pave way for further research and the academic pursuit, as an endeavour.

Author

Introduction

SAARC is the best example of small, but pretty and apparently insignificant, but really very important. SAARC is the first major step of a long journey towards the regional integration on the pattern of European Union. The increasing degree of regional cooperation among SAARC countries would prove to be of immense socio-economic and political importance to this region which is the ultimate aim and objective of SAARC. SAARC consists of seven countries, viz., India, Bangladesh, Pakistan, Bhutan and Nepal in Indian Subcontinent; and Sri Lanka and Maldives in Indian ocean. It was established on 8th December 1985 after about four and a half years of ground work. The basic aim of the Association is to accelerate the process of economic and social development in member countries through joint action in the agreed areas of cooperation.

The region of SAARC lies in the South of Himalayas surrounded by Hindukush mountains. The SAARC countries are of different sizes both geographically and population-wise, and have different resource endowments. They are the less developed countries of the world. They account about 21 per cent of the world population and only 3.5 per cent of total land area. However, their share in world output is a mere 1.3 per cent. Further, their share in world merchandise,trade is about 1 per cent only. About half of the world's poor inhabit this part of the world. Their per capita GNP range from US $ 180 (Nepal) to US $ 1000 (Maldives). The per capita GNP of all the members of SAARC taken together is barely around US $ 350 only. The economic structure of these countries is basically agrarian. About three-fourth of their total population subsists on agriculture. The imports of the SAARC countries are mainly composed of manufactured goods from the developed countries.

The irony of the sitiuation is that the position of their balance of trade and terms of trade follow an unfavourable trend. In fact, the existing international economic order has been operating against the basic interests of the poor countries due to the growing protectionist tendencies among the rich countries. In the world market, the products of the poor countries are facing tough competition with the products of the rich countries.

As a result, the share of the poor countries has been decreasing in the world market with the passage of time. On the other hand, the share of the rich countries has been increasing in the world market. The poor countries are left with only one option, i.e. to promote mutual cooperation in order to solve their socio-economic, and politico-ethnic problems and to achieve collective self-reliance. Thus, it is required that the South should explore seriously the ways of mutual cooperation and reduce its dependence on the North. Such cooperation is also beneficial to the poor countries in order to improve their prospects of cooperation with the rich countries in future. There is a great scope of regional economic cooperation among SAARC countries as they share many common concerns and are facing many problems of a similar nature.

The regional cooperation among these countries would not only lead to rapid economic development, but also strengthen their mutual relations. Normally the economic system among the SAARC countries, is the same as that of mixed economy because of their underdevelopment characteristics and adoption of planning process for their development. These countries are having various economic features in common like poverty, income inequality, large population, dependence on agriculture, low productivity and mass unemployment. Industrial backwardness further adds to the already existing underemployment and unemployment in this region. Industrial production accounts for about one-fourth of the gross domestic product and provides employment to less than 15 per cent of the total population of this region.

India among the SAARC nations, has the largest area, population and GDP among the SAARC countries, whereas Maldives has the smallest area, and least population and GDP. However, the annual growth rate of population was as high as 3 per cent in Maldives and as low as 1.4 per cent in Sri Lanka. Further, in case of Sri Lanka, life expectancy and literacy rate were also highest, i.e. 72 years and 89.3 per cent respectively, which were, however, lowest, i.e. 49 years and

SOME FACTS ABOUT SAARC COUNTRIES

Regional Performance figure	*Bangladesh*	*Bhutan*	*India*	*Maldives*	*Nepal*	*Pakistan*	Sri *Lanka*
Area ('000 Km. sq.)	144	47	3288	0.3	147.2	796	66
Population (million)	140	2.1	1025	0.3	23.6	145	19.1
Annual Population Growth (%)	2.17	2.3	2.14	3.0	2.3	2.82	1.4
Urban Population (%)	18	6	26	26	12	33	22
Life Expectancy (years)	56	49	61	64	54	62	72
Literacy Rate (%)	38.1	42	65.38	93	35.7	42.2	89.3
Per Capita GNP (US %)	245	415	335	1000[1]	180	495[1]	830[1]
Per Capita GDP, Purchasing Power Parity (US %)	1350	1475	1385	1373	1165	2235	3030
GDP (US $ billion)	31.9	0.3	294.7	0.24	4.7	65.6	16.26[1]
GDP Growth Rate (%)	4.7	5.4	7.1	7.2	6.1	6.1	3.7
Rate of Inflation, (%)	6.4	7.8	7.6	3.1	8.2	10.3	16.1
Per Capita Exports (US $)	26.1	50.8[3]	33.2	192	15.4	61.4	204.5
Per Capita Imports (US $)	54.1	68.4[3]	37.5	1373	35.3	88.0	324.5
Per Capita Foreign Exchange Excluding Gold	14.5	80.7[2]	23.9	243.7[3]	27.1[3]	6.1	118.2[3]
Per Capita Foreign Debt (US $)	139.2	55.2	98.6[3]	400[4]	90.9[4]	217.3[3]	353.6
Foreign Direct Investment (US $ million)	915.6	0.98[4]	2587[1]	915[5]	110	1102	272[1]
Currency	Taka	Ngultrum	Rupee	Rufiyaa	Rupee	Rupee	Rupee
Exchange Rate (Per US $ App.)	43.1	36.02	36.02	11.41[1]	57.25[1]	41.25	54.78[1]
People per Doctor	12500	4255	2165	5330	12612	2000	5888
People per Telephone	380	141.5	85	17.9	174	62.7	88.1
Tourist Arrivals ('000)	150	98	2124	324	346	528	451
Power Capacity Installed (MW.)	2208	360	83288[1]	15.19	296	12883	1409

Source: World Development Report; Far Eastern Economic Review; and SAARC SCAN (Various Issues).

27 per cent respectively in case of Bhutan. While Pakistan has 33 per cent urban population, Bhutan accounted only 6 per cent for the same. The per capita GDP in terms of purchasing power parity of the SAARC countries ranges from US $ 1165 (Nepal) to US $ 3030 (Sri Lanka). Their annual growth rate of GDP ranges from 7.2 per cent (Maldives) and 3.7 per cent (Sri Lanka). Sri Lanka appeared to be the most inflationary country among SAARC nations with the rate of inflation touching 16.1 per cent during 1995-96, whereas it accounted only 3.1 per cent in case of Maldives. Further, the per capita exports and imports are highest, i.e. US $ 192 and US $ 1373 respectively in case of Maldives and lowest, i.e. US $ 15.4 and US $ 35.3 respectively in case of Nepal. Thus, Nepal appears to be the least developed country of SAARC in terms of GDP and trade, which are the core areas of economic development. The per capita foreign exchange excluding gold of the SAARC countries are highest, i.e. US $ 243.7 in case of Maldives and lowest, i.e. US $ 6.1 in case of Pakistan. However, the per capita foreign debt ranges from US $ 400 (Maldives) and US $ 55.2 (Bhutan). If we examine the exchange rate of currency per US $ of each SAARC country, the value of Maldives's Refiyaa was the highest, i.e. 13.41 and Nepali Rupee was the lowest, i.e. 57.25.

For South Asia, the Report on Human Development, authored by the distinguished Pakistani economist, Mahbub-ul-Huq, speaks volumes about the low profile quality of life in this region. Fifty years after independence, about 500 million people in the region are destitutes; basic education is denied to some 1200 million individuals; and 260 million are without elementary health facilities. In terms of real per capita income, Pakistan ranks 119 and India 142 in the world. In the face of such a grim situation in the social sector, says the Report, the countries of South Asia are spending far too much money on arms and far too little in the social sectors. India ranks first in total arm imports and Pakistan tenth though India's per capita expenditure is far less than Pakistan's. While the global expenditure declined by 37 per cent during the last decades, military spending in South Asia has gone up by 12 per cent. NCAER's human development profile of India said that about 16 per cent of India's rural population earned Rs. 3 per day and another 18 per cent only about Rs. 5 per day. Accessibility of safe drinking water is denied to nearly 50 per cent of the villagers. UNDP introduced the human development index comprising life expectancy, educational attainments and income indicators to give a composite measure of human development. SAARC countries occupied low positions in this ranking. They were ranked as under: Sri Lanka (89), Pakistan (134), India (135), Bangladesh (143), Nepal (151) and Bhutan (158).

Under SAARC, the trade is one of the major priority areas of economic cooperation. In spite of various commonalities of SAARC countries, the intra-regional SAARC trade was 2.8 per cent of their global trade during 1985 which, however, picked up to 4 per cent till 1995. Then it progressed further. The operationalisation of SAARC Preferential Trading Arrangement (SAPTA) on 7th December 1995, a decade after the launch of SAARC was, of course, a positive step in the right direction. In fact, it was the real beginning of SAARC. But, at the same time, it was only a first step towards liberalisation and creation of SAARC trade block, that too, very modest. The consolidated National Schedules of Concessions containing the list of products furnished by the member countries for tariff concessions is not very impressive. In the first round of SAPTA negotiations, SAARC countries identified 226 items (484 tariff lines at six digit level) for exchange on tariff concessions ranging from 10 per cent to 100 per cent. India agreed to extend tariff concessions upto 50 per cent on 106 items, while Pakistan agreed to offer tariff concessions from 10 per cent to 20 per cent on 35 items, Sri Lanka on 31 items, Maldives 75 per cent on 17 items, Nepal 10 per cent on 14 items, Bangladesh 10 per cent on 12 items, and Bhutan 15 per cent on 11 items. However, during the Second Round of SAPTA negotiations which concluded in Kathmandu on 29-30th November 1996, items for exchange on tariff concessions picked up to 1972 tariff lines. India agreed to give tariff concessions on 911 items, while Pakistan offered tariff concessions on 386 items, Nepal on 277 tariff lines, Bangladesh on 241 tariff lines, Sri Lanka on 102 tariff lines, Bhutan on 47 tariff lines and Maldives on 8 tariff lines. The slow process of SAPTA is manifested with the fact that SAARC countries could finalise only 1972 tariff lines out of the 6000 tariff lines for tariff concessions. However, there was a proposal of transition from SAPTA to SAFTA (SAARC Free Trade Area) in the Eighth SAARC Summit in New Delhi with total elimination of all tariff and non-tariff barriers by 2005. Keen interest shown by all the member-countries of SAARC in the Ninth SAARC Summit held in Male during May 1997 advanced the deadline for the implementation of SAFTA from 2005 to 2001. India's proposal for SAEC (SAARC Economic Community) after attaining the goal of SAFTA had also responded positively in this summit.

The targets however could not be met and it was decided at the XIth Summit at Kathmandu that the goal should be attained by the end of 2002. The successful completion of Uruguay Round of GATT, and the establishment of WTO (World Trade Organization) to facilitate world trade system is a trend towards globalisation of world economy. On the other hand, the trend of forming regional trade blocks has also got momentum. The manifestations of this trend are EU, ASEAN, NAFTA (North American Free Trade Area), APEC (Asia Pacific Economic Cooperation), etc. WTO, which provides MFN (Most Favoured Nation) status to all its 128 members, has allowed 100 per cent discrimination under FTA (Free Trade Area) and CU (Customs Union) alongwith reduced consessional arrangement for the developing countries under tariff and subsidy reduction programmes.

Trade relations of WTO members are influenced by regional trade blocks. The emergence of these regional trade blocks is an attempt of these countries to operate in the global market with their increased economic strength. EU has 70 per cent intra-regional trade, whereas other trade blocks have average 50 per cent Intraregional trade. Further, ASEAN countries also tried to form regional PTA by 2000, but it could not be achieved. SAARC countries have deprived themselves from the changes occurred on the global economic scene. They have only 4 percent intra-regional trade and account for 1 per cent in the global trade, which speaks a lot on the opportunities that they have lost. SAARC region has remained underdeveloped due to isolation, in spite of the tremendous wealth in terms of human and natural resources. Nevertheless, the late realisation of the importance of regional trade cooperation on the part of political leadership had led to the modest attempt of forming SAARC trade block with SAPTA.

In view of an overwhelming support of business community of the SAARC region, SAARC is expected to augment the intra-regional trade of the region for the benefit of the peoples of this region. It is hoped that the next Round of SAPTA negotiations will lead to even greater progress. SAPTA Agreement should be looked at as a big pool of resources to be drawn from SAARC region. Now the SAARC Community looks ahead towards the XIIth Summit to be held at Islamabad.

PART 1

Small but Significant

ONE

Evolution and Development

SAARC is a small organisation, with only seven members, but this does not lessen its importance.

South Asian Association for Regional Cooperation (SAARC), includes as member states: India, Pakistan, Bangladesh, Sri Lanka, Nepal, Bhutan and Maldives. It's a regional entity, confined to South Asia only. It may not be as big as Arab League or African Union or as important as European Union, but its significance lies in the strategic location of the region, when its wings are spread.

All the seven member countries are separate nations, independent and sovereign and have their own identities. But, these nations have a common history. Five of these, viz. India, Pakistan, Bangladesh, Sri Lanka and Maldives have a shared colonial past. The rest two, viz., Nepal and Bhutan had managed to remain free of the shackles of direct slavery, but they were also under immense imperial pressure, bound by enforced treaties. Hence, a common past again.

Further, all the SAARC nations have a common heritage and culture. By and large, it's a homogenous region, more or less like Central Asia or Western Europe. However, it took almost four decades for the South Asian nations to conclude that they badly required a common platform for improving mutual relations and developing cooperation for their economic growth.

The Structure

SAARC, the South Asian Association for Regional Cooperation comprises the seven countries of South Asia, i.e. Bangladesh, Bhutan, India, the Maldives, Nepal, Pakistan and Sri Lanka. SAARC is a manifestation of the determination of the peoples of South Asia to work together towards finding solutions to their common problems in a spirit of friendship, trust and understanding and to create an order based on mutual respect, equity and shared benefits. The primary objective of the Association is the acceleration of the process of economic and social development in member states, through collective action in agreed areas of cooperation.

The Birth

The idea of regional cooperation in South Asia was first mooted in November 1980. After consultations, the Foreign Secretaries of the seven countries met for the first time in Colombo in April 1981. This was followed up, a few months later, by a meeting of the Committee of the Whole, which identified five broad areas for regional cooperation. The Foreign Ministers, at their first meeting in New Delhi in August 1983, adopted the Declaration on South Asian Regional Cooperation (SARC) and formally launched the Integrated Programme of Action (IPA) in the five agreed areas of cooperation namely, Agriculture, Rural Development, Telecommunications, Meteorology, and Health and Population Activities. Later, Transport, Postal Services, Scientific and Technological Cooperation, Sports, Arts and Culture were added to the IPA.

The Heads of State or Government at their First SAARC Summit held in Dhaka on 7-8 December 1985 adopted the Charter formally establishing the South Asian Association for Regional Cooperation (SAARC).

The objectives, principles and general provisions as mentioned in the SAARC Charter are as follows:

Objectives

- To promote the welfare of the peoples of South Asia and to improve their quality of life;
- To accelerate economic growth, social progress and cultural development in the region and to provide all individuals the opportunity to live in dignity and to realise their full potentials;
- To promote and strengthen collective self-reliance among the countries of South Asia;
- To contribute to mutual trust, understanding and appreciation of one another's problems;
- To promote active collaboration and mutual assistance in the economic, social, cultural, technical and scientific fields;

- To strengthen cooperation with other developing countries;
- To strengthen cooperation among themselves in international forums on matters of common interests; and
- To cooperate with international and regional organisations with similar aims and purposes.

Principles

- Cooperation within the framework of the Association is based on respect for the principles of sovereign equality, territorial integrity, political independence, non-interference in the internal affairs of other States and mutual benefit.
- Such cooperation is to complement and not to substitute bilateral or multilateral cooperation.
- Such cooperation should be consistent with bilateral and multilateral obligations of Member States.

General Provisions

- Decisions at all levels in SAARC are taken on the basis of unanimity.
- Bilateral and contentious issues are excluded from the deliberations of the Association.

The Setup

Summit: The highest authority of the Association rests with the Heads of State or Government, who meet annually at Summit level. To date, eleven Meetings of the Heads of State or Government have been held in Dhaka (1985), Bangalore (1986), Kathmandu (1987), Islamabad (1988), Male (1990), Colombo (1991), Dhaka (1993), New Delhi (1995), Male (1997), and Colombo (1998), respectively. The Eleventh SAARC Summit was held in Kathmandu (2002) while, the 12th Summit was slated to be held in Islamabad in 2003.

The Heads of State or Government during the Ninth SAARC Summit had agreed that a process of informal political consultations would prove useful in promoting peace, stability and amity and accelerated socio-economic cooperation in the region.

Council of Ministers: Comprising the Foreign Ministers of Member States, the Council is responsible for formulating policies;

reviewing progress: deciding on new areas of cooperation; establishing additional mechanisms as deemed necessary; and deciding on other matters of general interest to the Association. The Council meets twice a year and may also meet in extraordinary session by agreement of Member States. It has held twenty two regular sessions till January, 2002.

A Commemorative Session of the Council, to mark the First Decade of SAARC, was also held at New Delhi on December 18, 1995, during the Sixteenth Session of the Council of Ministers.

Standing Committee: The Standing Committee comprising the Foreign Secretaries of Member States is entrusted with the task of overall monitoring and coordination of programmes and the modalities of financing: determining inter-sectoral priorities; mobilising regional and external resources; and identifying new areas of cooperation. It may meet as often as deemed necessary but in practice normally meets twice a year and submits its reports to the Council of Ministers. The Committee has held twenty-seven regular sessions and two special sessions till January, 2002.

The Standing Committee may also set up Action Committees comprising Member States concerned with implementation of projects as per Article VII of the Charter.

The Standing Committee is assisted by a Programming Committee, an ad hoc body, comprising senior officials, to scrutinise the Secretariat Budget, finalise the Calendar of Activities and take up any other matter assigned to it by the Standing Committee. The Programming Committee has also been entrusted to consider the Reports of the Technical Committees and the SAARC Regional Centres and submit its comments to the Standing Committee. The Programming Committee has held twenty two sessions till December 2001.

Technical Committees: Comprising representatives from the Member States, the Technical Committees formulate programmes and prepare projects in their respective fields which make up the Integrated Programme of Action under SAARC. They are responsible for monitoring the implementation of such activities and submit their reports to the Standing Committee through the Programming Committee. There are currently eleven Technical Committees, the Chairmanship of which rotates among Member Countries in alphabetical order every two years.

Other Meetings: Since the establishment of the Association, several other important meetings have taken place in specific contexts. A number of SAARC Ministerial Meetings have been held, to focus attention on specific areas of common concern and have become an integral part of the consultative structure. Various meetings of Planners have been held so far. These meetings initiated cooperation in important areas such as Trade, Manufactures and Services; Basic Needs; Human Resource Development; Data base on socio-economic indicators; Energy Modelling Techniques; Plan Modelling Techniques and Poverty Alleviation Strategies.

The Ninth SAARC Summit had decided that the Environment Ministers Meeting would be held annually.

SAARC Secretariat

The SAARC Secretariat was established in Kathmandu on 16 January 1987. Its role is to coordinate and monitor the implementation of SAARC activities, service the meetings of the Association and serve as the channel of communication between SAARC and other international organisations. The Secretariat, being the headquarters of the organisation has recently been increasingly utilised as the venue for various SAARC meetings.

The Secretariat comprises the Secretary-General, seven Directors and the General Services Staff. Initially, the Secretary-General was appointed by the Council of Ministers upon nomination by a Member State on the principle of rotation in alphabetical order for a period of two years. The Ninth SAARC Summit (Male, May 1997) had decided that henceforth the tenure of the Secretary-General should be of three years.

Directors are appointed by the Secretary-General upon nomination by Member States for a period of three years which, in special circumstances, may be extended by the Secretary-General for a period not exceeding another full term, in consultation with the Member State concerned.

Funds and Finances

Member states make provision in their national budgets, for

financing activities and programmes under the SAARC framework, including contributions to the Secretariat budget and that of the regional institutions. The financial provision thus made is announced annually, at the meeting of the Standing Committee.

The annual budget of the Secretariat, both for capital as well as recurrent expenditure, is shared by member states on the basis of an agreed formula. The initial cost of the main building of the Secretariat, together with all facilities and equipment, as well as that of the annex building completed in 1993 has been met by His Majesty's Government of Nepal.

A minimum of forty per cent of the institutional cost of regional institutions is borne by the respective host governments and the balance is shared by all member states, on the basis of an agreed formula. Capital expenditure of regional institutions which includes physical infrastructure, furnishing, machines, equipment, etc., are normally borne by the respective host governments. Programme expenditure of regional institutions is also shared by member states, according to the agreed formula.

In the case of activities under the approved calendar, local expenses including hospitality are borne by the host Governments, while the cost of travel is met by the sending Governments.

Integrated Programme of Action

The Integrated Programme of Action (IPA) is a key component of the SAARC process and includes a number of important areas of cooperation. Technical Committees numbering eleven at present have been designated to coordinate work in the identified areas of cooperation.

In response to the emphasis given by successive Summits on the need to further consolidate and streamline IPA and to make it more result oriented, a comprehensive set of guidelines and procedures was adopted in 1992 for the rationalisation of SAARC activities. As a result of this, there is now a greater focus on activities that would bring tangible benefits to the people of South Asia.

The Secretary-General reports on the progress in the implementation of IPA to the Standing Committee, both at its inter-Summit and pre-Summit Sessions. The Standing Committee has also taken the initiative to review the institutional mechanisms and activities of the Association, including the evaluation of the functioning of the Technical Committees, amalgamation/alteration of their mandate and also a review of the role of the Secretariat. In this context, the Independent Expert Group set up by the Secretary-General has recently undertaken an extensive review of the functioning of IPA and come up with important recommendations presently under consideration of the Member States.

The highlights of the activities of the areas covered by the IPA under each Technical Committee are as follows:

Forestry and Agriculture

Agriculture was among the original five areas identified for fostering regional cooperation. The first meeting of Technical Committee was held in 1983. Subsequently, Forestry was also included in the functions of the Committee. (Committee was instrumental in the setting up of SAARC Agricultural Information Centre (SAIC) at Dhaka in 1988 - the first SAARC regional institution of its kind. Under the work of this Technical Committee, Member states have been exchanging Germ-plasm, Breeding Materials on Livestock and Fishery in accordance with the quarantine regulations in force in their respective countries. Prototypes of Farmtools and Equipment have been exchanged for trial and adaptation. Activities for improved livestock through exchange of animals, frozen semen and vaccine have also been undertaken. The responsibility of compiling lists of institutions and disciplines capable of offering training in member countries has been entrusted to SAIC. Rice and Wheat-breeding Programmes for enhancing productivity have been conducted while Multilocation trials for various crops are being undertaken.

Regular meetings of Counterpart Scientists is an important feature of the Committee's programmes. The list of Counterpart Scientists in the twelve agreed areas of crops and disciplines have been finalised for networking. These are: Rice (Millet); Wheat; Oilseeds; Horticulture (Potato) Vegetables and Fruits; Fisheries; Forestry; Transfer of Technology; Livestock (Animal Health and Production); Farm Machinery and Implements; Post Harvest

Technology; Agriculture Economics and Policies and Soils. Progress has been made towards establishing a network on Amelioration of Problem Soils. The programme for the 1990s focuses on Genetic Engineering and Bio-Technology (for crop and livestock improvement, agricultural and horticultural development, embryo transfer technology for livestock and conservation of endangered germ-plasm); Homestead Vegetable Production; Food Availability and Nutritional Balance; Data Base on Technology and Training facilities in agricultural science within the SAARC countries; and meeting of the Expert Group on Crop Diseases. Two important project proposals namely (i) Promotion of the "Bio-Villages, and (ii) Reaching the Million - Training of Farmers and Farm Women have recently been completed and future course of action on these proposals is underway.

Following its Sixteenth Meeting, the Committee initiated thematic discussion on one important agricultural topic annually. During the same meeting, the member countries had extensive discussion on the theme SAARC Agricultural Perspective to the year 2020. In the light of the discussion on the occasion, the Committee recommended that the member countries should step up efforts to strengthen regional cooperation as part of a comprehensive strategy to address the main challenges facing the agricultural sector in the SAARC region.

The Information Net

TC on Telecommunications and TC on Postal Services both established in 1983 were amalgamated into a single TC on Communications with effect from 1993. With a view to bringing about an overall improvement in the postal services in the region, the work programme in Postal sector includes training, seminars, workshops study tours, etc., covering a number of areas. Training programmes were held for First and Middle Level Officers and for Trainers as well as in Philately, International Postal Services, International Mail Accounting and Routing, Postal Management Services and Post Office Savings Banks. Seminars/Workshops were organized on Postal Operation and future challenges, Mechanisation of Postal Operations, Agency functions, Financial Services, Caring for Customer, Expedited Mail Service (EMS), Circulation System of EMS and Postal Marketing. Study tours on Agency Services, Safety and Security of Postal Articles, Postal Services in Hilly or Rural Areas and New Mail and Financial Service in Pakistan were undertaken to gain first-hand knowledge of problems and plans for improvement of postal services. SAARC Philatelic Exhibitions have been held to exchange/share knowledge and develop skills of philately.

Since 1985, Letter Writing Competitions have been held annually. Studies had been undertaken on Productivity Measurement Techniques applied in postal operations, Postal Delays in SAARC region, Integration of Postal Services with rural development and Concessional Mail Tariff and Mail Transmission. Other activities undertaken include issuance of commemorative stamps, postage stamp displays and philatelic exhibitions. Further studies are underway in various fields such as: Electronic Tracking and Tracing for EMS; introduction of a Professional Postal Management Course leading to Diploma; setting up of a Regional R&D Centre; and revision of accounting rates among SAARC countries. Within the overall objective of providing telecommunication services to majority of the rural population, the Committee has focused on efforts to promote technological and human resource development and management. There has been substantial progress in implementing the recommendations for the establishment of ISD, automatic telex, and bureaufax facilities, improvement of inter-country links, operation and maintenance of communication links, etc. Efforts are being made to further promote cooperation in improving transit facilities. An initiative has been taken to establish an Information Network among the member countries. Short-term activities in Telecommunications include Seminars/ Workshops on Data Transmission, Digital Switching, Network Management and Operations, Software maintenance, Adoption of new technologies in rural telecommunication systems, IDR satellite technology and improvement of rural telecommunications.

While recognising, the need for better and cheaper telecom links between SAARC countries, the Council of Ministers at its Seventeenth Session (December 1996), discussed several possibilities, including a SAARC satellite; updating, expansion and harmonisation of telecom hardware in the region. A high-level Expert Group on Telecommunications has been set up by the Secretary-General to address these issues, as well as to examine the possibility of bringing telecommunications tariffs between SAARC countries as close to domestic rate as possible. The SAARC Communication Ministers also met for the first time in Colombo in May 1998.

Promotion of Education

TC on Education (established in 1989) and TC on Sports, Arts and Culture (established in 1983) were amalgamated into a single TC on Education and Culture in January 1993. The Technical Committee was renamed Technical Committee on Education, Culture and Sports with effect from 1st January 1995. The priority themes identified for cooperation in the field of education are Women and Education; Universal Primary Education; Literacy, Post Literacy and Continuing Education; Educational Research; Science and Technical Education and Education for the Underserved Areas and Distance Education. The nominations of Nodal Agencies for each of the priority themes have been completed and appropriate Action Plans are being prepared.

Short-term activities in the field of Education include, Expert Group Meetings; Workshops/Seminars on the priority themes; Modernisation of Curriculum; Environmental Education including Population Education; Planning and Management of Education, Teacher Training, Higher Education and Book Production and Marketing. Publication of an Anthology of South Asian Poetry has been completed and preparation of an Anthology of short stories of SAARC countries is underway. The Committee is also engaged in the improvement and expansion of the SAARC Chairs, Fellowships and Scholarships Scheme. In this context, emphasis is being placed on augmenting the utility and effectiveness of the Scheme, exchanging detailed information on the Scheme particularly relating to offers, facilities, eligibility requirements, disciplines, etc., and reviewing and assessing the implementation of the scheme. Nodal Points for establishing a networking arrangement for sharing information on Mass Literacy Programmes have been identified. The modalities and operational framework for this purpose are being prepared.

Nature and Environment

TC on Meteorology and TC on Environment were merged as a single TC with effect from January 1996. Environment was identified as an area that called for the urgent attention of SAARC in 1987, during which year the Heads of State or Government decided to commission a Study on "Causes and Consequences of Natural Disasters and the Protection and Preservation of the Environment". Following this decision at the Third SAARC Summit in Kathmandu in 1987, National Studies were undertaken and subsequently consolidated into a Regional Study, which was approved by the Sixth SAARC Summit (Colombo, 1991). The other Regional Study conducted by SAARC relates to the "Greenhouse Effect and its Impact on the Region". This Study was completed in 1992 and approved by the Seventh SAARC Summit in Dhaka in 1993.

The Heads of State or Government during their Eighth Summit (New Delhi, 1995) stressed the importance of effective and speedy implementation of the recommendations of the two studies on Environment. Further, at their Ninth Summit, they also gave directives that SAARC Environmental Ministers Meeting would be institutionalized to focus more directly on the environmental concerns of the region. Accordingly, the conference of the SAARC Environment Ministers was held in Male in October 1997 which formulated an Action Plan for immediate implementation of recommendations contained in the two SAARC Studies on Environment. It also formulated a collective position on climate change which was subsequently presented to the Kyoto Conference in December 1997.

The Committee has identified measures for immediate action from among the recommendations in these two studies and decided on a number of modalities for their implementation. These include, improving climate monitoring capability through networking arrangement and through SAARC Meteorological Research Centre (SMRC); developing climate change and sea-level rise scenario through country specific studies and sharing of information data in this respect; making available to member states expertise on climate research and monitoring Greenhouse Gases emission; identification of training and research institutions and ongoing programmes; exchange of information and data; exchange of experience on strategies for developing mitigating and adaptive responses to climate change. The work programme of the Technical Committee also covers topics such as Approaches to Environmental Legislation, Regulations and

Standards in SAARC countries; Rehabilitation of Degraded Lands; Training Course on Wetlands Assessment and Management; Workshop on Alternate/Renewable Energy and Workshop of SAARC National Experts on Climate Change. The urgent need to establish a networking approach through identified nodal points/institutions has also been stressed.

A SAARC Environmental Ministers Conference was held in New Delhi in April 1992 to evolve a joint position on the issues related to the UN Conference on Environment and Development (UNCED). The Environment Ministers also met second time in New Delhi in April 1997 to coordinate their position before the Special Session of the UN General Assembly to be held in June, 1997 to review Agenda 21. In the field of Meteorology, a number of seminars/workshops have been organised in areas such as joint Inter-Comparison of Barometers, Meteorological Instruments, Agricultural Meteorology, Numerical Weather Prediction, Crop Weather relationship and Crop-Yield Forecast, Long Range Weather Forecasting, Radar Meteorology, etc. Training programmes have been conducted on Meteorological Telecommunications, Management and Establishment of National Data Centres, Monsoon Forecasting, etc. State-of-the-Art Reports on Western Disturbances, Tropical Cyclones including Prediction of Recurvature, Thunder Storms, Long Range Forecasting of Monsoon Rain, Short Range Prediction of Monsoon and Norwesters, Tornadoes and Water Sprouts, have been completed. Expert panels have been convened on specialized fields such as Agro-meteorology; Climatology and Data Exchange and Instrumentation.

An Annual Regional Award is given to a young scientist or a group of scientists for a research paper on meteorological topics to encourage research in the field of Meteorology. Another Award has been introduced since 1995 for senior scientists to encourage research work in the field of Meteorology. The Committee also addresses issues relating to the work of the SAARC Meteorological Research Centre (SMRC) established in Dhaka.

Welfare and Health

Health and Population Activities was one of the original five areas of cooperation identified by member states. The First Meeting of the Technical Committee assigned these subjects was held in 1984 and since then fifteen meetings have been held so far. The primary focus of the Committee has been on children, population welfare and policy, maternal and child health, primary health care, disabled and handicapped persons, control and eradication of major diseases in the region such as malaria, leprosy, tuberculosis, diarrhoea diseases, rabies, AIDS, and iodine deficiency disorder.

Important health issues have also been at the centre of SAARC's social agenda. The SAARC member states have thus taken a number of initiatives to address several key issues relating to population control, serious problems in the area of health care and disease control. Discussions on health issues have highlighted the need for strengthening efforts to combat problems posed by the resurgence of communicable diseases such as malaria, TB, water borne diseases and the emergence of AIDS as major health hazards. Stress has been laid on greater inter-country coordination and cooperation amongst the member states to enable them to make a frontal attack on the communicable and non-communicable diseases afflicting the region. Networking arrangements for training, research and eradication of malaria and regional approach for combating major diseases in the region have been undertaken. A Directory of training programmes in six priority areas, i.e. malaria, tuberculosis, leprosy, diarrhoeal diseases, human rabies and maternal and child health have been prepared and circulated. In addition, several status papers on important subjects relating to health have been circulated among the member states. Member States have also identified Centres such as the National Institute of Communicable Diseases, New Delhi and the National Institute of Malaria Training and Research, Lahore to act as focal points on the different diseases. Likewise, the SAARC Tuberculosis Centre, established in Kathmandu in 1992, has been specifically entrusted with the main objective to work towards the prevention and control of tuberculosis in the SAARC region by coordinating the efforts of the National TB Control Programmes of the Member Countries. The Centre is also proactive in training, research and dissemination of information in the region.

Child Care

The development and well-being of children is another principal area of cooperation identified by SAARC from its very inception. The objective of building a region-wise consensus on social action for achieving the rights of the child and the goals set for them within the framework of the survival, development and protection strategy was addressed during three Ministerial Conferences held in 1986, 1992 and 1996 respectively. The momentum generated during the First SAARC Ministerial Conference on Children has contributed in a major way to the convening of the World Summit on Children held in New York in September 1990. Ministerial Conferences of a thematic nature have also become a regular feature of SAARC. Among others, a Ministerial Conference on Women and Family Health was held in Kathmandu (1993) and a Ministerial Meeting on Disabled Persons in Islamabad (1993). In accordance with a decision of the Second SAARC Summit held in Bangalore in 1986, that the survival, protection and development of children be given the highest priority and the SAARC leader directed that annual reviews be undertaken on the situation of children in SAARC countries. Accordingly, the reviews which began in 1993 have become a regular feature of the work in the Technical Committee on Health, Population Activities and Child Welfare. The Annual Situation Reviews on children have been an important source of ascertaining the status of the indicators relating to the well-being of children in the SAARC countries. It has also revealed areas where progress had been slow and required urgent interventions.

The Ninth Summit has given a further impetus to cooperation, among the member states in tackling the important issues relating to women and children. Among many other, they resolved to implement appropriate polices at the national level to achieve the targets and objectives set out in the Rawalpindi Resolution adopted at the end of the Third SAARC Ministerial Conference on Children of South Asia held in August 1996, including the call to eliminate the evil of child labour by the Year 2010. They also recognised that the problems faced by children were inextricably linked to the prevailing socio-economic conditions and problems of the region, and therefore, called for a holistic approach to address them. They expressed the need to formulate a Convention on Regional Arrangements on the Promotion of Child Welfare in South Asia in launching the SAARC Decade of the Rights of the Child, from the year 2001 A.D. to 2010 A.D.

In the area of child development, SAARC has been very closely cooperating with international agencies such as UNICEF with which SAARC has signed an MOU in December 1993. The SAARC-UNICEF MOU envisages cooperation in implementing the relevant SAARC decisions relating to children through an annual agenda which include joint studies, exchange of documentation and monitoring of implementation. Other agencies such as WHO and UNFPA have also shown interest to cooperate with SAARC in advancing the social development agenda of SAARC.

Drug Abuse and its Protection

Since its establishment in 1987, the Committee has implemented a number of programmes in law enforcement, prevention, treatment and rehabilitation as essential elements of a coordinated regional strategy in combating drug trafficking and drug abuse. It contributed significantly towards the finalisation of the SAARC Convention on Narcotic Drugs and Psychotropic Substances in November 1990, which came into force in September 1993 upon its ratification by all member states. Cooperation among Drug Law Enforcement Agencies and officers is being developed through short-term activities such as seminars and Training Courses. Nodal Agencies in member states have been nominated to exchange information and intelligence on drug offences. The SAARC Drug Offences Monitoring Desk (SDOMD) has been established in Colombo to collate, analyse and disseminate information on drug offences. Efforts are afoot for further strengthening SDOMD. In the field of demand reduction, short-term activities such as workshops/seminars held so far have focused on the role of media in drug abuse prevention, community mobilisation against drug abuse, preventive education, school curriculum development, treatment and relapse prevention and exchange of information on indigenous and innovative methods of treatment. A networking arrangement among Nodal Institutions in drug abuse prevention is being established.

Meetings of selected NGOs involved in Drug Abuse Prevention have been held. A directory of such organisations has been compiled in order to promote greater interaction among them. The Colombo Plan Bureau's Project Proposal and the establishment of working relations between SAARC and the Colombo Plan Bureau were approved by the Standing Committee. This will promote and encourage cooperation among NGOs in SAARC countries involved in anti-narcotics activities. Efforts have been directed at promoting SAARC member states' accession to the relevant UN Conventions, conclusion of Regional and Drug Convention and harmonisation and consolidation of national drug laws. A Memorandum of Understanding for cooperation between SAARC and the United Nations International Drug Control Programme (UNDCP) has been signed.

Development of Villages

Rural Development is one of the five original areas identified for cooperation under the IPA. The first meeting of the Committee was held in 1984. Specific activities taken up by the Technical Committee include, exchange of information and literature among member states on issues relating to rural development, preparation of research studies on selected topics, compilation of lists of experts, training institutes, and institutions involved in transfer of appropriate technology in member states, with a view to exchanging expertise and sharing training facilities within the region. Several workshops/seminars and training courses covering practically all aspects of rural development including regional planning, poverty focused development, rural energy, design of agricultural projects, local level planning, inter-country comparisons, appropriate technology, disaster management, rural child development, rural sociology, peoples participation, rural water supply, employment generation, social forestry, rural communication and development of agricultural markets have been conducted in member states under the Committee.

The Technical Committee has identified a set of priority areas on which activities under its aegis would be carried out. These priority areas focus on income and employment generation on a sustained basis; creation of assets and enhancing availability of credit access to the same by the rural poor; human resource development in the rural areas; development and maintenance of rural infrastructure; development and introduction of appropriate technology to enhance productivity in the rural areas; rural environments; issues related to diversification of rural economies; mobilisation of resources for rural development; gender perspective of rural development: assured supply of inputs for rural production and improvement in the marketing facilities and improvement in the institutional environment for rural development.

The decision to establish a Shelter Information Network "SHELTERNET" is being followed up by the Committee which is now undertaking in-depth examination of the proposal including the operational modalities and funding. The Committee has also been entrusted with the implementation of the SAARC Youth Volunteers Programme (SYVOP), which had begun from November 1989.

Later, several concrete steps were taken to prioritise the activities of the TC on Rural Development and during its Fifteenth Meeting in Kathmandu in November 1996 an eleven-point priority list was drawn up to facilitate promotion of cooperation among the member countries on various issues germane to rural development in South Asia.

Promotion of Science

Since its establishment in 1983, Technical Committee on Science and Technology has undertaken a wide variety of programmes which include short-term activities such as seminars/workshops/meetings of experts, training programmes, joint research projects, preparation of state-of-the-art reports and compilation of directories.

Seminars/Workshops/Meetings of Experts held so far were on: Post Harvest and Food Technology; Renewable Energy Resources: Photovoltaic; Pesticides; Instrumentation; Maintenance and Calibration, Cultivation and Processing of Medicine and Aromatic Plants; Delivery System of Improved Stoves for Rural Users; Low Cost Housing Technology Diffusion in Rural Areas; Treatment of Drinking Water in Rural and Urban Areas; Science Policy; Low Cost Scientific

Educational Equipment; Bio-Fertilizer Technology; Bio-Mass Gasification; Recycling of Waste Water and Development of Technologies for Pollution Control; Technology Information and its Linkages; Biological Control of Plant Pests: Immunodiagnostics; Ore Benefication; Energy Modelling Techniques; Solar Thermal Technology; Technological Aspects of Low Cost Housing: Examination of Operational System of Rural Electrification Cooperative; Short-term Course on Technology Assessment and Technology Diffusion. Training Programmes have also been held for Scientists and Technologists on: Tannery Waste Management; Low Cost Housing: Development of Prawn Hatcheries; Electronics and Molecular Biology. In addition, Joint Research Projects on Design and Manufacture of Food Processing Equipment and Appropriate Post Harvest Food Technology for Perishable items have been carried out. State-of-the-Art Reports have been completed on: Bio-Gas: Mineral Resources Exploration; Producer Gas; Application of Remote Sensing Techniques; Use of Organic Fertilizers; Building Material and Housing Technologies; Selected Rural Technologies; Food Processing Technologies and Handicrafts; and Electronic Products.

Directories are being prepared on: Specialised Analytical Instrumentation Facilities and Techniques: Process Engineering/ Pilot Plant Facilities in Agro Food Processing. Networking Arrangements are being established in the fields of: (a) Biotechnology and Genetic Engineering; (b) Energy Modelling Techniques; (c) Technology Information; and (d) Low Cost Housing and Building Technologies. The Technical Committee also recommended the establishment of a SAARC Bio-technology Council.

Development of Tourism

The Committee was established in 1991 to promote cooperation in the field of tourism in the region. At its first meeting held in Colombo in October 1991, the Committee decided on an Action Plan on tourism to promote cooperation in the areas such as training programmes, exchange of information, joint promotion, joint-venture investment, intra-regional tourism, etc. The Committee is also charged with the responsibility of reviewing the progress on the SAARC Scheme for Promotion of Organized Tourism. These topics have formed an integral part of the agenda of the meetings of the Committee which have been held so far. Among others, activities of the Committee include training facilities by the member states in the field of tourism and hotel management; production of SAARC Travel Guide and SAARC tourism promotional film on the theme "A Unique Holiday with Diversity: From Top of the World to the Sunny beaches". Efforts are also being made by the Committee for early launching of the SAARC Scheme for Promotion of Organised Tourism.

On the recommendation of the Committee, Tourism Ministers of SAARC Countries met in Colombo in September 1997. The activities relating to the constitution of a group of experts on tourism to prepare a comprehensive strategic plan for the overall development of tourism for the next five-year period is in progress.

Structure of Transport

The Technical Committee on Transport, established in 1983, covers three major segments of transport, i.e. land transport, divided into roadways and railways; sea transport sub-divided into inland waterways and shipping; and air transport. The activities of the Committee cover exchange of data and information, preparation of status papers and compilation of data-base and directories of consultancy centres for transport sector. Seminars and workshops have covered areas such as Material and Cost of Road Construction, Maintenance of Roads, Rural Roads, Road transportation and safety; Containerization for Railways, Urban transportation, Inland Water Transport, Maritime Transport, etc.

Training courses have included Corporate Planning for Railway sector, Highway and Bridge Engineering. A Compendia of Information on Roads in the SAARC region has been completed and similarly data on Railway Transport has been compiled. Two important Directories - one on Centres of Excellence and the other on Consultants and Experts in the field of transport are being prepared. An important study on "In-depth examination of Transport Infrastructure and Transit Facilities so as to come up with viable proposals for Improvement" has been completed. The activities held under the Transport Sector have helped in fostering better cooperation among member countries and resulted in the dissemination and exchange of data, expertise, information and experiences.

The work programme for the 1990s included a number of activities related to rail, sea and air transportation. Recently, four new specific areas of cooperation in the Transport Sector namely—Transport Safety, Rural Transport, Environmental Aspects, and Energy Conservation have been identified by the Committee. Two proposals: "Establishing Joint Venture Operations to provide Container Liner Shipping Services for Long Haul Trade Routes" and "Consultancy/ Contracting Joint Ventures in the Transport Sector in the SAARC Region" are also being considered by the Technical Committee. Introducing a SAARC driving licence Scheme is being prepared. Transport has been recognised a vital area in providing access to products and markets and opening up new areas of productivity, particularly with the operationalisation of SAPTA.

Emancipation of Women

Women in Development was included as an area of cooperation under the IPA in 1986 and since then twelve meetings have been held so far. Specific issues taken up by the Committee include, preparation of a Regional Plan of Action for Women, effective dissemination of technical information relating to women in development generated by member states. So far, four SAARC Solidarity Journals have been published with the Fifth issue on the theme 'Violence Against Women" is to be published by Sri Lanka in time for the Tenth SAARC Summit. It may be noted that the previous issues have covered the subjects—Rural Development for Women; The Girl Child; and Women in the Informal Sector. One of the most important features of the work of the Technical Committee was designating 1990 as the SAARC Year of the Girl Child and 1991-2000 as the SAARC Decade of the Girl Child. A Plan of Action was also drawn up to observe the decade. A mid-decade review on the implementation of the Plan of Action for the SAARC Decade of the Girl Child was conducted in October 1996 in India which took into consideration priority concerns under Health and Nutrition, Education and Literacy and Marriage and Motherhood. Taking note of the mid-decade review of the SAARC Plan of Action on the Girl-Child, the Heads of State or Government expressed their determination to accelerate efforts at reduction of malnutrition and mortality rates, raising education and literacy rates, reduction of the proportion of early marriage among girls, and the postponement of the age of first pregnancy, thereby contributing to the increased welfare of the girl-child and reduction of population growth rates. An appraisal of the situation of Girl Children in Especially Difficult Circumstances (GCEDC) was also carried out in December 1996 where key common issues and concerns of SAARC Member States were identified and categorised into two groups, i.e. directly affecting GCEDC and indirectly affecting GCEDC. Recommendations were also made both on policy and programme issues.

At the Ninth SAARC Summit, the leaders had reaffirmed their commitment to take urgent action to alleviate the situation of Girl Children in Especially Difficult Circumstances (GCEDC), including those orphaned, disabled and/or exploited. In this context, they had endorsed the recommendations made by the Council of Ministers, aimed at the creation of a socio-economic environment in the SAARC region which would provide equal opportunities to children from all economic sections. Another important area which has received priority attention in the recent years has been the issues relating to trafficking in women and children within and between countries. During their Ninth Summit, the SAARC Leaders expressed their grave concern at the trafficking of women and children within and between countries and pledged to coordinate their efforts and take effective measures to address this problem. They had also directed the member countries to examine the possibility of formulating a Regional Convention on Combating the Crime of Trafficking in Women and Children for Prostitution.

SAARC has also been at the forefront of these issues with their commitment to issues of gender equality and to bring women into the mainstream of development. Two Ministerial Conferences were held one in 1986 in India and the other in Pakistan during 1990. A Regional Plan of Action has been drawn which has identified areas of concern and goals set for them. The Technical Committee on Women in Development is mandated with the task of reviewing progress every year on the implementation of the Plan of Action on Women.

Several short-term activities like seminars, workshops and training courses have been held in the areas of women in law, women and environment, women's education and training, women's employment, women in agriculture and extension, etc. Several activities related to different aspects of the Girl-Child have been held under the Committee. Exhibitions on Handicrafts and Design by Women have also been organised by member states.

A SAARC collective position on issues before the Fourth World Conference on Women in Beijing in September 1995 had been formulated at the "SAARC Ministerial Meeting on Women: Towards the Fourth World Conference on Women in Beijing" held in Dhaka, during July 1995.

Elimination of Poverty

Poverty Eradication has been placed high on the social agenda of SAARC since the Sixth SAARC Summit (Colombo, 1991). The Summit accorded the highest priority to the alleviation of poverty in South Asia and decided to establish an Independent South Asian Commission on Poverty Alleviation (ISACPA) consisting of eminent persons from member states to conduct an in-depth study of the diverse experiences of member states and report their recommendations on the alleviation of poverty to the Seventh Summit.

A consensus on poverty eradication was adopted at the Seventh SAARC Summit (Dhaka, 1993). The Summit welcomed the ISACPA report and expressed its commitment to eradicate poverty from South Asia preferably by the Year 2002 through an agenda of action which would, inter-alia, include a strategy of social mobilisation, policy of decentralised agricultural development and small-scale labour-intensive industrialisation and human development. The Summit also stressed that within the conceptual approach of "*Dal-Bhaat*", the right to work and primary education should receive priority. It also underscored the critical links between the success of national efforts at poverty alleviation and relevant external factors. The Summit urged major actors in the world economic scene to create an enabling atmosphere supportive of poverty alleviation programmes and expressed the need for a new dialogue with donors for this purpose.

The call for a new dialogue with donors has led to important initiatives in this respect, among which was the SAARC/World Bank Informal Workshop on Poverty Reduction in South Asia (Annapolis,

USA, October 1993). UNDP and ESCAP are formulating proposals for cooperation with SAARC in Poverty Reduction.

The Eighth SAARC Summit (New Delhi, 1995) endorsed the recommendations of the Finance/Planning Ministers (Dhaka, July 1994) to establish a three-tier mechanism for exchanging information on poverty eradication. India hosted the meetings of the first and the second tier in New Delhi (September 1995). The meeting of the first-tier which constituted the Group of Secretaries to the Governments in the Ministries/Departments concerned with poverty eradication and social development in SAARC countries, underscored the need to give a distinct status and top priority to pro-poor plans in member countries ensuring specific commitment of adequate resource and organisational support. It stressed the necessity to involve the poor in the formulation and implementation of plans meant for them through participatory institutions and process at grass root levels. The member states were also urged to evolve mechanisms to evaluate the efficacy of pro-poor plans and develop appropriate socio-economic indicators relevant for the purpose. On specific issues germane to poverty eradication, the meeting emphasised the need to pursue an integrated approach taking into account the critical linkages among various sectors. The Meeting of the second-tier, i.e. Finance and Planning Secretaries, endorsed the recommendation of the first-tier and emphasised that poverty eradication should be viewed in the overall context of accelerating economic growth resulting in employment generation in an environment of macro-economic stability with emphasis on human resource development. The meeting also put special emphasis on the need to improving the implementation of poverty eradication programmes through devolution of power and decentralisation. A special mention was also made in the meeting on the need to ensure the sustainability of poverty eradication programmes, especially through ensuring adequate funds for such programmes on a continuous basis. During the recent discussions on poverty eradication under the SAARC three-tier mechanism, Member Countries also discussed specific measures which they may take either individually or collectively to create the enabling condition for eradication of poverty within the time-frame agreed for the purpose. In this context, serious analytical exercise has also been initiated to identify the critical elements of pro-poor strategies in terms of their implications for fiscal and monetary policies of member countries, need for appropriate support infrastructure for the poor and their active involvement in the planning and implementation of the pro-poor programmes.

Economic Cooperation

SAARC has taken important steps to expand cooperation among member countries in the core economic areas. The completion of the Regional Study on Trade, Manufactures and Services (TMS) in 1991, was the first significant step which paved the way for SAARC to move forward in strengthening cooperation in this important field. The study outlined a number of recommendations for promoting regional cooperation in the core economic areas.

A high-level Committee on Economic Cooperation (CEC) comprising the Commerce Secretaries of Member States, was established in July 1991 to act as the forum to address economic and trade issues. The Committee is charged with the responsibility of, inter-alia, monitoring the progress in the implementation of decisions relating to expansion of trade and economic cooperation under the framework of SAARC. It considers the reports of Inter-Governmental Group (IGG) on trade liberalisation, Inter-Governmental Expert Group (IGEG) on transition to South Asian Free Trade Area (SAFTA), and Committee of Participants (COP), and other expert groups on customs, investments, and standardisation. It also reviews progress in the implementation of decisions of meetings of SAARC Commerce Ministers. At the Colombo Summit in December 1991, the Heads of State or Government approved the establishment of (IGG) to seek agreement on an institutional framework under which specific measures for trade liberalisation among SAARC member states could be furthered. The IGG evolved a draft Agreement on SAARC Preferential Trading Arrangement (SAPTA), which was subsequently signed by the Council of Ministers in Dhaka on 11 April, 1993 during the Seventh SAARC Summit, upon the recommendation of CEC.

After completion of procedural formalities by all SAARC member countries and subsequent to a notification issued by the Secretariat to this effect, as per Article 22 of the Agreement, the SAPTA

Agreement entered into force on 7th December, 1995 two years ahead of the time schedule envisaged initially. SAPTA contains provisions giving special and favourable treatment to the LDCs in the SAARC region. Additional measures in favour of LDCs including provisions for safeguard action and balance of payment measures are also incorporated in SAPTA to protect the interests of member states during critical economic circumstances.

With the operationalisation of SAPTA in December 1995, the IGG on Trade Liberalisation, embarked on its Second Round of Trade Negotiations, which was successfully concluded after four meetings of the Group in Colombo, Islamabad, New Delhi and at the SAARC Secretariat, Kathmandu in March, September, October and November 1996 respectively. The number of products enjoying preferential treatment at the conclusion of the Second Round is more than 2000. The non-tariff barriers in the way of expansion of intra-SAARC trade are also being identified and removed. The Third Round of Trade Negotiations under SAPTA is presently underway and is expected to be completed shortly. Following the ratification of SAPTA by all Member States, the Sixteenth Session of the Council of Ministers (New Delhi, December 1995) agreed that Member States should strive for the realisation of a South Asian Free Trade Area (SAFTA). An Inter-Governmental Expert Group (IGEG) on transition to SAFTA comprising experts from the Member Countries was set up as an ad-hoc body by the CEC to identify the necessary steps towards moving into a free trade area. The IGEG has met twice and held in-depth discussions and agreed on the draft terms of reference for the Group and has also drawn up a broad framework of Action Plan for achieving SAFTA. In order to give impetus to intra-SAARC trade under the SAPTA Agreement and to promote economic cooperation in the region, the Commerce Ministers of SAARC countries met in New Delhi in January 1996. Then, it was decided that the Commerce Ministers would meet annually.

The first SAARC Trade Fair was held in New Delhi in January 1996 with the theme "Cooperation for Growth". The Fair, organised as a part of the commemoration of the first decade of SAARC, was jointly inaugurated by the Commerce Ministers and leaders of delegations of Member States. The Fair provided a befitting venue for the representatives of the business and industry of SAARC member countries to discuss various issues connected with promotion and expansion of intra-SAARC trade.

The Heads of State or Government at the Ninth SAARC Summit had recognised the importance of achieving a free trade area by the year 2001 A.D., and reiterated that steps towards trade liberalisation must take into account the special needs of the smaller and the Least Developed Countries and that benefits must accrue equitably.

The Tenth SAARC Summit had decided to constitute a Committee of Experts with specific terms of reference to work on drafting a comprehensive treaty regime for creating a free trade area and emphasised the importance of finalising the text of regulatory framework.

Regional Centres

SAARC Agricultural Information Centre (SAIC): SAIC, the first regional institution, was established in Dhaka in 1988. Its Governing Board formulates policy matters, approves projects, recommends budget estimates, monitors and evaluates administrative and overall activities of SAIC. The SAIC Director is the Member-Secretary of the Board. SAIC serves as a central information institution having a network with relevant national information centres in each member state with a view to rapidly exchange regionally generated technical information and thereby strengthen agricultural research and development activities. SAIC has brought out several publications which contain information on various agricultural institutions in SAARC countries and current contents services on various subjects like fisheries, forestry, livestock, potato, rice, etc. SAIC also publishes a quarterly newsletter.

Some of the completed programmes are: Directory of Agricultural Institutions in SAARC Countries: Directory of Agricultural Scientists and Technologists of SAARC countries; Database on Fish Diseases in the SAARC Region; Database on Potato; Directory of Agricultural Periodicals of the SAARC Countries; Bibliography of Women in Agriculture in the SAARC Countries; Bibliography of Agro-forestry in the SAARC Region.

The on-going and future programmes of SAIC include: Selective Dissemination of Information (SDI); Preparation and Distribution of Selective Bibliographies; Acquisition of Books, Journals, Annual Reports, etc., produced in the SAARC countries; Directory of on-going Research Projects in SAARC member states: SAARC Agricultural Fact Book; Improved Farm Implements Currently used in the SAARC Countries; Procurement and Processing of Non-conventional Agricultural Information Materials; Abstracting and Indexing of Articles of Journals/Newspapers and other Periodicals.

SAARC Tuberculosis Centre (STC): Located at Thimi, Bhaktapur (Nepal), STC became operational in mid-July 1992. The Centre's main objective is to work towards the prevention and control of tuberculosis in the SAARC region through better coordination of efforts of the member states, especially their tuberculosis control programs. Institutional structure of the Centre consists of a Governing Board. A Director appointed to head the Centre is responsible for the implementation of the programmes and activities of the Centre. He is also the ex-officio Member-Secretary of the Board.

Since its inception, STC has undertaken a number of initiatives for the prevention and control of tuberculosis in the region. It has undertaken a number of important training programs for the medical practitioners in the relevant areas and also organised several seminars. Some of its notable activities included seminars on surgical aspects of tuberculosis, socio-cultural aspects of tuberculosis, tuberculosis control programme through primary health care approach, etc. The Centre has also organised a number of trainers training programs for tuberculosis in the region. Its other useful initiatives resulted in the compilation and printing of a SAARC list of TB hospitals, TB training institutes in the region, compilation of a similar list on TB and chest specialists in South Asia. The Centre is actively engaged in collation and distribution of information on national tuberculosis control programs in SAARC countries, networking arrangements among member countries on tuberculosis related subjects as well as circulation of information on research activities in the region on tuberculosis.

SAARC Documentation Center (SDC): SDC has been established at the Indian National Scientific Documentation Center (INSDOC) in New Delhi in May 1994. The SDC Director is responsible for the implementation of the programmes/activities of the Center and is also the Member Secretary of the SDC Governing Board which comprises a representative from each member state. The SAARC Documentation System (SDS) comprises the central facility i.e. SDC and its sub-units in member states which would act as the Center's repositories, the SAARC Secretariat and SAARC Regional Institutions. In fulfilling the need for ready access to information, SDC will focus on documents generated in member states, those generated elsewhere in the SAARC region and access to international data bases in the areas of biological, physical, chemical, engineering, and life sciences as well as in developmental matters.

SAARC Meteorological Research Centre (SMRC): The SMRC, established in Dhaka, was inaugurated on 2 January, 1995.

The Centre concentrates primarily on the research aspects of weather forecasting and monitoring rather than the operational aspects of the medium and long-range forecasting. The responsibilities of the Centre would include undertaking research relevant to weather prediction and compiling climatological information. In addition to monitoring special weather phenomena, developing a networking system among the member states would also receive priority in its work. SMRC has a Governing Board, comprising a representative from each member state.

Some of the important activities being undertaken by SMRC are collecting from national meteorological services of member states the available lists of up-to-date climatological information for compilation; compiling a Directory of Meteorological Professionals and Technicians available in the National Meteorological Services of member states; publishing newsletters regarding activities and programmes of the Centre; and collecting required meteorological data from sources outside the region for its research programmes and to disseminate it to member states.

SAARC Human Resource Development Centre (SHRDC): SAARC Human Resources Development Centre (SHRDC) is being set up in Islamabad. The Director of the Centre has already been appointed and member states have been invited to make nominations to the Governing Board which will draw up the Terms of Reference and Work Programme of the SHRDC. The Centre aims at developing human resources in member states, inter-alia, in social, economic, educational and environmental fields. The Centre will have a Governing Board comprising members from all SAARC countries.

Conventions and Agreements

Agreement on Establishing the SAARC Food Security Reserve: During the Third SAARC Summit (Kathmandu, 1987), an Agreement on establishing the SAARC Food Security Reserve was signed. The Agreement, which came into force on 12 August, 1988, provides for a reserve of foodgrains for meeting emergencies in member countries.

The SAARC Food Security Reserve Board (SFSRB) comprises representatives from each member country and meets once a year. The main functions of the Board are to undertake a periodic review and assessment of the food situation and prospects in the region including factors such as production, consumption, trade, prices, quality and stocks of foodgrains. Member countries are now actively considering the possibility to further improve the functioning of the Reserve.

SAARC Regional Convention on Suppression of Terrorism: The SAARC Regional Convention on Suppression of Terrorism was signed in Kathmandu in November 1987 during the Third SAARC Summit and came into force on 22 August, 1988 following ratification by all member states. The Convention provides a regional focus to many of the well-established principles of international law in this respect. Under its provisions, member states are committed to extradite or prosecute alleged terrorists thus preventing them from enjoying safe havens. Regional Cooperation is also envisaged in preventive action to combat terrorism through exchange of information, intelligence and expertise identified for mutual cooperation under the Convention. The SAARC Terrorist Offences Monitoring Desk (STOMD) has been established in Colombo to collate, analyse and disseminate information about the terrorist incidence, tactics, strategies and methods.

SAARC Convention on Narcotic Drugs and Psychotropic Substances: The SAARC Convention on Narcotic Drugs and Psychotropic Substances which was signed in Male during the Fifth SAARC Summit in November 1990 came into force on 15 September,

1993, following ratification by all member states. The Convention seeks to reinforce and supplement at the regional level, the relevant international conventions and promote regional cooperation among member states in both law enforcement and demand reduction. Incorporating the generally accepted principle of extradition or prosecution consistent with the respective national legislative regimes, the Convention envisages the widest measures for mutual legal assistance among member states in investigation, prosecution and judicial proceedings in respect of drug offences.

The SAARC Drug Offences Monitoring Desk (SDOMD) has been established in Colombo to collate, analyse and disseminate information on drug related offences in member countries. The implementation of the Convention is monitored by the Technical Committee on Prevention of Drug Trafficking and Drug Abuse, during its annual meetings.

Financial Resources

South Asian Development Fund (SADF): The idea of establishment of South Asian Development Fund (SADF) was mooted at the Sixth SAARC Summit in Colombo in December, 1991 to mobilise the global surpluses for the development of South Asia. The basic objective to establish SADF was to provide finances for industrial development, poverty alleviation, protection of environment and balance of payments support. The SADF was formally established in 1996 with the merger of the two earlier SAARC Funds namely: SAARC Fund for Regional Projects (SFRP): and SAARC Regional Fund (SRF).

The Fund is aimed at developing common economic interests among SAARC member countries by promoting economic projects involving more than one member country. SADF has three Windows for (i) Identification and Development of Projects (WIDFP); (ii) Institutional and Human Resource Development Projects (WIHRDP); and (iii) Social and Infrastructural Development Projects (WSIDP). The Fund has since provided finance for conducting feasibility studies for various projects.

SAARC-Japan Special Fund: The SAARC-Japan Special Fund has been established through a Memorandum exchanged between the two sides in Kathmandu on 27 September, 1993. The Fund established entirely with contribution of the Government of Japan consists of two components. The allocation under Component-I is to be used to finance selected programmes/activities identified and managed by the member states. Component-II is for the programmes/activities identified and managed by the Government of Japan.

TWO

People's Forum

Promotion of people-to-people contact in the region to strengthening mutual understanding and goodwill among the peoples of South Asia, has always received a high priority among SAARC leaders. In order to give effect to this concept a number of initiatives have been taken under the aegis of SAARC.

SAARC Audio-Visual Exchange (SAVE) Programme: The SAARC Audio Visual Exchange (SAVE) Committee, aimed at increasing the awareness of SAARC among the peoples of the region and disseminating information about member countries, was established by the Council of Ministers at its Third Session (New Delhi,June 1987). The Committee is entrusted with the task of producing and implementing the SAVE Programmes. SAVE programmes comprise regular TV and Radio Programmes. These are telecast/broadcast on the 1st and 15th of each month, respectively in all SAARC member countries. SAVE Radio and TV Quiz Programmes are also organised at regular intervals and have evoked keen interest among the youth. Other SAVE programmes include joint productions on specific themes such as Environment, Disabled Persons, Youth, Literacy and Participatory Governance. SAVE has proved to be an effective medium for promoting South Asian consciousness amongst the peoples of the region and for establishing people-to-people contact.

SAARC Scheme for Promotion of Organised Tourism: The SAARC Scheme for the promotion of organised tourism was initiated with the overall objective of strengthening people-to-people contact in the region. All issues relating to the Scheme are addressed by the SAARC Technical Committee on Tourism. The Scheme is specifically aimed at facilitating intra-regional tourism. It was envisaged that the Scheme would facilitate exchange of organised group tours between the member countries, with provision of concessional air-fare, and arrangement for limited convertibility of foreign exchange through a travel voucher system. The first meeting of SAARC Tourism Ministers held in Colombo in September 1997 decided to launch the Scheme with immediate effect.

SAARC Chairs, Fellowships and Scholarships Scheme: The SAARC Chairs, Fellowships and Scholarships Scheme was instituted with the aim of providing increased cross-fertilization of ideas through greater interaction among students, scholars and academics in the SAARC Countries. The Scheme was reviewed by an Expert Group recently and its recommendations are under consideration by the Technical Committee on Education, Culture and Sports.

SAARC Youth Volunteers Programme (SYVOP): The SYVOP is aimed at harnessing the idealism of Youth for regional cooperation programmes. The programme enables young people to work in other countries in the field of agriculture and forestry extension work. SYVOP is implemented by the Technical Committee on Rural Development.

SAARC Visa Exemption Scheme: In order to further promote closer and more frequent contacts among the peoples of the region, the SAARC Visa Exemption Scheme was initiated in 1988 and became operational on March 1, 1992. Under the Scheme, visa requirements are waived for specified categories of persons to travel within the region. Currently, there are 21 categories of persons who are entitled to the Scheme. In addition, a process of simplification of visa procedures and requirements is in place to assist business people to accelerate promotion of trade and tourism within the region.

SAARC Youth Awards Scheme (SYAS): The SAARC Youth Awards Scheme was established in 1996. The aim of the Scheme is to provide suitable recognition to extraordinary young talents and encourage the overall development of youth in the region. An annual award is presented to an outstanding youth selected from the member states.

South Asian Festivals: The holding of the South Asian Festival at regular intervals is regarded as a desirable activity by all member states to promote intercultural exchange, understanding and friendship among the artistes of the region.

Collaboration with NGOs

SAARC has emphasised the need for strengthening intergovernmental efforts with increased people-to-people contacts through greater participation of NGOs, including professional bodies in the private sector, to promote socio-economic and cultural development of South Asia. In appreciation of the contributions of the NGOs and professional bodies to the official SAARC process, SAARC has set in motion a process of granting recognition to such deserving bodies. These organisations fall under two categories: (a) SAARC Regional Apex Bodies, and (b) SAARC Recognised Bodies.

The Apex Bodies

SAARC Chamber of Commerce and Industry (SCCI): The SAARC Chamber of Commerce and Industry (SCCI) was granted the status of SAARC Regional Apex Body in December 1992. The SCCI brings together the national chambers of commerce and industry of the seven SAARC countries under one umbrella. The SCCI has played a significant role in promoting the core area of economic and trade cooperation in the region. It was instrumental in bringing into fruition the SAARC Preferential Trading Arrangement (SAPTA). SCCI has been very active in the promotion of trade and interaction of business community of the SAARC region. It organises the SAARC Economic Cooperation Conferences on a regular basis and so far has held two such conferences in New Delhi (November, 1996), and Islamabad (March, 1998). SCCI has also been organising SAARC Trade Fairs in Member Countries, the first of which was held in New Delhi in January 1996.

SAARC Law: SAARC Law is an Association for persons of the legal communities of SAARC countries. It was established in 1991 and was accorded recognition as a SAARC Regional Apex Body in July 1994. It was established with the twin objectives of bringing together the legal Communities of the region for closer cooperation and developing law as a source of social change for development. SAARC Law has been convening periodic conferences covering important areas of common interest to member states. These conferences focused on themes such as: law and development in the region; law as an instrument of social justice; law as an instrument of economic change; law and justice for the common people; and development through law; legal education; public interest litigation; money laundering: child abuse and violence against women and investment climate in the region. Since 1995, a parallel meeting of the Chief Justices of the Member States has also been held to coincide with the SAARC Law conference. SAARC Law aims at, inter-alia, exchange of legal professionals, establishment of SAARC Law libraries, and harmonisation of laws which offer mutual assistance within the judicial process. The Secretariat of the SAARC Law is located in Sri Lanka.

Recognised Bodies

South Asian Association for Regional Cooperation of Architects (SAARCH): The SAARCH was founded in 1991 in Colombo with the objective of assisting the development of national architectural bodies within the South Asian region so that it would provide opportunities for consultation on holding of conferences of architects to discuss professional matters and interchange ideas. SMRCH was granted SAARC Recognised Body status in May 1997. It has held several conferences in the region and also publishes a newsletter SAARCH. The SAARCH Secretariat is located in Sri Lanka.

Association of Management Development Institutions (AMDISA): AMDISA was established in June 1988 for the promotion of management education and management development activities in South Asian region. It has brought under its umbrella the leading institutions, both public and private, involved in the teaching, training and research in management and development oriented fields. SAARC Recognised Body status was granted to AMDISA in May 1997 in recognition of its contribution to management and development education fields. AMDISA has held several fora on management development related topics. Its general office is located in India.

SAARC Federation of University Women (SAARCFUW): SAARCFUW was established in July 1995 in Colombo with the objectives of, among other things, bringing together the university women of the region to promote understanding and cooperation and share responsibility in society for the social upliftment in the region. SAARCFUW was granted the status of SAARC recognised body in

May 1997. At present, it has national chapters in Bangladesh, India, Nepal, Pakistan and Sri Lanka. It publishes a newsletter SAARCFUW. SAARCFUW Secretariat is currently located in Sri Lanka.

South Asian Federation of Accountants (SAFA): SAFA was established in 1984 with the objective of developing a coordinated accountancy profession in the region. Its membership is open to accountancy bodies in the South Asian region. At present the Institutes of Chartered Accountants and/or the Institutes of Cost and Management Accountants in Bangladesh, India, Pakistan and Sri Lanka are the members of SAFA. SAFA was granted the status of SAARC Recognised Body in May 1997. Its Secretariat is located at South Asian Federation and Accountants, Institute of Chartered Accountants of India.

SAARC Association of Town Planners: SAARC Association of Town Planners was granted SAARC recognition in August 1998. The main objective of the Association is to promote coordinated town planning in the region. At present, its country chapters are in Bangladesh, India, Pakistan and Sri Lanka. Its headquarters are located in Colombo.

SAARC Cardiac Society: SAARC Cardiac Society was granted the status of SAARC recognised body in November 1998. The main objectives of the Society is to foster cooperation and exchange of information in the field of cardiovascular science including its research, training and rehabilitation programmes. It has country chapters in Bangladesh, India, Nepal, Pakistan and Sri Lanka. Its headquarters are located at Dhaka.

Association of SAARC Speakers and Parliamentarians: The Association of SAARC Speakers and Parliamentarians was formally launched in 1992 in Kathmandu. The Heads of State or Government at their Seventh SAARC Summit (Dhaka, April 1993) had welcomed the initiative of the Speakers of Parliaments of SAARC countries in forming the Association.

Extended Cooperation

UNCTAD: A Memorandum of Understanding on the Trade Analysis and Information System (TRAINS) was signed between SAARC and UNCTAD in February 1993. This was the first Agreement of cooperation to be signed by SAARC with an international organisation. Under this Agreement, since 1993, UNCTAD has been providing updated copies of its Trade Analysis and Information System (TRAINS) to the SAARC Secretariat on a regular basis. TRAINS, which is now available on CD-ROM, contains latest data on trade control measures prevailing in ninety-one developed and developing countries. Under the MOU, it is the responsibility of the SAARC Secretariat to update UNCTAD database on trade control measures in respect of the SAARC Member Countries and forward the same to UNCTAD Secretariat, Geneva on computer floppies for final incorporation in the forthcoming updated versions of TRAINS CD-ROM.

UNICEF: A Cooperation Agreement between SAARC and UNICEF, was signed in December 1993. The Agreement envisages cooperation in implementing the relevant SAARC decisions relating to children through an annual agenda which include joint studies, exchange of documentation and monitoring of implementation. In pursuance of the Cooperation Agreement, the SAARC Secretariat and UNICEF Regional Office for South Asia in Kathmandu hold regular consultations on all child related issues including the Annual Review of the Situation of Children in the SAARC Countries; and implementation of the decisions taken at the Ministerial Conferences on Children of South Asia held at the various SAARC capitals. SAARC and UNICEF have been at the forefront of efforts of the global community for the survival, protection and development of children.

APT: The SAARC-APT Memorandum of Understanding (MOU) signed in February 1994 envisages cooperation between the two organisations to promote the growth of telecommunications in order to accelerate economic and social development in the region. SAARC and APT exchange information, publications and documents on their respective activities in this field. They will also exchange technical and operational details of plans for improvement of national, regional and international telecommunications network. Collaboration is also envisaged in planning and development of networks, transfer of technology, promoting international standards, development of human resources and application of telecommunications in sectors such as health, education, environment, transport, and tourism.

ESCAP: A Framework Agreement for cooperation between SAARC and Economic and Social Commission for Asia and the Pacific (ESCAP) was signed in February 1994. The Agreement provides for cooperation on development issues through joint studies, workshops and seminars and exchange of information and documentation in poverty alleviation, human resource development, trade promotion, foreign direct investment, environmental protection and prevention of drug trafficking, infrastructure development, etc. Since then, there has been regular interaction between the SAARC and ESCAP both bilaterally and under the aegis of the Consultative Meetings of the Executive Heads of Sub-regional Organisations in Asia and the Pacific and ESCAP.

UNDP: The SAARC-UNDP Memorandum of Understanding (MOU) was signed in July 1995 and embodies a general agreement for broad- based collaboration with the aims and purposes of promoting sustainable human development for eradicating poverty, preservation and protection of environment, regeneration of natural resources, employment creation, and the goals of women in development; undertaking periodic consultation for joint activities; publishing studies on priority concerns and exchanging relevant reports. Cooperation between SAARC and UNDP has been particularly close in the area of poverty eradication. UNDP has initiated programmes in specific locations in six member countries of SAARC to promote social mobilisation with a view to eradicating poverty under its programme RAS/96/600. UNDP and SAARC have been maintaining regular contacts on the implementation of these programmes. A UNDP Advisory Committee on its Poverty Eradication Programmes in South Asia was formed in 1996. Recent SAARC-UNDP cooperation also covered issues relating to training of SAARC officials in specific disciplines and consideration of specific proposals for the strengthening of the institutional capacity of the SAARC Secretariat. UNDP arranged a specialised training for SAARC officials in the important area of Media and Communication. SAARC and UNDP are also maintaining close contact on the possibility of further UNDP assistance to meet some of the important requirements of the SAARC Secretariat for greater professional and expert services in a number of specialised areas.

UNDCP: SAARC signed the MOU with UNDP in August 1995 to coordinate efforts in combating drug trafficking and drug abuse in the region. The Memorandum envisages mutual consultation and exchange of information between the two organisations, development and implementation of such activities as human resource development; improving regional cooperation on drug intelligence through the SAARC Drug Offences Monitoring Desk; legislation; financial investigation; money laundering; precursor control; and the establishment of a networking arrangement among existing institutions in drug abuse prevention, etc. A UNDCP-SAARC Workshop for policy makers of the member states on Drug Trafficking and Drug Abuse was held in Colombo on 1996.

EC: Since the conclusion of the MOU on Administrative Cooperation with the EC in July, 1996, the Secretariat has been in regular touch with the European Commission to concretise SAARC-EC cooperation through the implementation of specific projects/ programmes. The MOU mainly focuses on exchange of information, institutional support and training, and technical assistance. The MOU envisages cooperation between the two organisations in the areas of staff training of SAARC Secretariat and SAARC institutions, technical assistance for institutions and institutional support to strengthen the capacities and effectiveness of SAARC Secretariat and SAARC institutions. The two organisations have identified specific areas where cooperation was feasible. The South Asia Rinderpest Eradication Campaign Support Project (SAREC SP) proposed by EU is under consideration by the Member States. The Foreign Ministers of SAARC Countries, during the period of the annual UNGA Session in New York would meet the Troika of EU to carry toward the process of consultation between the two organisations.

ITU: The Memorandum of Understanding (MOU) between SAARC and International Telecommunications Union (ITU) was signed in March 1997. Providing a framework agreement for ensuring closer cooperation and coordination of efforts between SAARC and ITU. The areas covered by the MOU include development of telecommunications and telematic services as well as improvement of the quality of voice and non-voice telecommunication services in the region. Member States of SAARC and ITU would jointly work towards improving the productivity and efficiency of the telecommunication organisations and networks in the region.

CIDA: SAARC and the Canadian International Development Agency (CIDA) signed a Memorandum of Cooperation in July, 1997 for promotion of cooperation and mutually beneficial relationships between the two organisations in the core areas of mutual concern, which, among others, include poverty eradication; economic and trade cooperation; social and human resource development; sustained economic growth; and sustainable development. For the purpose of cooperation in these areas, the Memorandum envisages establishment of an annual programme of cooperation and regular interaction for coordination, exchange of information, and review of cooperation activities, between the two contracting parties. The Memorandum also intends to encourage cooperation between SAARC and CIDA through involvement of mutually agreed upon regional institutions and non-governmental organisations.

RULES AND REGULATIONS

The rules shall apply to the meetings of the Council of Ministers, the Standing Committee, the Programming Committee, the Technical Committees or any other ad hoc SAARC bodies that may be set up by the Heads of State or Government, or the Council of Ministers, or the Standing Committee.

Composition of Delegation

Rule 1: 1. Each State participating in the Meeting shall be represented by a Head of Delegation and other representatives of the State, as may be required. 2. The names of the representatives shall be submitted to the host country and the Secretary-General as early as possible, preferably not less than one week before the date fixed for the opening of the Meeting.

Appointment of Officers of the Meeting

Rule 2: The Meeting may appoint the following officers from among the representatives of the States participating in it: a Chairperson, a Vice-Chairperson and other officers for subcommittees, working groups, drafting groups.

Acting Chairperson

Rule 3: 1. If the Chairperson finds it necessary to be absent from a meeting or any part thereof, he/she shall designate the Vice-Chairperson to take his/her/place. 2. The Vice-Chairperson acting as Chairperson shall have the same powers and duties as the Chairperson.

Participation by the Secretary General

Rule 4: The Secretary General, or, in his/her absence, an officer of the Secretariat who shall be designated by the Secretary General, shall act in that capacity at the Meeting.

Statement by the Secretariat

Rule 5: The Secretary General, or any officer of the Secretariat designated by the Secretary General for the purpose, may, subject to Rule 10, make statements concerning any questions under consideration.

Conclusions of the Meeting

Rule 6: The Meeting shall adopt a report at the conclusion of its session.

Conduct of Business

Rule 7:* The Chairperson may declare a meeting open and permit the debate to proceed only when the representatives of at least five member-states are present. The presence of all the member-states shall be required for any decision to be taken.

* This Rule shall not apply to bodies established with a membership less than the total membership of SAARC.

General Powers of the Chairperson

Rule 8: 1. The Chairperson shall preside over the Meeting.. He/she shall declare the opening and the closing of each sitting, direct the discussions, ensure observance of the Rules of Procedure, accord the right to speak and announce decisions. He/she shall rule on points of order. The Chairperson, subject to these Rules, shall have complete control of the proceedings and over the maintenance of order thereof. 2. The Chairperson in the exercise of his/her functions remains under the authority of the Meeting.

Points of Order

Rule 9: During the discussions on any matter, a representative may at any time raise a point of order which shall be immediately decided by the Chairperson in accordance with these Rules.

Speeches

Rule 10: 1. No one may address the Meeting without having previously obtained the permission of the Chairperson. Subject to Rule 9, the Chairperson shall call upon speakers from member-countries in the order in which they signify their desire to speak. 2. Debate shall be confined to the question before the Meeting and the Chairperson may call the speaker to order if his/her remarks are not relevant to the subject under discussion. 3. The Meeting may limit the time allowed to speakers and the number of times participants may speak on a question.

Basic Proposals

Rule 11: All draft proposals or reports submitted to the Meeting following its last session shall constitute the basic proposals for consideration by the Meeting.

Submission of other Proposals and Substantive Amendments

Rule 12: Other proposals and substantive amendments shall normally be introduced in writing and handed over to the Chairperson of the Meeting for circulation to delegates in the language of the Meeting. As a general rule, no proposal shall be discussed unless copies of it have been circulated to all delegations. The Chairperson may, however, permit discussion and consideration of amendments even though these have not been circulated in advance, if the Meeting so decides.

Decision Making

Rule 13: The Meeting shall adopt its decisions and make recommendations on the basis of unanimity.

Language of the Meeting

Rule 14: 1. English shall be the language of the Meeting. 2. A representative may deliver his/her statements in his/her national language if he/she provides for interpretation into English.

Record of Meetings

Rule 15: Sound recordings of the meetings of the plenary may be kept:

Public and Closed Meetings

Rule 16: 1. All the meetings under SAARC shall be closed meetings. 2. If it is decided to have inaugural and closing ceremonies of some of the meetings, these shall be held in public.

Status and Participation of Invitees

Rule 17: 1. Representatives of the international organizations of the United Nations System or those international organizations outside the System with which SAARC has reached an agreement for co-operation shall be admitted as invitees to inaugural and closing ceremonies. 2. They may also be invited to be present during discussions on proposals or projects involving collaboration with their organizations.

THREE

Regional but Important

India and Pakistan became independent in 1947 and Sri Lanka in 1948, Bangladesh took birth by abandoning Pakistan in 1971. Nepal and Bhutan were already free of all influence. Only Maldives gained independence in 1966. The reason prevailed in early eighties, the South Asian nations agreed to have a regional association of their own and in 1985, SAARC became a reality.

Notably, South Asia, comprising seven states—India, Pakistan, Sri Lanka, Bangladesh, Nepal, Bhutan and Maldives, has been one of the greatest cradles of human civilization and a birth place of two great religions like Buddhism and Hinduism and later a great centre of Islamic activities. The region has left an indelible impact upon the culture of Asian mainland.

The post-independent political history of South Asia has been full of vicissitudes that have ranged from problems relating to demarcation of boundaries, disputed lands and waters, illegal immigrations to persistent fears of hegemony by the core nation toward the peripheral states.

Almost all the South Asian states are ascriptive in character owing to low level of socio-cultural and economic conditions. Consequently, their regional policies have been naturally influenced by their religious and linguistic traditions. The ethnic and cultural diaspora in the region where minorities are scattered under the jurisdiction of different states provides a ready-made potential for sparking off fanatical outbursts and turmoils. This is a dangerous issue against which the region should be on guard and where SAARC can play a decisive role. The majority-minority character based on religion, language, race and ethnic configuration is a major variable that has a profound impact upon the intra-regional relations in South Asia.

Political Factors

Political and security factors such as Pak entry into western sponsored military alliance system, Indo-Russian alignment, Indo-China and Pak-China relations have to a large extent influenced the foreign policy perceptions of the major states of South Asia.

Diversity of opinion prevails from country to country in the region regarding the security issue. While India, the core state, is inclined to evolve a security framework in regional terms, the majority among the rest of the states tend to be guided more so by intra-regional rivalries and fear perceptions, leading to trans-regional linkages. Thus, Pakistan's security frame has been conditioned by its antagonism towards India and of late, by Afghan issue. Nepal and Bhutan have the problem of weak buffer states. Bangladesh is moved by powerful emotion of nationalism, independent identity, being almost surrounded by India. Sri Lanka is an Island Republic, whose orientations have been not only bound by its status as a South Asian state but also by the Great Power politics in the Indian Ocean.

Thus, while some states in the region have in the past pursued policies that have admitted various forms of foreign interests, India, in line with its policy of opposing foreign involvement in the regional affairs and partly motivated by its close ties with Russia, has been opposing it. Nevertheless, it too had to conclude a Friendship Treaty with the erstwhile Soviet Union, which although not ostensibly a defence pact, had acted as one and was a source of weaponry supply to it. In later years, however, India came closer to USA also. Thus, the situation changed to a great extent. Besides Pakistan, Sri Lanka and Bangladesh have also been displaying a pro-West inclination, while Nepal has been showing desires to consolidate links with external powers including China and United Slates. Maldives, the only South Asian state without any bilateral-regional differences, has close ties with certain extra-regional powers including the United Slates. Nevertheless, the states of the region have, on occasions also displayed some collective and cooperative orientations in their external relationships. For example, in 1950's India, Pakistan and Sri Lanka cooperated in promoting Colombo powers and later the Afro-Asian Movement. All the states of South Asia are members of Non-alignment Movement and subscribe to its objectives.

It follows, therefore, that the states in South Asia despite some collective initiatives have more or less exhibited asymmetrical and combative attitudes towards each other. They have not been able to settle their territorial disputes, boundary disputes and disputes over sharing of river waters. They have failed to evolve a common regional policy in the United Nations regarding declaring South Asia as a Nuclear Weapon Free Zone or a common stand on Non-proliferation Treaty (NPT). Instead, they have engaged in efforts to win support for their goals from nations outside the region. Pakistan, for instance, has been canvassing for the support of West Asian countries in its dispute with India over Kashmir. The latter, no doubt, have been voicing sympathy for Pakistan's position, but have not attempted to intervene in any tangible way. Even on occasions, Pakistan has been raising questions of safety of minority rights in India in international forums like OIC. The two neighbours were unable to respond coherently to Afghan imbroglio or Iraq's aggression against Kuwait in the neighbouring gulf region. Likewise, Sri Lanka has been trying to elicit support from the countries outside the region with respect to India's intervention in its internal affairs.

Role of other Powers

From South Asian regional integration point of view, the involvement of extra-regional powers in the regional affairs has more negative than positive sides. The feeling that the extra-regional links of small South Asian states would balance India's dominant position in the region cannot be compatible with the regional understanding in South Asia, to which India's role is central.

Drastic as the recent external changes are, they have disrupted the familiar cold war patterns, and have till recently done very little to reduce the rivalry between India and Pakistan, the two major states in the region. Each continue to be plagued by an array of political and security crisis, regime instability, secessionist movements of an explosive potential. Each alleges to be a victim of 'low intensity war' and subversion by the other.

Faced with the challenges of this magnitude, the task of resolving them in a manner which can ensure lasting goodwill and harmony has been no doubt a daunting one. That amply provides the reason why the leaders of the region had to evade this challenge under the cover of avoiding bilateral and contentious issues, in the SAARC forum. However, the time has come when this can no longer be a sensible course, no other reason other than the economic situation will not permit it. The countries in the region, now with the change in the standing and influence of the great powers, would need to reassess their policies. Earlier, they have fully exploited the cold war tensions between the super powers to achieve their ends, usually in the opposite directions in the past. The new situation now demands each to adjust its posture significantly. The leaders of South Asia are the masters of the destiny of their respective countries and if they lack the courage to undertake effort, no other can do it on their behalf. Whatever hesitation there has been in the past, it is no longer excusable because of the existence of SAARC. Its scope has to be widened to the extent that security questions are put in its care. In SAARC lies as good an opportunity as any to undertake this task, utilizing it as a medium to conduct and stage-manage the intricate and protracted initiatives and remedial measures the task will entail. SAARC's ultimate objective, in fact, is not merely to increase regional cooperation in the economic spheres, but by adopting this functional approach also to contribute to mutual trust and understanding among the member states, which would lead to cooperation among them in political sphere too.

Not withstanding the fact that in spite of cold war consideration, which made it to enter into a virtual alignment with Moscow, India, on its part, has been vocal on the need for a regional unity. Indian leaders ever since the attainment of independence from the colonial yoke have remained wedded to the philosophy of South Asian unity. Jawaharlal Nehru was the initiator of the first Asian Relations Conference under the auspices of Indian National Congress in New Delhi, followed by the Conference on Indonesia and then of a bigger conference at Bandung, Indonesia. In fact, India has carried the message of international unity for peace and cooperation all the time. Non-interference and respect for the sovereignty of others has been the very philosophy that has been ingrained in India's outlook through the ages. It was again under the leadership of Nehru, the first Prime Minister that India laid the foundations of a foreign policy based on the doctrine of Panchsheel and non-alignment. It has always resisted being drawn into the vortex of great power rivalry and avoided becoming enmeshed in their ideological webs.

In no other region of the world, do we have such a big country as India, surrounded by a number of small ones. It has the major concentration of mineral resources of the region and far more advanced technological base and structure of production, covering the entire range of modern industry than the rest of-the countries of the region, who are almost in an infant stage of industrial development. In view of such peculiar features of India relative to the rest of the region, there can be no worthwhile regional cooperation without full Indian participation in such an endeavour. Thus, it would not be an exaggeration to say that as India goes, so goes South Asia. South Asia is not likely to go very far in any direction, unless India is also headed in the same direction. Its size, economic dynamism, political stability, military power, contrive to assure that the major regional influences which originate within are going to emanate from that nation. In other words, India is to be central to the future of cooperation in South Asia.

Expansion Required

In the South Asian Regional Cooperation context, the thinking in New Delhi is that cooperation within the SAARC framework should be expanded and that the existing level is not an end in itself. India views this cooperation as a means of ensuring broader mutual understanding in the region. The strategy of policy makers in India has been that the organisation needs to move forward cautiously in this direction from certain elementary steps to more well defined objectives.

India is in a position to meet many of the capital goods requirements of the member states. The capacity of its capital goods industry remains under-utilized for lack of sufficient domestic demand. There is, nevertheless, a potential market for the Indian capital goods in other countries of the region. But the potential remains under utilized because of the fear among the countries of the region that trade with India would become heavily unbalanced, if they allow an unrestricted import of these goods from India. This is because the

Indian policy of self-reliance in consumer goods implies that India does not provide a market for the consumer goods which these industrially less developed states of the region could produce.

Thus, a modification in the Indian policy of self-sufficiency in respect of such consumer goods can create a market for such goods in India that could be manufactured in the less developed countries of the region. If these countries can increase their exports to India, they would have the means to pay the larger imports of capital goods from India and, thereby, a balance in trade can be maintained in the region.

In the SAARC context, India on its part, has been promoting cooperation in the region by providing member states with financial assistance, helping them in setting up industries and joint ventures. Being far ahead in the scientific and technological know-how in the region, it has been deputing large number of experts to the neighbouring states and also receiving trainees and students from them.

Some of the countries bordering India, rightly or wrongly harbour all sorts of misgivings about it and often accuse it of being a big bully. Whether it is the case of an apprehensive Pakistan or the other neighbours who are just suspicious, the political strategy by India should be to go all out to convince the states of the region about India's bona-fides and friendly intentions towards them and its genuine desire to join them in developing and consolidating regional integration in South Asia. The overwhelming edge that India enjoys in its size, population and economical and technical base makes it imperative that instead of showing up the inferiority or weakness of the smaller states of the region, it should demonstrate an attitude of accommodation and of concern for their apprehensions.

It is a tribute to the sagacity and statesmanship of late Zia-ur-Rehman, that he put forward in 1981 a proposal for closer economic cooperation among the states of South Asia. He saw in the context of regional cooperation in South Asia a potential for peace keeping and if executed in good faith by all the participants, likely to offer not only economic but also political dividends. The idea received immediate approval of the peripheral states of the region. Sri Lanka, which had by that time explored without success the possibility of joining ASEAN could see the point in joining a large economic grouping and along with Nepal supported the proposal. Likewise Maldives and Bhutan found no reason to be hesitant about their participation in the proposed forum. However, the two core countries in the region—India and Pakistan were in two minds about the exercise. India, no doubt, recognised the desirability of a cooperative relationship in South Asia but was not quite sure if all the states of the region were really committed to the concept. Pakistan, in spite of its own vision of what its own economic expression and identity should be, accepted it, having recognized the fact that by doing so, it was likely to bring India round to the need for dealing with other states of the region on the basis of equality and not of domination.

Between the time, the idea of South Asian Regional Cooperation was first spelt out and the holding of the first summit in Dhaka in December 1985, drastic changes had taken place in the domestic power structure in South Asia. A coup had overthrown Zia-ur-Rehman. An assassination had removed Indira Gandhi. Their successors, however, persevered with the idea and drove their bureaucrats to prepare the way for the first summit.

The meeting at Dhaka saw the seven leaders of the seven states of the region get together for the first time for a multilateral summit and for informal consultations at bilateral levels. This was, indeed, a good augury. In order to promote the quality of life in South Asia, the summit highlighted the urgency to accelerate economic growth, social progress and cultural development among the member states, besides urging the member countries to contribute to the mutual trust, understanding and appreciation of each others problems in their region.

Area of Cooperation

Since then, the successive summits of the heads of government of the SAARC states have led to the expansion of the areas of cooperation to a number of result oriented programmes that are likely to confer tangible benefits on the peoples of the region. Apart from formal consideration of an agenda for cooperation in agreed areas, these meetings facilitate informal discussions on bilateral issues. These exchanges outside the conference venues are perhaps even more useful and significant than the regular sessions of various bodies, for they serve to diffuse tensions, remove misunderstandings and enable remedial measures when problems or conflict of interests are encountered. As a corollary of the regular meetings and contacts, an awareness of the commonality of problems within the member countries and learning from each others' experience has developed.

No doubt, the scope of economic cooperation achieved so far by the member states through SAARC has remained limited to certain relatively non-controversial areas owing to the existing wide disparities in the resource potential among them. Vital subjects such as Trade, Industry, Transfer of technology, Investment and monetary cooperation have so far not been included within the scope of SAARC activities. SAARC partners particularly Pakistan have remained wary of the inclusion of core economic areas in the SAARC activities on the ground that such a course would lead to greater dependence on India. Nevertheless, the Islamabad SAARC summit succeeded in making a breakthrough of sorts in view of softening of stands on the issue from both India and Pakistan. The Indians on their part sought to allay Pakistani fears of economic dominance when Indian Prime Minister Rajiv Gandhi declared in Islamabad that India was fully conscious of its special responsibilities and that it would not 'seek to secure any unfair advantage at the expense of any other partner' Accordingly, Pakistan responding positively to the issue, hoped that the study already being conducted in the areas of trade, manufacture and services would lend itself to enhanced economic exchanges and harmonisation of economic efforts towards the socio-economic progress of the peoples of the region.

Thus, in the successive summits after the Islamabad SAARC summit, an inclination to include core economic areas within SAARC activities has been distinctly observed. In keeping with this desire, the SAARC members can begin by promoting cooperation in regional scheme in less controversial, though of necessity, more limited core areas. These can include, for instance, schemes for transfer of technology, establishment of joint ventures, besides expanding bilateral trade relations. Though there exists a certain lack of complementarity, the scope of trade can be expanded considerably if the misgivings of the smaller states and their problems in achieving a modicum of balance with potentially advanced members can be overcome. SAARC needs, indeed, to integrate the economic resources of the region to increase the level of growth of intra-regional trade. In this direction, a series of gradual steps need to be taken to stimulate the trade within the region, starting with Preferential Trade agreements, followed by measures to keep the bilateral arrangements equitable and to prevent excessive benefits to the more advanced economies. These measures would not only be in association with the SAARC objectives but also in keeping with the spirit of South-South cooperation.

As in the case of trade, there is a great scope for regional cooperative efforts through SAARC in international forums to redress the common grievances of the member states. SAARC has to lead the member states to create a joint front vis-a-vis developed world in their demand to improve their deteriorating terms of trade with the developing world. The SAARC is likely to add to the bargaining power of the member states by reducing their dependence on the industrialized North, enhance their horizontal linkage with the developing world and can create a set of equitable relations within the region. Already some progress has been recorded in the path of strengthening cooperation with other developing countries and the like-minded organizations on economic and political issues affecting the Third World. The SAARC leaders have been at various summits identifying common problems and advocating the improvement of regional trade with and terms of assistance from the developed world. Committees of experts have been established to recommend ways and means of negotiating with multilateral, agencies such as GATT and UNCTAD on problems facing the region. While SAARC has been showing its strong support to international bodies such as Non-alignment movement and the United Nations, its utmost disregard for nuclear arms race, resort to use of force and external intervention in the affairs of other states can never be under-emphasized.

For South Asia where regional cooperation was non-existent, it has been indeed a welcome sign that some efforts have been undertaken. So far whatever has been done, no doubt, constitutes a small beginning, but perhaps an irreversible movement has begun which in due course may develop into a substantially mutual beneficial activity. It is a fact that South Asia has many things in common, culturally, geographically, socially and economically but unfortunately not politically. It is up to the states of the region now that it has in

SAARC a ready-made instrument to use it as a medium for laying the foundations for an enduring peace and prosperity. This calls for political goodwill on part of SAARC leaders, getting rid of distrusts, mutual suspicions and fear perceptions, besides sorting out conflicting policies which give rise to them. This means appreciation of sensitivities and responsible behaviour, instead of fanning flames, which they so far have been doing. Of particular importance is India's role due to its centrality in terms of location, size and power resources, which has, no doubt, made it a 'critical variable' in the viability of any regional cooperation in South Asia. India will have to provide assurance to its neighbours of its economic and political goodwill if the regional cooperation in South Asia has to expand beyond the limits identified so far.

FOUR

The Goal for Unity

Basically, SAARC is a cultural, economic and commercial association, aimed at creating a free zone, which may ultimately turn into a unified geographical entity, like European Union. However, it's a distant dream, at the moment, as the pace of advancement towards such goals have been very slow.

The very idea of regional cooperation was first proposed through 'a regional forum' by Bangladesh in 1980, with a view to holding periodic, regional-level consultations among countries in South Asia on matters of mutual interest and possible cooperation in economic, social, cultural and other fields. The rationale was primarily predicated on the premise that regional experiences elsewhere in the globe had been highly successful and that the countries in the South Asian region would benefit enormously from such cooperation as it would strengthen their competitive position, both individually and as a group.

The Bangladesh proposal argued that inherent logic strongly justified regional cooperation, particularly among South Asian countries, because the countries in the region enjoy geographical contiguity, historical, social, cultural and ethnic affinities which would act as centripetal forces and thus, contribute substantively to facilitate coordination and to reducing of transaction costs. The Foreign Secretaries of the seven South Asian countries accordingly agreed at their first meeting in Colombo (21-23 April, 1981) to pursue cooperation in five broad areas, namely agriculture, rural development, telecommunications, meteorology, and health and population services. The Foreign Secretaries also agreed to set up a Committee of the Whole comprising senior officials from the seven countries to identify and report on other areas of possible cooperation. At the first Meeting of this Committee in Colombo (31 August - 2 September 1981), the need to expand economic relations, and the need for cooperation in international economic negotiations were discussed.

In 1983, (24-25 January) the first meeting of the representatives of *National Planning Organization* was held in New Delhi. This was in fact, the first 'economic' meeting at a regional level among the South Asian countries. The meeting focussed on three areas viz. first, national planning models and techniques; second, poverty alleviation programmes and third, the global economic situation. The meeting agreed on the need for regular consultations and exchange of information, but more importantly, it called for the systematic exploration of the scope for intra-regional economic cooperation.

Aims and Objectives

The SAARC Charter mentions that among the objectives of the Association shall be acceleration of economic growth, social progress and cultural development in the region, promotion of active collaboration and mutual assistance in the economic, social, cultural, technical and scientific fields and strengthening of cooperation among the Member States in international fora on matters of common interest. Regional cooperation agreements in other parts of the world identified economic cooperation as constituting the very heart, as it were, of cooperation among the countries, without which the extent and accruant benefits may be severely constrained. However, within the SAARC region a fundamental asymmetry among the Member States, their varied levels of development, including administrative procedures and rules, suggested that economic cooperation, while important, was likely to be a complex and gradual process. Accordingly, the first SAARC Summit in Dhaka (1985) primarily focussed on regional cooperation in areas such as health, population activities and child welfare; culture and sports.

This does not imply that the Association had decided to leave out economic cooperation. In fact, in 1986, the first Ministerial Meeting on International Economic Issues was held in Islamabad (31 March - 3 April). The Declaration of this Ministerial Meeting stressed the need for intensifying economic cooperation among SAARC countries and also agreed that SAARC countries should coordinate their positions at the various headquarters of regional and international organizations, as well as in relevant international conferences to further the common objectives of member countries.

In 1987, the representatives of the National Planning Organisations met for the second time in Islamabad (11-14 October) and recommended that in view of the adverse international economic situation facing the region, there was a need to pool resources for long-term regional cooperation. Recognizing asymmetries at the development levels and the fact that the share of SAARC in world trade was relatively small, the Meeting recommended that analytical studies need to be earned out in the first instance to facilitate identification of priority areas for economic cooperation. As a result of this recommendation, a consultant was commissioned to carry out a Study on Trade, Manufactures and Service (TMS) in the South Asian region. Meanwhile, the National Planning Organizations continued to meet and agreed on a series of initiatives which would intensify the consultative process particularly in basic needs programmes and poverty alleviation.

The TMS Study, which was completed in 1991, considered economic cooperation among the countries of the SAARC region as an inevitable imperative for promoting all-round development of the region. In May 1991, the Council of Ministers at their Ninth Session at Male endorsed the Study and established a high-level Committee known as the Committee on Economic Cooperation (CEC) comprising Commerce/Trade Secretaries of the SAARC Member States.

The CEC was mandated to formulate and oversee implementation of specific measures, policies and programmes within the SAARC framework to strengthen and enhance Intraregional cooperation in the fields of trade and economic relations. With the creation of the CEC, regional economic cooperation was formally institutionalized. To date, the CEC has held ten meetings.

Over the years, the CEC has emerged as one of the most important groups within the SAARC having a mandate over economic and trade issues. The CEC has provided recommendations and guidance in identifying new areas for cooperation on economic and trade related matters as well as considering reports of constituted groups. In fact, the mandate of the CEC includes monitoring cooperation in areas such as standards and measurement; customs and the harmonization of procedures; preferential trading arrangement; rules of origin; agreements for the promotion and protection of investments within the SAARC Region as also for the avoidance of double taxation; setting up of a SAARC Arbitration Council; sharing information on economic and trade related matters; taking note of special circumstances of Least Developed Countries within the region; and formulation of joint strategies to be adopted in multilateral negotiating fora. The recommendations of the CEC are submitted to the Standing Committee (of Foreign Secretaries) and through it to higher bodies, namely the Council of Ministers and the Summit. In December 1991, the Sixth Summit held in Colombo approved the establishment of an Inter-Governmental Group (IGG) to formulate an agreement to establish a SAARC Preferential Trading Arrangement (SAPTA) by 1997. Given the consensus within SAARC, the framework Agreement on SAPTA was finalized in 1993, and formally came into operation in December 1995, well in advance of the date stipulated by the Colombo Summit. The Agreement reflected the desire of the SAARC countries to promote and sustain mutual trade and economic cooperation within the SAARC region through exchange of concessions. Three Rounds of Trade Negotiations have so far been completed under SAPTA. In SAPTA-I, trade concessions were offered to 226 commodities by all the countries. In SAPTA-II, trade concessions were offered to 1868 products reflecting an increase by almost ten fold over SAPTA-I. In SAPTA-III, trade concessions were increased to 3456 commodities reflecting almost a doubling over SAPTA-II. During the First and Second Round, trade negotiations were conducted on a product-by-product basis. In the Third Round, the negotiations were also conducted chapter-wise. For the Fourth Round, it had been decided that the negotiations would as far as possible, be conducted on Chapter-wise, Sectoral and Across-the-Board basis.

The Tenth Summit (Colombo, 1998) had decided that in order to accelerate progress in the next round of SAPTA negotiations, deeper tariff concessions should be extended to products which are being actively traded, or are likely to be traded, among members; that discriminatory practices and non-tariff barriers should be simultaneously removed on items in respect of which tariff concessions are granted or have been granted earlier. Measures to remove structural impediments should also be taken in order to move speedily towards the goal of a South Asian Free Trade Area (SAFTA). The Summit also directed that the domestic content requirements under SAPTA Rules of Origin be reduced. The Summit affirmed that benefits of the process be equitably shared by all member states. One of the core principles of the SAPTA Agreement is that there should be special treatment for Least Developed Countries through the consideration of additional measures. It was accordingly decided in 1999 to reduce the domestic content requirement further under the SAPTA Rules of Origin to enable the smaller and Least Developed Countries to benefit equitably from economic liberalization. This reduction would apply to all products covered so far in the trade negotiations. Recognizing the important role economic cooperation plays in South Asia, the first meeting of SAARC Commerce Ministers was held in New Delhi (8-9 January, 1996). Since then, two more Ministerial Meetings (29-30 April, 1998 in Islamabad and 2-3 February, 1999 in Dhaka) have been held focussing on enlarging the scope and coverage of regional economic cooperation.

SAPTA was envisaged primarily as the first step towards the transition to a South Asian Free Trade Area (SAFTA) leading subsequently, towards a Customs Union, Common Market and Economic Union. In 1995, the Sixteenth session of the Council of Ministers held in New Delhi (18-19 December) agreed on the need to strive for the realization of SAFTA and to this end an Inter-Governmental Expert Group (IGEG) was set up in 1996 to identify the necessary steps towards moving into a free trade area. The Male Summit in 1997, had recognised the importance for achieving a Free Trade Area.

Free Trade Area

Recognizing the need to address asymmetries in development and other complexities that may stand in the way of such a tight schedule, the Colombo Summit directed that the text of the regulatory framework for creating a Free Trade Area in the Region should be finalized. In this connection, a Committee of Experts has been constituted to draft a comprehensive treaty which has, following its first meeting in Kathmandu (July 1999) worked out its broad terms of reference. Eventually, the treaty would incorporate, inter alia, binding time frames for freeing trade, measures to facilitate trade, protection of LDCs including mechanisms for compensation of revenue loss, etc. With the setting up of the Committee of Experts, the IGEG was wound up.

SAARC has also initiated action on a series of practical measures to facilitate the process of economic integration. A Group on Customs Cooperation was set up in 1996 and so far, has held three meetings. It was *interalia* decided to harmonize HS lines and customs rules and regulations; simplify procedures for intra-regional exports; upgrade infrastructural facilities and provide training facilities. A Customs Action Plan was drawn up in Islamabad (April 1997) and agreed to by all Member States.

The need to improve the transport infrastructure and transit facilities in the region was recognized and the 11th Session of the SAARC Council of Ministers in Colombo (8-9 July 1992) directed the CEC to take appropriate steps in this regard. Accordingly a study was commissioned to assess the existing transport infrastructure and transit facilities, including procedural and documental issues in the region in relation to volume and composition of the existing trade in the region and to make recommendations for their improvement, with a view to enhancing trade within and outside the SAARC region. The study was completed in 1994 and had made farreaching recommendations.

It is relevant to mention at this stage that the Technical Committee on Transport was established in 1983, covering three major segments of transport, i.e. land transport, divided into railways and roadways; sea transport sub-divided into inland waterways and shipping; and air transport. Seventeen meetings of this Committee have been held. Subsequently, according to new arrangements of the Integrated Programme of Action (IPA), the Technical Committee on Transport has been merged with Communications forming a single Technical Committee on Transport and Communications effective from January 2000.

A draft Regional Investment Agreement is under consideration of the member states and is meant to create conditions favourable for promoting and protecting investments in member states by investors from other member states of the region. The objective is to finalize the Regional Investment (Promotion and Protection) Agreement prior to the commencement of the implementation of SAFTA.

Linked to the Regional Investment Agreement is the setting up of a SAARC Arbitration Council for which proposals are under examination by Member States. Discussions have also commenced on harmonizing tax laws within the Region to assess the possibility of having a Regional Agreement for the Avoidance of Double Taxation. Recognizing the importance of standards and measurement. Standards, Testing and Certification Bodies of the Member States met in New Delhi (June 1999) to identify how national standards may be harmonized and regional standards agreed upon.

In the area of trade and tariff which are critical to individual member states and to the region as a whole, particularly those relating to multilateral negotiations in World Trade Organization (WTO), World Customs Organization (WCO), World Intellectual Property Organization (WIPO) etc., regular consultations are held not only at the headquarters of such international organizations, such as Geneva, but also in the member states themselves, so as to effectively coordinate, project and protect their collective interests. This process of consultations has been intensified so that wherever possible, a regional position may be taken which is compatible with the overall principles of SAARC, and which reflects the needs and requirements of the LDCs in the region through the provision of special and more favourable concessions. In this regard, SAARC Commerce Ministers issued a Declaration on the eve of the Second WTO Ministerial Conference (Geneva 1998). Consultations were also held with regard to the WTO Ministerial Conference held in Seattle (30 November to 3 December 1999) and the SAARC Commerce Ministers had issued a preliminary Joint Statement on the issues to be considered at that Meeting.

Role of Chambers of Commerce

The important role played by the Chambers of Commerce and Industry in the region has been given special emphasis. The SAARC Chamber of Commerce and Industry (SCCI) was set up in 1992 as the first recognized regional Apex Body. SCCI brings together under one umbrella the national chambers of commerce and industry of the member states and is actively engaged in the promotion of trade and the interaction of the business community within the SAARC region. SCCI has been involved not only in increasing public awareness through workshops and studies they have been commissioning, including the publication of books and other material, but also through the interactive sessions between government and industry aimed at providing pertinent input to the process of regional economic cooperation. The SCCI also holds regular consultations with the SAARC Secretariat. The SCCI recently brought out a book tided *SAARC Means Business: Opportunities for Partnership* which highlights sectors of cooperative advantage within the region.

Indeed, it was in recognition of the positive role played by the SCCI that the member states decided to wind up the Technical Committee on Tourism (which was set up in 1991) to replace it with SCCI Tourism Council based on inputs from the SAARC Chamber of Commerce and Industry. This Council which represents the private sector perspective towards enhancing and gainfully exploiting the tourism potential of the region would provide policy and other inputs for the consideration of the Committee on Economic Cooperation (CEC).

Organizing SAARC Trade Fairs has become a regular feature since 1996 when the first Trade Fair was held in India. The Second SAARC Trade Fair was held in Colombo 1998. Pakistan is to host the next SAARC Trade Fair. The trade fairs have succeeded not only in projecting the potential of the region but also in promoting the wide variety of products the region produces which match international quality and standards. The SAARC Secretariat has also set up stalls at Trade Fairs to inform the public of SAARC activities. At the Colombo Summit, there was consensual recognition of the need to strengthen the individual financial systems of the SAARC countries through the enhancement of their institutional capacity, surveillance mechanism, as well as through closer consultations on, and coordination of, macroeconomic policies where appropriate. It was felt that the region needs to enhance the collective capacity of SAARC in respect of policy analysis with specific emphasis on international financial and monetary, trade and investment issues along with their domestic ramifications. In this regard, meetings of finance officials of the SAARC countries have been held, including among the Governors of Central Banks to not only put into position early warning mechanisms, but also to coordinate policies to respond to global financial and economic developments that affect the region.

It was also agreed at the Colombo Summit in 1998 to establish a Network of Researchers comprising members of the private sector, central banks, planning ministries, research institutes and eminent economists nominated by Governments to identify, analyse and help SAARC face up to current global financial and economic issues affecting the region. Such a network has since been set up and has decided on an immediate and longer-term research agenda which would help identify areas of common concern, as also new areas of cooperation among the member countries. The Network has also brought out a South Asian Economic Journal and would be bringing out a Directory of Research Institutes in South Asia focussing on global financial and economic issues. Successive Summits have acknowledged the importance of SAARC pursuing mutually beneficial cooperation with regional, UN and other international organisations on the Association's agreed areas of cooperation.

Memorandum of Understanding

In terms of external linkages, SAARC and United Nations Conference on Trade and Development (UNCTAD) signed a Memorandum of Understanding in February 1993 on UNCTAD Database on Trade Control Measures and Trade Analysis and Information System (TRAINS). As envisaged under the MOU, the UNCTAD Database is updated for the SAARC Member States by the SAARC Secretariat. The latest issue of CD-ROM TRAINS (Spring 2000 Version 7.0) contains trade control measures of 113 countries of the world including 51 tariff schedules of 1999 as well as 1998 import data by origin at the Harmonized System 6-digit level for 49 countries. The data in respect of all SAARC countries, except, the Maldives, is also available in the CD-ROM TRAINS. Similarly, a Framework Cooperation Agreement was signed between SAARC and Economic and Social Commission for Asia and the Pacific (ESCAP) (February 1994) to provide for cooperation on developmental issues through joint studies, workshops and seminars and exchange of information and documentation in poverty alleviation, human resource development, trade promotion, foreign direct investment, environmental protection and prevention of drug trafficking, infrastructure development, etc. ESCAP has also established an institutional mechanism of Consultative Meetings of the Executive Heads of Sub-regional Organisations in Asia and the Pacific (SAARC, Economic Cooperation Organization (ECO), Association of South East Asian Nations (ASEAN), South Pacific Forum) and ESCAP.

A Memorandum of Understanding on Administrative Cooperation between SAARC and the European Commission (now European Union was) entered into (July 1996). The Secretary-General was authorised by the Twenty-sixth Session of the Council of Ministers in Nuwara Eliya, (18-19 March 1999) to discuss with EC, specific areas of possible cooperation under the MOU. Agreement has been reached on four programmes as follows:

(a) facilitating access into the Single European market;
(b) implementation of the EU-GSP Scheme including cumulative rules of origin;
(c) drawing on the EU experience for the SAFTA process; and
(d) evolving common SAARC standards and harmonisation with international obligations including certification, testing, etc.

Since 1998, SAARC has had an informal Ministerial-level dialogue with ASEAN and the European Union on the sidelines of the UN General Assembly in New York. Informal discussions of an exploratory nature at the level of Secretary-General have also been initiated with the Gulf Cooperation Council.

Among the various areas of cooperation within SAARC, economic cooperation appears to have gained considerable momentum. This is derived to some measure from the changing global economic environment and its apparent unpredictability. The Tenth Summit Declaration (Colombo, 1998) had expressed serious concern over the severe distortions produced by the process of unrestrained globalization as has been evidenced in the downturn of economies of several Asian states. At the same time, negotiations in the multilateral economic fora appear to disadvantage developing and Least Developed Countries and there is urgent need to not only develop joint positions and strategies but also to find ways and means of protecting natural resources, heritage and knowledge. In addition to both the above compulsions is the recognition within the region that it is indeed blessed with considerable resources, both natural and human, which not only identifies it as a market but also as a major trading partner provided it is in a position to build on its competitive and comparative advantages.

Tapping the Potential

The SAARC brings together countries which, in combination, offer a wide range of opportunities for development.

The region is already the powerhouse for manpower to the Middle East and to the burgeoning economies of South-East Asia. It would be fair to say that labour inputs from SAARC nations provided the boost these economies needed in order to reduce manpower costs and to remain competitive. The SAARC region is already a significant provider of:

•agricultural produce from tea to exotic fruits to coconut oil, •manufactured goods from garments to gloves to industrial machinery, •services from tourism to construction to software development. However, much of the potential in all these areas remains untapped.

The SAARC region represents an untapped market of over a billion people, the majority of whose incomes have now started to rise. An integrated approach towards development, which SAARC hopes to promote with the establishment of SAPTA and SAFTA, would finally provide access to the whole of South Asia, as a common market.

FIVE

The Major Player (India)

India is the major player in the arena of SAARC. With its population and area, India is the largest country in the SAARC region. It has an area of thirty-two lakh eighty-eight thousand square kilometers and its share in the region's area is around 73.4 per cent. The country lies south of the Himalayas and extends to the Indian Ocean. India is located between latitude 8° 04' and 37°18' North and longitude 68° 08' and 97° 24' East. It is bordered by four SAARC countries namely Pakistan, Nepal, Bhutan and Bangladesh besides China and Burma. The other two SAARC countries namely Sri Lanka and Maldives, though not connected by common border being Islands, can be also considered as border countries. Thus India stands as a center of the SAARC region both location-wise and area-wise.

Population

The population of India had crossed 1000 million by the time of the census of 2001 and it was over 77 per cent of the total population of the region. The annual exponential growth rate of population during the period 1991-2001 was around 21.3. The life expectancy at birth is estimated to be 62.3 years during 2000-01. In 1990, the crude birth rate per thousand was 26.4 and crude death rate per thousand was estimated to be 69. The percentage of literacy rate was 65.38 in 2000-01. The density of population per Sq. km. is around 324 according to the census 2001 in the country.

Agriculture based Economy

India is an agriculture-based country sharing nearly 31 percent of the GDP in 2001. While the share of industry is 30 per cent, the manufacturing sector alone contributes nearly 20 per cent in 2001. The analysis of the share of GDP exhibit that the share of agriculture is decreasing, while the share of industry and manufacturing is increasing. This indicates that the country is shifting to developing and industrial economy. The per capita income of the country was estimated at 2230 US Dollars in 2001 and the real growth rate estimated for the last decade, 1990-2000 was 3.5 per cent. But the real growth rate during the period 2000-2001 was only 2.9 per cent. This was because of the adverse impact of the Gulf crisis. High oil prices, the return of migrant workers and the embargo on trade with some countries of Middle East have slowed the economy and exacerbated the macro-economic imbalances. Though during the various Plans, the growth target was comfortably achieved, the macro-economic imbalances deteriorated significantly with the emergence of persistent fiscal and balance of payments deficits and high level of external and domestic debt.

Fiscal Situation

The strained fiscal situations of the late eighties reached a critical situation in 1990-91 by the deteriorated foreign exchange reserves, the decline in exports and the high inflation deepened the crisis. But the timely initiation of the efforts by the government in 1991-92 brought the economy back on the rails. As a corrective measure the government tried to encourage indigenous industries and improve the competitiveness of the industrial sector particularly export-oriented industries. The important policy initiatives comprised reduction in fertilzer subsidy, abolition of Cash Compensatory Support (CCS) for exports, abolition of subsidy on sugar disinvestment in selected public sector undertakings. A reduction of 4.5 per cent over the previous year was initiated in the provision for non-plan expenditure.

The process of fiscal consolidations continued in 1992-93. The economic growth was only 1.2 per cent in 1991-92 and it was significantly lower than the growth of 2.5 per cent of the previous year's projection. 1992-93 was also not a year without set backs. The irregularities in securities trading, the riots and communal tension prevailed in the country in December 1992. This disrupted the transporting system, slowed the growth of exports and industrial productions and reduced the revenue. Though, without these setbacks, there would have been faster recovery in the economy, the prospects for the year 1992-93 were distinctly better than 1991-92 and the GDP was expected to grow more than four per cent. Even in later years, the process was continued, but it is still needed to continue the initiated reforms in the industrial and trade policies to enhance the efficiency of the economy and to improve the international competitiveness of India's exports.

Position of Trade

Exports: The main components of India's exports are readymade garments, leather and leather products, handicrafts, gems and jewellery, chemicals and allied products, machinery, transport equipments, engineering goods, metal products, iron and steel, cotton, iron ore, fish and fish preparations, etc. India is considered as an agriculture-based country and the export of agricultural and allied products constituted nearly 31 per cent of the total exports during the period 1980-81 and earned foreign exchange worth $ 2601 million during the period. In this category, tea and mate was the single largest commodity sharing nearly one-fifth and 6.3 per cent of the total export earnings But the share of agriculture and allied products in the total exports came down to 27.7 per cent in 1985-86 and further to 19.4 per cent in 1990-91. The share of agriculture and allied products came down to 18.7 per cent in 1991-92, even though nearly 30 per cent increase was recorded in rupee terms. This was because of the sharp decline in the export of raw cotton by 74 per cent and marginal decrease of 17.4 per cent in the exports of tea and mate in dollar terms. Though the export of tea and mate increased marginally in rupee terms, raw cotton declined in rupee terms also.

Fish and fish preparations was the largest foreign exchange earner in this classification and earned $ 585 million in 1991-92 recording nearly 9.3 per cent annual growth rate. The share in total exports was 8.9 per cent in 1991-92 while it was only 3.2 per cent in 1980-81 thus showing a significant increasing trend.

The export of tea and mate was nearly 6.3 per cent of the total exports in 1980-81 though, the value of export marginally increased by 10.7 per cent during this period. But in 1991-92, its share in the total exports was only 2.75 per cent and the value of exports also decreased by 17.4 per cent from the previous year.

The export of raw cotton was nearly 2.5 per cent of the total exports in 1980-81 and marginally increased only to 2.6 per cent in 1990-91 even though, the value of exports increased from $ 209 million to $471 million during the period. But in 1991-92, the export of cotton came down to $ 124 million and as a result the share of its exports declined to 0.7 per cent.

The export of ores and minerals constituted nearly 6.2 per cent of the total exports in 1980-81 and increased to 7.2 per cent in 1985-86. But in 1990-91, the share in the total exports declined to 4.6 per cent even though the exports increased from $ 641 million in 1985-86 to $ 834 million in 1990-91. In 1991-92, the exports of these items declined by 1.3 per cent over the previous year and the share of exports remained at 4.6 per cent due to decline of exports by 1.5 per cent in dollar terms.

Foreign Trade

(Rs. in crore)

Year	*Exports*	*Imports*	*Total value of foreign trade*	*Balance of trade*
1990-91	32,557.63	43,192.86	75,750.49	-10,635.23
1991-92	44,041.81	47,850.94	91,892.65	-3,809.03
1992-93	53,688.25	63,374.52	1,17,062.77	-9,686.27
1993-94	69,751.39	73,101.01	1,42,852.40	-3,349.62
1994-95	82,674.11	89,970.66	1,72,644.77	-7,296.55
1995-96	1,06,333.34	1,22,678.14	2,29,031.48	-16,324.80
1996-97	1,18,817.08	1,38,919.68	2,57,736.76	-20,102.60
1997-98	1,30,100.64	1,54,176.30	2,84,276.94	-24,075.66
1998-99	1,39,753.14	1,78,331.85	3,18,084.99	-38,578.71
1999-2000	1,59,561.00	2,15,528.00	3,75,089.00	-55,967.00
2000-2001	2,01,674.00	2,27,512.00	4,29,246.00	-25,898.00

The components of manufactured goods are textile fabrics and manufactures, leather and leather manufactures, handicrafts, chemicals and allied products and machinery and transport equipments. The share of manufactured goods in the total exports was nearly 55.8 per cent in 1980-81 and increased to 58.5 per cent in 1985-86. The share further increased to 73 per cent in 1990-91 and to 74.2 per cent in 1991-92. This exhibits a continuous and significant increase in the exports of manufactured goods.

The single largest foreign exchange earner in the manufactured goods is textile fabrics and manufactures. It was nearly 14 per cent of the total exports in 1980-81 and increased to 16.5 per cent in 1985-86. In 1990-91, the share of its exports stood at 21.3 per cent of the total exports and readymade garment alone constituted 12.3 per cent while cotton yarn and fabrics shared 6.4 per cent. In 1991-92 the share of readymade garments remained at 12.3 per cent while the cotton yarn and fabrics increased to 7.3 per cent of the total exports. As a result, the share of textile fabrics and manufactures to total exports increased to 22.9 per cent in 1991-92 and it constituted nearly 31 per cent of the total manufactured goods exported.

Handicrafts is another important component constituting nearly 25.5 per cent of the manufactured goods and its share in the total exports was 14.2 per cent in 1980-81. It increased to 17.3 per cent in 1985-86. The share of its exports increased to 19 per cent in 1990-91 and almost remained at the same level in 1991-92. In Handicrafts, Gems and Jewellery alone constituted 85 per cent in 1990-91 and nearly 81 per cent in 1991-92. The share of exports of gems and jewellery was around 16 per cent of the total exports in 1990-91 and marginally declined to 15.3 per cent in 1991-92 while the export of these items was only 9.2 per cent of the total export in 1980-81.

The share of export of machinery, transport equipments, engineering goods, metal products and iron and steel constituted nearly 12.3 per cent of the total exports in 1980-81 and marginally declined to 11.9 per cent in 1990-91. But in 1991-92 its share in the total exports were around 12.5 per cent.

The main component of India's exports to Bangladesh is cotton yarn and fabrics and it amounted at Rs. 31655.28 lacs in 1991-92. The share of its exports to total exports to Bangladesh stood at 39.1 per cent in that year. The other main items of exports to Bangladesh during 1991-92 are machinery and instruments (8.9%), fruits and vegetables (8.7%), spices (6.2%), man made yarn, fabrics and made ups (5%), drugs, pharmaceuticals and fine chemicals (3.9%), rubber manufactured products (3.5%) and transport equipments (3.1%). The total of other insignificant export items constituted nearly 21.6 per cent of the total exports in 1991-92.

The main component of India exports to Bhutan is transport equipments and it amounted to Rs. 124.48 lacs in 1991-92, which were nearly 42.1 per cent of the total exports to that country. The other items of exports to Bhutan in 1991-92 were miscellaneous processed items (14.1%), primary and semi-finished iron and steel (9.9%), machinery and instruments (3.1%), manufactures of metals (3%), tea (2.1%) and ores and minerals (1.8%). The total of other insignificant items constituted nearly 23.9 per cent of the total exports in 1991-92.

The major component of India's exports to Maldives is cotton yarn, fabrics and made ups. It amounted to Rs. 267.81 lacs in 1991-92 and its share of exports to the total exports to Maldives stood at 22.8 per cent in that year. The composition of other items and their respective shares in the total exports are manufactures of metals (9.4%), fruits and vegetables (8.2%), drugs and pharmaceuticals (7.8%), and raw cotton and accessories (6.1%).

The largest component of India's exports to Nepal is transport equipments. The export of this item amounted to Rs. 3485.12 lacs in 1991-92 and its share in the total exports to Nepal was 17.7 per cent. The composition of other items of export and their respective share in the total exports to Nepal during the year 1991-92 are drugs and pharmaceuticals (11.9%), machinery and instruments (8.8%), glass, glassware, ceramics, and cement (8.8%), paper and wood products (6.8%), unmanufactured tobacco (5%), wheat (3.4%), coal (2.7%), processed items (3.5%), cotton yarn, fabrics and made ups (2.7%) and rubber manufactured products (3.4%).

Iron ore constituted nearly 21.1 per cent of India's total exports to Pakistan in 1991-92 and it amounted to Rs. 2077.68 lacs in that year. The other components of exports to Pakistan and their respective share in the total exports are oil meals (13.8%), dyes, tar and chemicals (9.6%), spices (9.2%), paint, enamel and varnish (7%), ores and minerals (5.3%), drugs, pharmaceuticals and fine chemicals (4.8%), as well as machinery and instruments (2.8%) during 1991-92.

Nearly one-fourth of the exports of India to Sri Lanka was

transport equipments during 1991-92. It amounted to Rs. 10409.49 lacs and its share in the total exports to that country stood at 24.3 per cent. Cotton yarn fabrics and made ups constituted 12.9 per cent and sugar and molasses, 7.3 percent during the same period. The other components are drugs, pharmaceuticals and fine chemicals (6.8 per cent), spices (6.4 per cent), fruits and vegetables (5.3 per cent), paper and wood products (3.9 per cent), man made yarn, fabrics, and made ups (4.4 per cent) and machinery and instruments (4.6 per cent).

The main components of India's imports are petroleum oil and lubricants, chemicals, pearls, precious and semi-precious stones, iron and steel, non-electrical machinery, fertilisers and fertiliser materials, non-ferrous metals.

Imports: The largest component of India's imports is petroleum, crude oil and petroleum products. It amounted to $ 6656 million in 1980-81 and its share in the total imports was nearly 42 per cent in that year. In 1985-86 the import of this item declined by 38.7 per cent in terms of dollar from 1980-81 and hence the share also declined to 25.4 per cent. In 1990-91 the annual growth rate was nearly 60 per cent and the imports amounted to $ 6028 million which was nearly 25 per cent of the total imports of the country. In 1991-92 the imports of this item declined by 11 per cent in terms of dollar and the share in the total imports increased by 27.6 per cent and this was due to the import curbs earned by the foreign exchange crisis. The imports of this item for April-November 1992 registered a 38.2 per cent increase over the corresponding previous period in terms of rupee.

Another important component of India's imports is the capital goods. In 1980-81 it amounted to $ 2416 million and it was 15.2 per cent of the total imports in that year. In 1985-86 the imports increased to $ 3503 million which was 21.8 per cent of the total imports. In 1990-91 the imports of this item recorded an annual growth rate of nearly 10 per cent and the share also increased to 24.2 per cent. But the annual growth rate in 1991-92 was 27.4 per cent as the imports declined to $ 4233 million and as a result the percentage share in the total imports also declined to 21.8 per cent. However, the items under this group increased by 33.8 per cent during April-

November 1992 over the corresponding previous period in terms of rupee.

Non-electrical machinery apparatus and appliances formed nearly 38.5 per cent of the total Capital goods imported in 1991-92. The import of this item was nearly 8.4 per cent of the total imports of 1991-92 while its share in 1990-91 was 9.8 per cent. The value of the import also declined by nearly 31 per cent in 1991-92 over the previous year. Pearls, precious and semi-precious stones are another major component of India's imports. In 1980-81, their import amounted to $ 527 million which was only 3.3 per cent of the total imports. But in 1985-86 their share in the total imports increased to 5.5 per cent and further increased to 8.7 per cent in 1990-91. Though their import declined by 6 per cent in terms of dollars in 1991-92 but in rupee terms it increased by 29.1 percent and the percentage share increased to 10.1 per cent. During April-November 1992, the import of gems amounting to Rs. 4271.98 crores increased by 35.9% over the corresponding period of the previous year.

Iron and steel which constituted nearly 6.8 per cent of the total imports in 1980-81 increased to 7.1 per cent in 1985-86. But in 1990-91 the import of this item declined by 14.9 per cent over the previous year and the share of its imports also declined to 4.9 per cent. In 1991-92 there was a sharp decline of import of iron and steel and also as a result of decline of total imports, the share of imports declined to 4.1 per cent. But during April-November 1992 the import of this item registered an increase of 38.1 per cent in terms of rupee.

Chemicals and chemical materials which is another major component of India's imports sharing nearly 2.9 per cent of the total imports in 1980-81. Though the share of import of this item increased to 5.5 per cent in 1985-86, the share declined marginally to 5.3 per cent in 1990-91. In 1991-92 the annual growth rate in respect of this item was 8.1 per cent over the previous year and its share in the total imports increased to 7.1 per cent. During April-November 1992 the import of this item registered an increase of 51.7 per cent over the corresponding period of the previous year.

News print imported from Bangladesh constituted nearly 29.1 percent of the total imports in 1991-92 and it is the single largest item imported from that country. Organic Chemical's share in the total imports was around 4.7 per cent in the same year. The other items imported from Bangladesh include metalifers ores and metal scrap, textile yarn and fabrics, transport equipments, non-ferrous metals, pearls, precious and semi-precious stones, etc. But none of these items had significant share in the imports from that country.

The share of wood and wood products was nearly 39 per cent of the total imports from Bhutan, during 1991-92. In the same year the import of inorganic chemicals stood at Rs. 45.14 lacs and its share in the total imports was 38.9 per cent. Coal, coke and briquettes another component of imports from Bhutan constituted nearly 6.9 per cent of the total imports from that country in 1991-92.

The imports from Maldives was not significant during 1991-92 and hence no single commodity was substantial enough to analyse although the imports from that country amounted to Rs. 6.47 lacs.

Printed books, newspapers and journals constituted the single largest items of import from Nepal and its share in the total imports from that country was around 17.11 percent in 1991-92. The share of vegetable oil in the total imports was nearly 7.7 per cent and the share of oil seeds was around 4.3 per cent during 1991-92. The cereal preparations constituted nearly 1.5 per cent of the imports from Nepal. The other components of imports such as crude minerals, wood and wood products, sugar, cereals, etc., did not have significant share in the total imports from Nepal.

The largest components of India's imports from Pakistan are fruits and their total amounted to Rs. 3188.26 lacs which was nearly 20.8 per cent of the total imports from that country. Nearly 9.2 per cent of the imports was constituted by textile yarn, fabrics and made up articles. The composition of other items of imports are metalifers, ores and metal scrap, crude minerals, wool, pearls and semi-precious stones and it did not have significant share in the total imports from that country.

The largest component of India's imports from Sri Lanka is metalifers, ores and metal scraps and it amounted to Rs. 709.07 lacs. The share of its total imports from Sri Lanka was around 25.3 per cent during 1991-92. The share of organic chemicals in the total imports was 13.3 per cent while the share of natural rubber was around 11.5 per cent. The composition of other items of imports and their respective share in the total imports are iron and steel (9.3 per cent), machinery (2 per cent), manufactures of metals (1.5 per cent), pulp and waste paper (1.5 per cent) and synthetic and reclaimed rubber (1.3 per cent).

External Trade: Trends

India being the largest economy among the SAARC countries has the largest volume of trade. The exports amounted to $ 8441 million in 1980, these increased by 4.6 per cent in 1981 and by 9.1 per cent in 1982. In 1983 it amounted to $ 9681 million which was less than a half per cent increase over the previous year. But in 1984, the exports declined by nearly 15 per cent for the first time during the decade and the increasing trend bounced back in 1985 with an annual growth rate of 0.4 per cent. The export performance in terms of volume of growth was 2.7 per cent per annum during the period 1980-85 i.e. the Sixth Five Year Plan period and the exports as per cent of GDP was 5 per cent during the same period. The overall exports during the pre-SAARC period i.e. 1980-85 was showing a negative trend as the exports in 1985 was less 0.3 per cent of 1980.

In 1986 the exports amounted to $ 9135 million, which was 10.5 per cent more than the previous year. Since then the exports were on an increasing trend. The annual growth rate increased to 18.2 per cent in 1986 and further to 20.2 per cent in 1988. Though the exports increased to $ 17814 million in 1990 from $ 15365 million of 1989. The annual growth rate declined to 15.9 per cent in 1990 from 18.4 per cent of the previous year. During the period 1985-90 i.e. the Seventh Five Year Plan period the volume of growth in exports was around 6.3 per cent per annum. Although the share of exports to GDP has been raising, the performance for the Seventh Plan period as a whole has not been distinctly better and the exports as a percentage of GDP rose only to 5.1 per cent during the same period.

In 1991, the exports amounted to $ 20,491 million and the annual growth rate was nearly 15 per cent during the year. But the exports during 1992 declined by nearly 1.5 per cent in terms of dollars while in terms of rupee it increased by 35.3 per cent. But the exports recorded a 5.5 growth rate in terms of dollars during the first six months of 1992-93 i.e. April to September over the same period of the previous year. The new trade promotion policies introduced in the nineties started yielding results and they should be allowed to continue without any constraints in the years to come.

Direction of Foreign Trade

(Rs. in crore)

Region/Sub-Region	*Exports*		*Imports*	
	1999-2000	*2000-2001*	*1999-2000*	*2000-2001*
West Europe	43,310.79	51,333.49	59,446.65	61,431.15
European Common Market	39,257.55	45,900.58	45,635.55	44,730.07
European Free Trade Area Countries	2,952.46	3,744.04	13,383.03	16,694.76
Rest of Europe	1,100.78	1,688.87	428.07	6.32
Asia and Oceania	60,062.93	75,899.96	1,01,925.92	62,357.44
Africa	8,167.98	10,723.46	28,648.91	9,333.86
America	41,737.03	50,081.68	21,139.26	17,872.69
North America	38,833.70	45,378.36	17,092.42	14,576.17
South America	1,669.98	2,749.41	3,594.77	2,936.39
Other America	1,233.35	1,953.90	452.07	360.13
East Europe	5,605.78	5,978.98	4,275.65	3,854.75

The imports amounted to $ 14,882 million in 1980 and they significantly increased by 21.5 per cent in 1981. Though there was a marginal increase of less than one per cent in 1982 the annual growth rate was negative in 1983 and 1984 and it was 7.6 per cent and 9.6 percent respectively. In 1985 the imports increased to $ 16,329 million and this was more than eight per cent of the previous year. The volume of growth of imports during the period 1980-85 i.e. the 6th Plan period was 6.9 per cent and the imports as a per cent of GDP was 8.1 per cent during the same period. Though the imports exhibited a mixed trend during the pre-SAARC period under the study, the average annual growth rate was 1.9 per cent.

The imports amounted to $ 15051 million in 1986 and the annual growth rate was negative at 7.8 per cent. But in the following years of the decade the imports recorded an increasing trend. In 1987 the annual growth rate was 11.9 per cent while in 1988 it was 13.6 per cent. Though the imports grew only by 0.6 per cent in 1989, it sharply increased to $ 23529 million in 1990, which was the highest recorded since 1980 and the average growth rate was 22.3 per cent. The volume of growth of imports during the Seventh Plan was 9.8 per cent and the imports as a per cent of GDP was 7.3 per cent. The average annual growth rate recorded during the decade was 5.8 per cent while in the Seventh Plan alone it was 8.8 per cent.

In 1991, the imports amounted to $ 21687 million which was 7.8 per cent less than the imports of the previous year. This was due to the severe pressure on the balance of payment caused by the gulf crisis and political instability in the country. During 1991-92, the imports declined by nearly 19.4 per cent over the previous year while in terms of rupee it increased. But the data available for the period April to September in the year 1992-93 states that there is an increase in imports by 22.5 per cent over the previous period. The new trade policy implemented by the present Government, the full convertibility offered and the bringing back of economy on the rails forced the imports to move upwards.

The balance of trade was always unfavourable to India and it was $ 6441 in 1980 this increased to $ 9253 in 1981. This was due to the higher growth rate recorded in the imports than the exports. The adverse position began to decline since then and came down to $ 6884 million in 1984. But in 1985 the adverse position bounced back to $ 8064 million. The adverse balance of trade, though exhibited a mixed trend, it came down to $ 3874 million in 1989. Though it increased by 47.5 per cent over the previous year as there was higher growth rate recorded in respect of imports over exports in 1990, the adverse balance of trade declined by nearly 79 per cent in 1991 and the trade deficit was $ 1195 million in 1991. This was because of the negative growth rate of imports by 7.8 per cent while the exports in that year increased by nearly 15 per cent over the previous year. The trade balance as a per cent of GDP was negative 3.4 per cent for 1980-85 i.e. pre-SAARC period and marginally declined to negative 3.2 per cent for 1985-90, i.e. the post-SAARC period. In 1990-91 the trade balance as a per cent of GDP was 2.9 per cent.

India's trade with SAARC countries was not substantial during the last decade and the position also did not have substantial change in the post-SAARC period. The exports to SAARC countries was never above 5 per cent of the total exports of India. The exports to SAARC countries amounted to $ 3.7 million in 1980 and it was 3.6 per cent of the total exports in that year. The exports to the region declined by more than 25 per cent in 1981 and by 14 per cent in 1982 and it forced the percentage of total exports to decline to 2.6 per cent and 2 per cent respectively. But in the following two years the annual growth rate was on an increasing trend. In 1985 the exports to SAARC countries amounted to $ 270 million which was nearly 14.3 per cent less than the exports of the previous year. The exports to SAARC as a percentage of total exports also declined from 3.8 per cent in 1984 to 3.3 per cent in 1985. During the pre-SAARC period, i.e. 1980-85, though the exports exhibited a mixed trend, they actually came down by nearly 2 per cent and also the percentage to total exports by 0.3 per cent.

During the post-SAARC period exports to SAARC were showing an upward trend. The exports to the region was $ 277 million in 1986, they increased by 10.5 percent in the following year and the annual rate of growth in 1988 was nearly 19 per cent. In 1989, the growth in exports declined to 4.1 per cent. This was because of the decline of exports to Nepal, a major trading partner in the region, due to the strained trade relationship. In 1991, the exports amounted to $ 949 million and the rate of growth recorded was 94.9 per cent against 28.5 per cent of the previous year. The reason for this substantial increase in the exports to SAARC was because of sharp increase in the exports to Maldives. In the post-SAARC period the trend was upwards and the exports to the region more than doubled during the period. But the proportion to total exports increased only marginally because of the increase in the total exports.

The imports from SAARC countries were not significant for India and it amounted to $ 141 million in 1980 and marginally increased by 6.4 per cent over the previous year in 1981. But in the following two years the imports declined considerably and the annual negative growth rate was 20 per cent and 25.8 per cent in 1982 and 1983 respectively. The upward trend shown in the beginning of eighties again bounced back and in 1984 the imports increased by 18.7 per cent over the previous year. The imports from the region amounted to $ 112.02 million in 1985 and the annual growth rate came down to 6 per cent in that year. Though the imports from SAARC countries exhibited a mixed trend the imports actually declined by 5.1 per cent annually during the pre-SAARC period.

Import of Principal Commodities

(Rs. in crore)

Commodities	*1999-2000*	*2000-01*	*Percentage Change*
A. Bulk Imports	85,400.34	95,224.84	11.50
i) Cereals	961.50	85.17	(-)91.14
ii) Fertilizers	6,062.74	3,407.41	(-)43.80
iii) Newsprint	960.07	1,189.48	23.89
iv) Petroleum Crude & Petroleum Products	54,648.60	71,496.52	30.83
v) Edible Oil	8,046.05	5,932.76	(-)26.27
vi) Pulp and waste paper	1,105.64	1,274.40	13.26
vii) Non-Ferrous metals	2,369.84	2,404.41	1.46
B. Pearls precious and Semi-precious Stone	23,555.78	21,966.90	(-)6.74
C. Machinery	19,850.05	19,675.59	(-)4.92
D. Project Goods	4,272.61	2,901.28	(-)32.10
E. Other items:	82,449.75	88,004.87	6.74
i) Organic and Inorganic chemicals	12,420.28	11,139.87	(-)10.31

ii) Coal, coke and briquettes	4,368.36	5,039.99	15.37
iii) Medicinal and pharmaceutical products	1,616.22	1,701.47	5.27
iv) Artificial resins, etc.	3,117.68	2,529.36	(-)18.87

Export of Principal Commodities

(Rs. in crore)

Commodities	*1999-2000*	*2000-2001*	*Percentage Change*
Plantations	3,219.52	3,164.57	(-)1.71
Agricultural and allied products	15,880.01	17,666.38	11.25
Marine products	5,124.56	6,36.9.37	24.27
Ores and Minerals	3,969.78	5,290.12	33.26
Leather and manufactures	6,890.87	8,915.23	29.38
Sports goods	290.16	314.66	8.45
Gems & Jewellery	32,509.43	33,760.71	3.85
Chemical and related products	21,285.75	28,249.86	32.72
Engineering goods	19,005.78	26,111.62	37.39
Electronics hardware	3,148.89	5,112.63	62.36
Project goods	170.68	123.42	(-)27.69
Textiles	39,733.22	49,318.18	24.12
Handicrafts	2,897.37	3,053.09	5.37
Carpets	2,795.36	2,656.03	(-)4.96
Petroleum products	129.91	8,309.97	6,296.71
Unclassified exports	1,966.86	3,870.15	96.77

In 1986, the imports from the region declined to more than one-third over the previous year and the imports amounted $ 73.02 million in that year. Though the imports increased in the subsequent two years they declined by 41.3 per cent over the previous year in 1989. This was because of the sharp decline in the imports from-Nepal due to the strained trade relationship. The increasing trend bounced back in 1990 and the annual growth rate in that year was 79.6 per cent and further increased by 20.6 per cent in 1991. The imports in 1991 amounted to $ 117 million which was 4.4 per cent more than the imports of 1985. This analysis of the import data exhibits that unlike the pre-SAARC period, the imports in the post-SAARC though showed a mixed trend, and they actually increased marginally with an average annual growth rate less than one per cent.

The exports to SAARC countries as a proportion of total exports stood at 3.6 per cent in 1980 and marginally declined in the early eighties. In 1985, the share of exports to SAARC countries stood at 3.3 per cent to the total exports, and a declining trend was observed during the second half of the last decade. Though the share of exports to SAARC was only 2.7 per cent in 1990, they increased to 4.6 per cent in 1991 which was the highest recorded since 1980. The current position of exports to SAARC countries is less significant. Hence, it is vital for the economic development of the country to promote exports to SAARC countries and it is expected to reap the benefit of SAPTA by India, being the largest economy in the SAARC region.

The degree of relationship between the exports to SAARC countries and India's total exports is established by the concurrent deviation method of correlation. The calculation of the correlation between the set of variables during the post-SAARC period show that there is a perfect correlation. But during the pre-SAARC period there is a high degree of negative correlation to the extent of 0.8. As a result, the degree of relationship between the total exports and SAARC exports during the period 1980-1991 was showing a moderate correlation of 0.8.

The imports from SAARC as a percentage of total imports stood at 0.95 per cent in 1980, these declined to 0.69 per cent in 1985. As a result of higher growth rate recorded in the total imports than the imports from SAARC, the imports from the region as a proportion of the total imports declined further to 0.54 per cent in 1991. This reveals that the imports from SAARC both in terms of value as well as the proportion to total exports had declined from 1980 to 1991.

The degree of relationship between the imports from SAARC countries and India's total imports is established by the concurrent deviation method of correlation. The calculation of the correlation between the imports from SAARC countries and total imports shows that there is a moderate amount of positive correlation during the post-SAARC period as the value of correlation is 0.44. But during the pre-SAARC period the value of correlation was -0.44. As a result, the value of correlation for the period under study, i.e. 1980-91 stood at negative 0.3 showing a negative relationship between the two set of variables.

India had favourable balance of trade with SAARC countries. The favourable balance stood at $ 166 million in 1980. But due to decline in the exports to the SAARC region and the imports increasing marginally, the favourable position declined by 52.4 per cent in 1981 and further by 2.5 per cent in 1982. The upward trend of exports and the marginally declining trend in imports pushed the favourable balance of trade upwards in the subsequent years. The favourable balance of trade was $ 157.98 million in 1985, this increased to $ 271.98 million in 1988. But in 1989 the favourable balance of trade increased by 19.5 per cent over the previous year, though the exports increased only by 4 per cent. This was attributed to the sharp decline in the imports from SAARC countries. An upward trend was also exhibited in the early nineties. In 1980 the favourable balance of trade increased by 20 per cent over the previous year while in 1991 it almost doubled. The trend of balance of trade with SAARC countries indicates that the favourable positions actually declined during the pre-SAARC period, i.e. 1980-85 by almost 4.8 per cent while it increased by almost four times during the period of 1985-91. In later years, the trend continued in a positive direction, though the results have not been satisfactory.

SIX

India's Trade with SAARC Nations

Bangladesh

India had substantial trade relations with Bangladesh during the last decade. India's exports to Bangladesh amounted to $ 106 million in 1980 and these were nearly 34.5 per cent of the exports to the SAARC region though they were only 1.3 per cent of the total exports made during the year. The exports to that country showed a declining trend in the early eighties. The negative growth rate recorded in respect of exports to Bangladesh was 45.3 per cent in 1981 and in 1982 the negative growth declined to 32.8 per cent. The exports to Bangladesh as a proportion of exports to the SAARC also declined and in 1983 they were around 14.6 per cent of the exports to the region. In 1984 the exports increased almost one and half times over the previous year and since then they exhibited an upward trend. The share in the exports to the region also began to rise and it was 38.5 per cent in 1985 while the exports to that country amounted to $ 104 million which was 1.9 per cent less than the exports of 1980. The above analysis indicates that the exports to Bangladesh were on a declining trend during the pre-SAARC period, i.e. 1980-85. The exports to Bangladesh were having an increasing trend during 1985-90. The exports amounted to $ 113 million in 1986 and increased at an annual growth rate of 28.3 per cent in 1987. Though the exports had only a growth rate of 17.2 per cent in 1988, they sharply increased in 1989 and as a result the annual rate of growth increased to 50 per cent in that year. The increasing trend continued in 1990 at a growth rate of 16.5 per cent and the exports in that year amounted to $ 297 million and these were the highest recorded during the last decade. But in 1991, the increasing trend reversed back and the exports declined by 46.5 per cent over the previous year. Though the exports amounted to only $ 159 million in 1991, they were 52.9 per cent more than the exports of 1985 and the overall analysis of the exports to that country exhibit an increasing trend during the post-SAARC period. The imports from Bangladesh stood at $ 12 million in 1980 and they increased by 83 per cent in the following year. There was no annual rate of growth in 1982, and it declined by 64 per cent in 1983. But in 1984, the imports from that country doubled over the previous year and the imports stood at $ 27 million. The figure of 1985 exhibits an increasing trend of 7.4 per cent over the previous year. The overall analysis of the imports during the pre-SAARC period, i.e. 1980-85 indicates that it increased with an average annual growth rate of 23 per cent during the period. But in the post-SAARC period, the trend of imports from Bangladesh exhibited a different trend. The imports came down to $ 8 million in 1986 which was nearly 72.5 per cent less than the previous year. Though the increasing trend bounced back in the following two years, it again declined by 6.7 per cent in 1989. In the early nineties the imports from that country increased. In 1991 they amounted to $ 26 million against the figure of $ 15 million of 1990 and the annual rate of growth in 1991 was 73.3 per cent against 7 per cent of the previous year. Though the imports were on a declining trend during 1985-91 by 1.7 per cent annually, the imports during 1980-91 were on an increasing trend with an average annual growth rate of 10.6 per cent. The exports to Bangladesh as a proportion of exports to SAARC countries stood at 40.8 per cent in 1986 and they increased to 47.4 percent in the following year. The percentage rose to 67.3 per cent in 1989 and the percentage share came down to 61 per cent in 1990 even though the exports to that country increased. This was because of the increase of exports to other SAARC countries. In 1991 the proportion of exports sharply declined to 16.5 per cent and this was the result of decline in the exports to that country as well as sharp increase in the exports to other SAARC countries particularly to Maldives. The imports from Bangladesh as a proportion of imports from SAARC countries stood at 8.5 per cent in 1980 and they increased in the early eighties. In 1983, the percentage of imports declined to 0.9 per cent from 18.3 per cent of the previous year. This was because the declining rate of imports from that country were more than that of the declining rate of imports from SAARC region. But in 1984 and 1985 the percentage was more than one-fourth of the imports from SAARC and it stood at 25.7 per cent and 25.9 per cent respectively. Though the percentage declined during the later half of the eighties, it bounced back in 1989 to 25.9 per cent. In 1990 the percentage of imports from Bangladesh as a proportion of imports from SAARC declined to 15.5 per cent and it was due to sharp increase in the imports from SAARC region. As a result the rate of growth of imports from that country was more than the imports from SAARC region, the proportion of imports increased to 22.2 per cent. The trade with Bangladesh was favourable to India during the last decade. The favourable balance amounted to $ 94 million in 1980 and declined sharply in the early eighties and in 1982, it amounted $ 17 million. In 1983, the trade balance increased to $ 26 million and since then was on a continuous upward trend upto 1990, when the favourable trade balance reached at its maximum of $ 282 million which was the highest recorded during the decade. This was because of the upward trend shown in the exports to that country and a fluctuating declining trend shown in the exports from that country. But in 1991 and later, the favourable trade balance declined to $ 133 million which was nearly 52.8 per cent less than the previous year. This was because of the decline of exports by 46.5 per cent and increase in the imports by 73 per cent.

Bhutan

India is the only country in the SAARC region which has substantial trade relation with Bhutan. More than ninety per cent of Bhutan's external trade was with India. Bhutan's total exports amounted to 131.5 million Ngultrum in 1980 increased to 272 million Ngultrum in 1985 exhibiting an increasing trend during the pre-SAARC period. During the post-SAARC period the exports of that country increased substantially and almost two-fold increase was recorded. The exports of Bhutan amounted to 1387.6 million Ngultrum in 1990 and out of this nearly one-third constituted for electricity. The imports of Bhutan which stood at 394.6 million Ngultrum in 1980 increased to 1041.6 million in 1985 and further to 1243.9

million in 1990 even though the rate of growth of imports was showing a declining trend in the late nineties. The balance of trade was always unfavourable to Bhutan during the pre-SAARC period and the adverse position increased during the same period. The trade deficit continued in the early post-SAARC period and in 1990, the country had a favourable balance of trade for the first time. The exports of India to Bhutan was not significant during the last decade. It was well below one per cent of the total exports to the region. The exports amounted to Rs. 2.96 crores during 1991-92 out of which nearly 42 per cent was transport equipments. According to the figures available for the period April-July 1992, the exports to Bhutan amounted to Rs. 1.89 crores showing an increasing trend in the exports to that country. Like exports, the imports from Bhutan were not significant and as far as India is concerned, it was negligible though the trend was increasing. During 1991-92 the imports from Bhutan stood at Rs. 1.16 crores, out of which nearly two-third were for the import of wood and wood products.

Maldives

India's trade with Maldives has been substantial during the last decade. The amount of exports amounted to $ 3 million in 1980 and declined to $ 1 million in 1985 after the exhibition of steady trend during the early eighties. The exports to Maldives as a proportion of exports to SAARC countries was only one per cent and in 1985 it was not at all significant, i.e. 0.37 per cent. But in the post-SAARC period the exports to that country exhibited an increasing trend. The exports amounted to $ 2 million in 1986 which increased to $ 3 million in 1988. But in the following year the exports to that country doubled to reach $ 6 million. Though there was a decrease of 16.7 per cent in the exports to Maldives in 1990, there was a tremendous increase in the exports to that country in 1991 to become the largest export market of India in that year. More than half of the exports to the SAARC countries were to Maldives and its share stood at 61.6 per cent in 1991. In 1991-92 the exports to that country amounted to Rs. 11.71 crores and the provisional figures available for 1992-93 (April-Aug.), i.e. only for first five months recorded the exports at 12.99 crores. The present trend is encouraging especially the trend of exports in the post-SAARC period and this can be further enlarged if export potential to that country is further identified and promoted. India's imports from Maldives were not substantial and not even significant during the last decade. However, the establishment of Indo-Maldives Joint Economic Commission and its first meeting held at Male in January 1990 yielded its results in early nineties. The imports from that country amounted to Rs. 0.06 crores in 1991-92. There was an increasing trend in the nineties and according to the figures available for the first five months, i.e. April to August, the imports from that country increased to Rs. 0.13 crores. The specific steps for promoting Indo-Maldives trade were discussed in the Second Meeting of the JEC's which was held al New Delhi in 1992 and it is hoped that it will further expand the trade between these countries.

Nepal

India's exports to Nepal were significant in the early eighties. They were nearly $ 95 million in 1980 and almost remained stagnant in 1981. But in 1982, the annual growth rate was negative and tht exports to that country came down by nearly $ 10 million. Though the exports bounced back to $ 95 million in 1984, the recorded annual growth rate was again negative in 1985 and it was around 13.7 per cent in that year. Thus, the figures available for the pre-SAARC period under the present study exhibit that though there was a mixed trend during the period, the exports to that country declined to almost 2.7 per cent annually from 1980 to 1985. The pre-SAARC period trend continued upto 1988 in the post-SAARC period. The exports to that country were $ 82 million in 1986 and remained at the same figure in 1988, though there was a decline of nearly 11 per cent in 1987. But in 1989, the exports to Nepal sharply declined by nearly 61 per cent over the previous year and it was due to the worsened trade relations with that country. But in the early 90's the exports picked up by 25 per cent in 1990 and 12.5 per cent in 1991. This was because of the improved trade relations with that country. The exports to that country during the post-SAARC period showed a declining trend and the declining rate during the period 1986-91 was around 9 per cent annually, and the trend continued. The imports from Nepal amounted to $ 21 million in 1980 and almost remained stagnant in the following year. But in 1982, the imports from that country declined by 9.5 per cent. In 1984, the imports almost doubled and the increasing trend continued in 1985 also. Thus, the import figures exhibit an increasing trend during the pre-SAARC period and the average annual growth rate in the imports during 1980-85 was around 27.6 per cent. But the post-SAARC period began with a declining trend and the imports declined by 20 per cent over the previous year in 1986, though a marginal increase was recorded in the following two years. The imports from Nepal came down to $ 3 million in 1989 from $ 44 million in 1988 and this was due to the adverse trade relation which existed between these countries in 1989. But due to improved trade relations in 1990 the imports from that country made almost a fourfold increase and increased further by 20 per cent in 1991. Thus, the trend that was declining in the late eighties, improved in early nineties. Though the imports declined from $ 40 million in 1986 to $ 18 million in 1991, the trend show in the early nineties was encouraging, which continued in a positive manner. The share of exports to Nepal as a proportion of exports to SAARC countries was significant in the early eighties. It was nearly 31 per cent in 1980 and sharply increased to 41.5 per cent in 1981. This was not because of the increase in the exports to that country, but due to a sharp decline in the exports to SAARC countries. As a result of a fall in the rate of growth in the total exports to SAARC there was a fall in exports to Nepal, the percentage again rose to 43.2 per cent in 1983 which was the highest recorded during the last decade. Since then the share of exports to Nepal was declining. In 1985 it declined to 30 per cent and further to 22.5 per cent in 1988. But in 1989 the share sharply dipped to 8.4 per cent and further to 4.7 per cent in 1991. In 1990 and later, the fall in the share of exports to that country was not only because of the fall in the exports to that country but also due to the annual rate of growth of total exports to SAARC was more than the rate of growth of exports to Nepal. The share of imports from Nepal as a proportion of imports from SAARC was nearly 15 per cent in 1980 and increased throughout the pre-SAARC period. The main reason attributed to it is the decline in the imports from other SAARC countries and increase in the imports from Nepal during the period. But the picture was not the same during the post-SAARC period. Nearly 55 per cent of India's imports from the SAARC region was from Nepal in 1986 and in the post-SAARC period the percentage started decreasing and came down to as low as 5.6 per cent in 1989 and this was due to the strained trade relationship between these two countries. But the share of imports from that country improved in 1990 to 15.5 percent. But due to the higher growth rate recorded in respect of imports from other SAARC countries apart from Nepal, the percentage marginally declined to 15.4 per cent in 1991 and in later years. India was having a surplus in trade with Nepal since 1980. In 1980, the trade surplus was around $ 74 million favourable to India and remained at the same figure in the following year. The favourable position which India was enjoying started declining in the following year. In 1983 it came down to $ 66 million and further to $ 32 million in 1985. Thus, the trade surplus began to decline in the pre-SAARC period under the study itself. In the post-SAARC period also the declining trend continued. Though, there was a marginal rise in 1986 to $ 42 million, the trade surplus declined to $ 38 million in 1988 and further to 25 million in 1990. Later due to more increase in the exports than the imports from Nepal the favourable position of India increased to $ 27 million setting an upward trend favourable to India. Nepal was the largest export market of India among the SAARC countries during the pre-SAARC period. But in the post-SAARC period the share of exports to Nepal as a proportion of exports to SAARC declined considerably and in the early nineties the share of exports was negligible. As regards the imports, percentage share as well as the total imports increased in the mid-eighties but declined significantly in the early nineties. The declining trend should be reversed to have more trade between these countries.

Pakistan

India's exports to Pakistan were not significant in the early eighties. They were nearly $ 2 million in 1980 and around $ 6 million in 1983. They again increased by 83 per cent over the previous year in 1984 and marginally by 9 per cent in 1985. Thus, the figures available for the pre-SAARC period indicates that during the pre-

SAARC period the exports to Pakistan were having a continuous increasing trend as the exports almost increased five times from the figure of 1980 to 1985. But the picture was not the same during the post-SAARC period. Though the exports to that country increased by 8 per cent in 1986, they came down by nearly 8 per cent in 1987. But in the succeeding three years there was significant increase in the exports to that country and the exports almost increased by more than three times. The highest exports since 1980 were recorded in 1990 and they amounted to $ 43 million in that year. But in 1991, the exports to that country recorded a negative annual growth rate of nearly 12 per cent as the exports came down to $ 38 million. In fact, India's exports to Pakistan have never been constant, due to uncertain relationship, and tension, every now and then. India's imports from Pakistan were not only significant but also substantial among the SAARC countries earlier. The imports amounted to $ 76 million in 1980 and since then a downward trend was observed during the early eighties. During the pre-SAARC period under study, only in 1985 there was an upward trend in the imports from Pakistan and it increased by nearly 40 per cent over the previous year. But in 1986, the negative annual growth rate bounced back to 46 per cent and the lowest amount of imports were recorded in that year. But, after that the imports from that country had a continuous increasing trend. The imports from Pakistan increased to $ 51 million in 1991 from $ 45 million of the previous year and thereby recording an annual growth rate of more than 13 per cent. The trend continued till the relations between the two countries got spoiled again. The share of India's exports to Pakistan as a proportion of total exports to SAARC was not only less substantial but also insignificant. It always stood well below 10 per cent throughout the decade. It was less than one per cent of the total exports to SAARC countries in 1980 and even though, the percentage share of exports to Pakistan continuously increased during the SAARC period under the study, it never reached 5 per cent. The increasing trend of percentage of exports to Pakistan exhibited a mixed trend during the post-SAARC period under the study. Though the share increased to 4.7 per cent in 1986, it declined to 3.9 per cent in 1987 and the increasing trend continued upto 1990 where the share of its exports to Pakistan stood at 8.8 per cent. But due to sharp increase in the exports to other SAARC countries and due to decline in the exports to that country the percentage of exports came down to 4 per cent in 1991 itself and the trend continued later also. The percentage of imports from Pakistan as a proportion of imports from SAARC stood at 54 per cent in 1980. As the imports were declining, the share of imports from Pakistan also declined considerably. The percentage declined to 46.7 per cent in 1982 and further to 19 per cent in 1984. In 1986, the declining rate of imports from Pakistan was more than the declining rate of imports from SAARC and hence the percentage dipped from 25 to 20.5 per cent. Since then, the percentage share of imports from Pakistan improved during the late eighties. But in 1990, though the imports increased by nearly 73 per cent, the total imports from SAARC countries increased by 79.6 per cent and as a result the share of imports from Pakistan declined to 46.4 per cent in 1990 from 48.1 per cent of 1989. Due to the same reason the share further dipped to 43.6 per cent in 1991 itself. Trade with Pakistan was always unfavourable to India during the later decades. During the early eighties the adverse position was very high and it was due to insignificant exports to Pakistan. But as exports picked up and the imports declined the trade deficit with Pakistan began to decline. The adverse position which was $ 74 million in 1980 declined to $ 25 million in 1983. Though the trade deficit declined to $ 9 million in 1984 it increased to $16 million in 1986. Thus, the trade deficit in the pre-SAARC period itself declined considerably, though there were heavy variations in the trade deficit during the post-SAARC period. The adverse position even came down to $ one million in 1989. But in 1990 the adverse position increased to $ 2 million and it was due to the higher growth rate recorded in respect of imports from that country. In 1991 there was a sharp increase in the trade deficit and it was due to 13 per cent annual growth rate recorded in the imports from Pakistan while the exports to that country declined annually by 11.6 per cent in that year. As a result, the adverse balance of trade increased to $ 13 million in 1991, and the trend continued in the coming years. India's imports from Pakistan had been substantial; but its exports to that country were not significant. The discriminatory policy adopted by Pakistan had been constraining India's trade with Pakistan. While India accorded

MFN status to Pakistan, Pakistan did not grant MFN status to India even after several rounds of discussions in this matter. It was due to the apprehension that the Pakistan's domestic markets would be flooded by Indian goods if it encouraged imports from India. Though there was a Sub-Commission on Trade headed by the Commerce Ministry in the Indo-Pakistan Joint Commission, it had not achieved its results. The existing political hostility between these two countries should be reduced to have meaningful economic co-operation and Pakistan should be willing to offer MFN status to India to improve the trade relation with India especially in reducing India's trade deficit with that country.

Sri Lanka

India had significant trade relations with Sri Lanka during the last decade. The exports to that country amounted to $ 101 million in 1980 and it was nearly one-third of the total exports to the region. In 1981 the exports to that country declined by nearly 30.7 per cent and further declined by 5.7 per cent in 1982. But the following two years exhibited an upward trend of 59.1 percent and 11.4 percent respectively. The declining trend bounced back in 1985 and the exports amounted to $ 71 million which were 39.3 per cent less than the previous year. During the Sixth Plan period i.e. during 1980-85 which is also considered as the pre-SAARC period under the study, the exports to Sri Lanka though exhibited a mixed trend, actually declined by 5.9 per cent per annum on an average basis. The declining trend continued in 1986 and the exports to Sri Lanka declined marginally by 5.6 per cent over the previous year. But in 1987 the exports increased by 10.5 per cent and further by 21.6 per cent in 1988. In 1989 the exports to that country amounted to $ 61 million which were the lowest recorded since 1980 and they were 32.2 per cent less than the exports of the previous year. The nineties began with an encouraging note. In 1990, the exports increased by 67.2 per cent over the previous year. In 1991, they increased to $ 122 million against $ 102 million of the previous year and the annual growth rate was 19.6 per cent of that year. During 1986-91 i.e. the post-SAARC period, the average annual growth rate of exports to Sri Lanka was 16.4 per cent against, the declining rate of the pre-SAARC period. India's imports from Sri Lanka amounted to $ 32 million in 1980 and marginally increased by 3 per cent in 1981. But in 1982 the imports from that country declined by 30.3 per cent, though the annual rate of growth in 1983 was 34.8 per cent. The declining trend bounced back in the following two years and it was 54.8 per cent in 1984 and 64.3 per cent in 1985. The analysis of the Sixth Plan period data exhibits that the imports from Sri Lanka declined considerably during the pre-SAARC period and they came down to $ 5 million in 1985 and the average annual negative growth rate was 16.9 per cent during 1980-85. Unlike in the pre-SAARC period, the imports from Sri Lanka showed an increasing trend except in 1987 where they decreased by 40 per cent over the previous year. The imports from that country stood at $ 11 million in 1989 and they doubled in 1990. The imports from Sri Lanka remained stagnant in 1991 and as they did not decline it was favourable sign of the regional co-operation, the trend continued in later years. During the early eighties, nearly one-third of India's exports to the region were to Sri Lanka. In 1983, the exports to this country stood nearly 45 per cent of the total exports to SAARC countries and this proportion was the maximum recorded during the decade. Though the percentage fluctuated during the pre-SAARC period it never came down below one-fourth of the exports. But during the post-SAARC period the trend of proportion of exports to Sri Lanka declined sharply. Later, the proportion came down to 12.9 per cent from 20.9 per cent of the previous year though the exports to that country increased by nearly 20 per cent over the previous year. The imports from Sri Lanka as a proportion of imports from SAARC stood at 22.7 per cent in 1980 and in the early eighties the percentage of imports declined marginally. In 1983, more than one-third of India's imports from the SAARC region were from Sri Lanka. As the imports from that country fluctuated and declined considerably the percentage of imports also declined significantly. In 1985 the percentage came down to 4.5 per cent, which was the largest recorded during the decade. But the percentage of imports marginally improved as the imports from that country increased. The percentage increased to 20.4 percent in 1989 from 7.6 percent of the previous year and this was due to the increase in the imports from that country by 57 per cent over the previous year and also due to the decline in the total imports from the SAARC region by 41.3 per cent over the previous year. Though the imports doubled in 1990, the share in the percentage of imports marginally increased to 22.7 per cent in 1991, later, and it declined to 18.8 per cent while the imports from that country remained stagnant. India was having a favourable trade balance with Sri Lanka throughout the last decades. The favourable position stood at $ 69 million in 1980. Though it came down to $ 39 million in 1981, due to a fall in the exports to that country, the favourable position improved further in the following three years. The maximum favourable position was recorded in 1984 when it reached at $ 103 million. Though the favourable position continued in the post-SAARC period as in the case of the pre-SAARC period, the favourable position was fluctuating and it was due to an inconsistent growth of imports and exports and even some times was due to a decline in the amount of trading. The favourable position which stood at $ 83 million in 1988 declined to $ 50 million in 1989. But it rose to $ 80 million in 1990 and further to $ 100 million, later, and went on rising. The increasing trend in the exports should be encouraged and also efforts should be made to increase the proportion in the exports to the region. To have a meaningful co-operation, the expansion of exports can be facilitated by the identification of the export potential products, which helps in the diversification of export products to Sri Lanka. India has found a market in Sri Lanka but it is yet to become a source of import among the SAARC countries. Though the exports to that country was rising, the imports from that country almost stood stagnated. While looking for export potentials India should identify the products that can be imported and adequate attention should be given to the imports to have better trade with that country. The analysis of India's composition and trend of trade exhibits that the trade recorded reasonably good growth rates and the economy diversified its industrial base and it provided a high degree of economic self-reliance. The exports as well as imports, increased considerably during the last decade. But due to gulf crisis and global economic recession, the exports kept a low profile. The instability of the government in the early nineties and the internal disturbances in December 1992 also added to the crisis. The foreign exchange crisis which the economy faced in the early nineties forced the government to curb the imports. But due to more liberalisation of the economy and the new export-import policy, the international trade started picking up. This is evident from the fact that the exports during the period of April 1992 to January 1993 increased by 2.2 per cent over the corresponding period of the previous year. The analysis of India's trade with SAARC countries exhibits that there exists a high degree of instability and commodity concentration. Now, SAPTA is hoped to enhance the country's trade with other member. countries of SAARC by reducing the tariff barriers and eliminating the non-tariff barriers.

PART 2

Summits

SEVEN

Eleven Summits

I. DHAKA SUMMIT

SOUTH ASIAN ASSOCIATION FOR REGIONAL COOPERATION DECLARATION

The Dhaka Declaration of the Heads of State or Government of the Member Countries of South Asian Association for Regional Cooperation issued on 8th December 1985.

INTRODUCTION

1. The President of Bangladesh, the King of Bhutan, the Prime Minister of India, the President of Maldives, the King of Nepal, the President of Pakistan and the President of Sri Lanka met in Dhaka on 7 and 8 December 1985.
2. The Heads of State or Government underscored the historic significance of their first ever South Asian Summit meeting. They considered it to be a tangible manifestation of their determination to cooperate regionally, to work together towards finding solutions towards their common problems in a spirit of friendship, trust and mutual understanding and to the creation of an order based on mutual respect, equity and shared benefits.
3. They recognized that periodic meetings at their level were central to the promotion of mutual trust, confidence and. cooperation among their countries.
4. The Heads of State or Government reaffirmed that their fundamental goal was to accelerate the process of economic and social development in their respective countries through the optimum utilization of their human and material resources, so as to promote the welfare and prosperity of their peoples and to improve their quality of life. They were conscious that peace

and security was an essential prerequisite for the realization of this objective.

5. The leaders of the South Asian countries reaffirmed their commitment to the UN Charter and the principles governing sovereign equality of States, peaceful settlement of disputes, non-interference in internal affairs and non-use or threat of use of force against the territorial integrity and political independence of other States. They reiterated that the United Nations constituted the most important forum for the resolution of all issues affecting international peace and security.
6. They also reaffirmed their deep conviction in the continuing validity and relevance of the objectives of the Non-aligned movement as an important force in international relations.
7. The Heads of State or Government acknowledged that the countries of South Asia, who constituted one-fifth of humanity, were faced with the formidable challenges posed by poverty, underdevelopment, low levels of production, unemployment and pressure of population compounded by exploitation of the past and other adverse legacies. They felt that, bound as their countries were by many common values rooted in their social, ethnic, cultural and historical traditions, regional cooperation provided a logical response to these problems. They were conscious of their individual and regional strengths, their potential as a huge market, their substantial human and natural resources and the complementarities of their economies. They were confident that with effective regional cooperation, they could make optimum use of these capacities for the benefit of their peoples, accelerate the pace of their economic development and enhance their national and collective self-reliance. They were convinced that their countries, which had made important contributions to the enrichment of human civilization, could together play their due role in international relations and influence decisions which affected them.
8. The Heads of State or Government emphasised that strengthening of regional cooperation in South Asia required greater involvement of their peoples. They agreed to increase interaction and further promote people-to-people contacts at various levels

among their countries. To this end, they decided to take steps to create awareness and public opinion in the region.

9. The Heads of State or Government welcomed the progress already made in the implementation of the Integrated Programme of Action in the nine mutually agreed areas. They expressed their desire to consolidate and further expand cooperative efforts within an appropriate institutional framework in a spirit of partnership and equality.
10. The leaders were convinced that they could effectively pursue their individual and collective objectives and improve the quality of life of their peoples only in an atmosphere of peace and security. In this context, they expressed concern at the deteriorating international political situation. They were alarmed at the unprecedented escalation of arms race particularly in its nuclear aspect. They recognized that mankind today was confronted with the threat of self extinction arising from a massive accumulation of the most destructive weapons ever produced. The arms race intensified international tension and violated the principles of the UN Charter. The leaders called upon the nuclear weapons-states for urgent negotiations for a Comprehensive Test Ban Treaty leading to the complete cessation of testing, production and deployment of nuclear weapons. In this connection, they welcomed the recent meeting between President Reagan and General Secretary Gorbachev in Geneva and expressed the hope that the meeting would have a positive effect on international peace and security.
11. The Heads of State or Government expressed deep concern at the continuing crises in the global economy. They underscored that deteriorating economic and social conditions had seriously retarded developing countries. Sharply falling commodity prices, deterioration in the terms of trade, intensification of protectionist measures, spiralling debt burden and a decline in the flow of external resources, especially concessional assistance, had caused a serious setback to the economic development of the developing countries. These had been compounded by natural disasters and precarious world food security situation affecting developing countries. They also expressed concern over the diminishing

capacity of international financial and technical institutions to respond effectively to the needs of the disadvantaged and poorer countries and regretted that the spirit of multilateral cooperation had begun to falter and weaken. This was particularly disturbing in the face of increased interdependence of developed and developing countries and the fact that economic revival of North was closely linked to economic progress in South. They believed that developments during the past decades had clearly demonstrated the structural imbalances and inequities inherent in the existing international economic system and its inadequacy to deal with problems of development.

12. They strongly urged that determined efforts should be made by the international community towards realization of the goals and targets of the International Development Strategy as well as the Substantial New Programme of Action for the Least Developed Countries. They called for urgent resumption of the North-South dialogue and early convening of an International Conference on Money and Finance for Development with universal participation.

13. The Heads of State or Government were conscious of the historic importance of the Dhaka Summit and reiterated their conviction that the launching of the South Asian Association for Regional Cooperation (SAARC), which they had established at this meeting, would place regional cooperation on a firm foundation, play an important role in accelerating the pace of economic and social development of their countries, promote the objectives of individual and collective self reliance and further the cause of peace, progress and stability in their region and the world.

14. The Heads of State or Government of Bhutan, India, Maldives, Nepal, Pakistan and Sri Lanka were deeply appreciative of the exemplary Chairmanship of their Meeting by the President of Bangladesh. They expressed their profound gratitude for the warm and gracious hospitality extended to them by the Government and the people of Bangladesh and for the excellent arrangements made for the meeting.

JOINT PRESS RELEASE

Joint Press Release Issued at the Conclusion of the First SAARC Summit in Dhaka on 7-8 December 1985 The President of Bangladesh, the King of Bhutan, the Prime Minister of India, the President of Maldives, the King of Nepal, the President of Pakistan and the President of Sri Lanka met in Dhaka on 7 and 8 December, 1985. The Heads of State or Government signed a Charter of the South Asian Association for Regional Cooperation on the 8th of December, 1985. They also adopted the Dhaka Declaration. They approved that the Standing Committee should set up a Study Group to examine the problem of terrorism, as it affects the security and stability of Member States of SAARC. They further directed the Council of Ministers to consider the report of this Study Group and submit recommendations to them as to how best the Member States could cooperate among themselves to solve this. They also approved that a similar exercise be carried out with regard to the problem of drug trafficking and abuse. They decided that the Member Governments should concert their views on the ongoing discussions on New International Economic Order and the improvement of the World Trading System through GATT taking particularly into account the interest of the least developed among the developing countries. For this purpose it was decided to convene a Ministerial level meeting. The Standing Committee should convene a meeting to prepare for it. The Heads of State or Government gratefully accepted the offer of the President of Pakistan to host both these meetings. The Heads of State or Government emphasized that women should increasingly participate in activities at the regional level within the framework of SAARC and that Programmes and Projects should be devised to ensure their active participation in the development process. They therefore directed the Standing Committee to convene a Ministerial Level Conference on the subject to identify the areas of activities and plan a Programme of Action. They gratefully accepted the offer of the Prime Minister of India to host such a conference. The Heads of State or Government who have decided that the Association shall have a Secretariat directed the Foreign Ministers to consider details regarding its location, structure, functions and financing and submit those for the consideration of Heads of State or Government. The Heads of State or Government decided to hold their next meeting in November, 1986. They gratefully accepted the offer of the Prime Minister of India to host that meeting. They also gratefully accepted the offer of the King of Bhutan to host the Annual SAARC Summit of 1987. The Heads of State or Government unanimously accepted the recommendation of the Fourth Meeting of Foreign Ministers on the emblem of SAARC.

II. BANGALORE SUMMIT

SOUTH ASIAN ASSOCIATION FOR REGIONAL COOPERATION DECLARATION

The Bangalore Declaration of the Heads of State or Government of the member countries of the South Asian Association for Regional Cooperation issued on November 17, 1986.

INTRODUCTION

1. The President of Bangladesh, the King of Bhutan, the Prime Minister of India, the President of Maldives, the King of Nepal, the Prime Minister of Pakistan and the President of Sri Lanka assembled at the second SAARC Summit in Bangalore on 16 and 17 November, 1986.
2. The Heads of State or Government reiterated their desire of promoting peace, stability, amity and progress in the region through strict adherence to the principles of the United Nations Charter and Non-alignment, particularly respect for the principles of sovereign equality, territorial integrity, national independence, non-use of force and non-interference in the internal affairs of other States and peaceful settlement of disputes.
3. The Heads of State or Government reaffirmed the will of their peoples and Governments to work together in accordance with the SAARC Charter to devise common policies and approaches for finding common solutions to the shared problems that all of them face. They stressed that mutual trust, goodwill and understanding must animate their cooperative effort under SAARC. Progress and prosperity in each country would redound

to the benefit of others. This was what constituted the SAARC spirit.

4. The leaders reaffirmed that the principal goal of SAARC was to promote the welfare of the peoples of South Asia, to improve their quality of life, to accelerate economic growth, social programmes and cultural development in the region and to provide all individuals the opportunity to live in dignity and to realize their full potential.
5. The Heads of State or Government recalled that the countries of South Asia had been linked by age-old cultural, social and historical traditions. These had led to enriching interaction of ideas, values, culture and philosophies. These commonalities constituted solid foundations for regional cooperation for addressing more effectively the economic and social problems.
6. The Heads of State or Government recalled that the South Asian Association for Regional Cooperation was the most populous regional grouping in the world. The countries of the region had large, rich and varied human and natural resources. They expressed their determination to achieve the optimum utilization of these resources by intensifying their cooperation, bearing in mind the immense present and potential complementaries among their economies. They recognised that this would require increasing exchange among their countries, on the basis of mutual benefit, of ideas, experience and technology as well as goods and services, which utilize and enhance the productive capacity of each of their countries and build their collective self reliance. They were convinced that the countries of South Asia which had been the cradle of human civilization and culture could, acting together cooperatively and cohesively, once again play their due role in the comity of nations.
7. The Heads of State or Government reiterated the great importance of the increasing involvement of the people for ensuring the success of regional co-operation. They emphasized the need for promoting greater contacts among the peoples of the region through such action as regular and frequent interchange of scholars, academics, artists, authors, professionals and

businessmen as well as facilitation of tourism.

8. The Heads of State or Government noted with satisfaction that considerable progress had been achieved in the implementation of SAARC Integrated Programme of Action. They expressed their firm commitment to consolidate and streamline further the implementation of the IPA. They agreed that a progressive movement towards more concrete and action-oriented projects and programmes was essential to ensure more tangible benefits from SAARC to the peoples of the region. The Heads of State or Government emphasized the importance of expanding cooperative endeavours under SAARC. They welcomed the establishment of the Technical Committees on Women in Development, and on the Prevention of Drug Trafficking and Drug Abuse.

9. The Heads of State or Government welcomed the signing of the Memorandum of Understanding on the establishment of the SAARC Secretariat by the Council of Ministers and their decision to locate the Secretariat in Kathmandu and appoint Ambassador Abul Ahsan of Bangladesh as the first Secretary-General of SAARC. They were convinced that the establishment of the Secretariat would assist in the coordination of SAARC activities and more fruitful implementation of its programmes and projects.

10. The Heads of State or Government recognised that meeting the needs of all children was the principal means of human resources development. Children should, therefore, be given the highest priority in national development planning. The Heads of State or Government underlined the importance of enhancing public consciousness and building a national political consensus on the rights of the children. In this context they called for an early conclusion and adoption of the UN Convention on the Rights of the Child. They subscribed to the goals of universal immunization by 1990, universal primary education, maternal and child nutrition, provision of safe drinking water and adequate shelter before 2000 A. D. They also believed that it should be possible to ensure at the end of the century, that no child be in need or be denied development, for reasons of material poverty in the family. They directed the Standing Committee to undertake

annual reviews of the situation of children in the SAARC countries, monitoring of programmes and exchange of experience.

11. The Heads of State or Government agreed that co-operation among SAARC States was vital if terrorism was to be prevented and eliminated from the region. They unequivocally condemned all acts, methods and practices of terrorism as criminal and deplored their impact on life and property, social economic development, political stability, regional and international peace and cooperation. They recognized the importance of the principles laid down in UN Resolution 2625 which among others required that each State should refrain from organizing, instigating, assisting or participating in acts of civil strife or terrorist acts in another State or acquiescing in organized activities within its territory directed towards the commission of such acts.

12. The Heads of State or Government expressed their concern at the crisis facing the United Nations system. They reiterated their deep commitment to the purposes and principles of the United Nations Charter and their support for and faith in the United Nations as the most important international forum for addressing issues of peace, disarmament and development and an essential instrument for bringing about justice and equity in international political and economic relations. They resolved to concert their efforts in all multilateral fora within the United Nations system to preserve and strengthen the Organisation and to prevent erosion of its role, functions and principles.

13. The Heads of State or Government reiterated their deep commitment to the principles and objectives of the Non-aligned Movement and underlined the historic role the Movement had been playing in strengthening international peace, promoting development, establishing equitable and just economic relations and strengthening international cooperation in all fields. The success of the Harare Summit of the Non-aligned countries was yet another demonstration of the strength and unity of the Movement and the increasing respect 'that it had come to command in the international community. They affirmed full

support for the decisions adopted at the Summit and called for their early implementation.

14. The leaders of the South Asian countries were convinced that an environment of peace, security and respect for international law was essential for their growth and stability. Unfortunately, this environment had become increasingly adverse for the pursuit of their cherished goals. The international political scene was marred by strife and tension due to Great Power policies and practices of domination and intervention as well as the increased resort to the threat or use of force, aggression, occupation, pressure, economic coercion and interference in flagrant violation of the principles and purposes of the Charter of the United Nations. The arms race, particularly the nuclear arms race, had escalated to a point where it jeopardizes the most fundamental of all human rights - the right to live.

15. The Heads of State or Government noted with deep disappointment that the promise held out by the Reykjavik Summit could not be realized. They, however, noted with satisfaction that the proposals made at the Summit were still on the table. They expressed the earnest hope that the negotiations would be resumed without delay so that a decisive step could be taken towards realizing the ultimate goal of eliminating nuclear weapons altogether. The Heads of State or government called for the early conclusion of a Comprehensive Test Ban Treaty.

16. The Heads of State or Government were deeply concerned that the world economy continued to be in the throes of crisis, with particularly harsh and severe consequences for the economies and development prospects and aspirations of the developing countries. They endorsed the Declaration of the SAARC Ministerial Meeting on International Economic Issues held in Islamabad and its analysis of the exceptionally adverse external economic environment which retards the development of the South Asian and other developing countries. These negative factors include depressed commodity prices, rising protectionism, global recession, lower export earnings, net outflow of financial resources from developing countries and

an aggravated debt crisis.

17. The Heads of State or Government noted that the rates of growth in the developed countries had turned out to be much lower than what was earlier projected and that the projection for future growth in these countries was not at all encouraging. They expressed their concern at the implications of these trends for the development prospects of the developing countries. They welcomed the recent recognition by the developed countries that the chronic problems of massive payment imbalances, high interest rates, unstable exchange rates and high unemployment are structural in nature. In view of global interdependence, the coordination of macroeconomic policies, contemplated at the Tokyo Summit of the seven major industrialized countries, cannot be effective in achieving sustained global economic growth unless it encompasses the developing countries.

18. The leaders urged that the recent retreat from multilateralism should be urgently reversed through a revival of the North-South dialogue which is responsive to the changed circumstances in the world economy. This must include a process of reform of monetary and financial system, through an International Conference on Money and Finance for Development, and urgent measures for preserving and strengthening the multilateral trading system. In the search for revival of global growth, priority must be accorded to exploiting the vast potential for expanded production, consumption and trade which exists in the developing countries. In all these endeavours, high priority should be accorded to supporting the development of the least developed countries, in particular, through the full and effective implementation of the Substantial New Programme of Action for the Least Developed Countries for the 1980s.

19. The Heads of State or Government noted with satisfaction that at the SAARC Ministerial Meeting on International Economic Issues a number of priority objectives of the SAARC countries have been identified. These include: enlarged concessional assistance, the doubling in three years of the financial flows for the development of developing countries, amelioration of official debts, trade liberalization, especially in textiles and agriculture, commodity

price stabilization, transfer of technology and special treatment for least developed SAARC countries. The Heads of State or Government agreed that the SAARC members should closely and regularly consult and cooperate in relevant international economic conferences and institutions in order to promote the above mentioned objectives. They recognised that an important opportunity in this context would be provided by UNCTAD VII.

20. The Heads of State or Government were of the view that the forthcoming New Round of Multilateral Trade Negotiations posed a challenge for their countries as well as an opportunity to accelerate their development through the expansion of their exports. They underlined the importance of the effective implementation with immediate effect and continuance until the formal completion of the negotiations, of the commitment to observe a standstill on protectionist measures and to roll these back under multilateral surveillance. They also expected that the principles of transparency and differential and more favourable treatment for the developing countries would be applied systematically and in concrete terms in the negotiations. They decided to concert their positions in these negotiations with a view to deriving maximum benefits from them in accordance with their national objectives and priorities.

21. The Heads of State or Government expressed their conviction that the Bangalore Summit had helped in consolidating the gains of regional cooperation activities so far undertaken by SAARC while, at the same time, exploring new avenues and possibilities for such cooperation. The Bangalore Summit had made a significant contribution to strengthening and streamlining the institutional basis for such cooperation.

22. The Heads of State or Government reiterated their determination and will to expand and strengthen their cooperation under SAARC. They underlined their belief that SAARC reflected a resurgence of the South Asian consciousness which had inspired the peoples of this region over several millennia. The leaders expressed their deep conviction that South Asian regional cooperation would not only have a salutary effect on bilateral relations between the countries of the region, but also impart

strength and stability to these relations.

23. The Heads of State or Government of Bangladesh, Bhutan, Maldives, Nepal, Pakistan and Sri Lanka were deeply appreciative of the exemplary manner in which the Prime Minister of India discharged his responsibilities as Chairman of the Meeting. They expressed their profound gratitude for the warm and gracious hospitality extended to them by the Government and people of India and for the excellent arrangements made for the Meeting.

JOINT PRESS RELEASE

Joint Press Release Issued an November 17, 1986 at the End of the Second SAARC Summit, Bangalore.

1. The President of Bangladesh, the King of Bhutan, the Prime Minister of India, the President of Maldives, the King of Nepal, the Prime Minister of Pakistan and the President of Sri Lanka met in Bangalore on 16 and 17 November, 1986.
2. They issued the Bangalore Declaration. A Memorandum of Understanding on the Establishment of the SAARC Secretariat was signed by the Foreign Ministers of the SAARC countries in their presence.
3. They welcomed the announcement by His Majesty's Government of Nepal that the Secretariat would be inaugurated in Kathmandu on 16 January, 1987. They decided that the first Secretary-General of the SAARC Secretariat, His Excellency Mr. Abul Ahsan, would assume charge of this office from that date.
4. They also considered several new ideas for expanding and strengthening the cooperative programmes under SAARC. While approving the following ideas in principle they directed that these be elaborated and concretized through expert level examination to be completed by March 1987, so that the reports thereon could be considered at the next Meeting of the Council of Ministers :
   (a) A South Asian Broadcasting Programme covering both radio and television should be launched.
   (b) In keeping with the emphasis that the Heads of State or Government have laid on people-to-people contacts

concrete steps should be taken to facilitate tourism in the region, including facilities for limited convertibility of national currencies for tourists from SAARC countries.

(c) The Heads of State or Government emphasized the importance they attach to students, scholars and researchers in their countries having ready access to reliable and upto-date information on technical, scientific and developmental matters. This need could be best met by a SAARC Documentation Centre as the repository of such information.

(d) The Heads of State or Government considered that it was essential to promote increasing cross-fertilization of ideas through greater interaction among students, scholars and academics in the SAARC countries. They, therefore, directed that a concerted programme of exchange of scholars be formulated and action taken for an early institution of SAARC scholarships, SAARC Fellowships and SAARC Chairs.

(e) The Heads of State or Government stressed that the idealism of youth must be harnessed for regional cooperative programmes. Nothing would be more conducive to the resurgence of South Asian consciousness than the involvement of the youth of each country with the development programmes of the other. An Organized Volunteers Programme should be established in SAARC under which volunteers from one country would be able to work in other countries in the fields of agriculture and forestry extension work.

5. The Heads of State or Government recalled that the planners of the SAARC countries had met in 1983. This had provided a useful opportunity for an exchange of ideas and experience in the formulation of development strategies and methods of plan implementation. They directed that another meeting of the planners of the SAARC member countries be convened at the earliest.

6. The Heads of State or Government took note of the recommendations of the Standing Committee on the financing of the institutional costs of regional institutions. They decided

that for regional institutions where all the Member States are directly involved and benefit, the formula proposed by the Standing Committee should be used. However, in the case of projects which affect only a certain number of Member States, the formula should be used as an indicative one, which could be suitably modified on the basis of consultations among the Member States.

7. The Heads of State or Government also decided that the next Meeting of the Council of Ministers would be held in India in May 1987. They directed that this Meeting should undertake a detailed review of the proposals for the establishment of regional institutions. The member countries which have undertaken to prepare concept papers, pre-feasibility or feasibility studies on these proposals, should complete them well before the convening of the Meeting. The SAARC Secretariat should establish and submit to the Ministers, an order of priority among these proposals having regard to their costs, benefits, readiness for implementation, and other relevant factors.
8. The Heads of State or Government gratefully accepted the offer of the King of Nepal to host the Third SAARC Summit in 1987.
9. They also accepted with gratitude the offer of the President of Sri Lanka to host the Fourth SAARC Summit in Sri Lanka in 1988.

III. KATHMANDU SUMMIT

SOUTH ASIAN ASSOCIATION FOR REGIONAL COOPERATION DECLARATION

The Kathmandu Declaration of the Heads of State or Government of the member countries of the South Asian Association for Regional Cooperation issued on November 4, 1987.

INTRODUCTION

1. The President of Bangladesh, the King of Bhutan, the Prime Minister of India, the President of Maldives, the King of Nepal, the Prime Minister of Pakistan and the President of Sri Lanka assembled for the Third Summit of the South Asian Association for Regional Cooperation (SAARC) in Kathmandu on 24

November, 1987.

2. The Heads of State or Government recalled with pleasure the launching of SAARC which marked the beginning of a new era of regional cooperation for the promotion of peace and progress, mutual trust and goodwill in South Asia and underlined the importance of annual meetings at their level, as a prime mover, in consolidating and accelerating the pace and process of overall social, economic and cultural development in the region. They renewed their commitment to the SAARC Charter. They reiterated their desire of promoting peace, stability, amity and progress in the region through strict adherence to the principles of the United Nations Charter and Non-alignment, particularly respect for the principles of sovereign equality, territorial integrity, national independence, non-use of force and non-interference in the internal affairs of other States and peaceful settlement of disputes.
3. The Heads of State or Government emphasized that a fundamental goal of SAARC was to promote the welfare of the peoples of South Asia and to provide them with the opportunity to live in dignity and realise their full potential. They were conscious of the formidable tasks ahead of eradicating poverty, hunger, disease, illiteracy and unemployment and alleviation of environmental degradation facing South Asia today. They were convinced that the peoples and governments of South Asia could, acting in unison, surmount these challenges.
4. The Heads of State or Government expressed their faith in and commitment to the principles and purposes enshrined in the United Nation Charter. They further believed that the United Nations has an important role to play in promoting universal trust, understanding and concerted actions for the attainment of lasting peace, global development and general disarmament. They reiterated their concern at the crisis facing the United Nations. They expressed their commitment to the multilateral negotiating process and called upon all states to help strengthen the UN system. They reaffirmed their belief that SAARC will reinforce this process by promoting South Asian cooperation.
5. The Heads of State or Government also reaffirmed their deep

commitment to the principles and objectives of the Non-Aligned Movement. They underscored the validity of its philosophy and the historic role the Movement has been playing and continues to play in strengthening world peace and harmony as well as in promoting development with justice and equity. They also noted that institutionalization and strengthening of regional cooperation in South Asia had further nurtured the spirit of South-South cooperation on the basis of mutual respect, equity and common benefit. They expressed satisfaction over the result of the Ministerial Conference on Non-aligned Countries held in Pyongyang in June 1987 and urged the Non-aligned and other developing countries to take action to implement effectively the Pyongyang Declaration and Plan of Action on South-South Cooperation.

6. The Heads of State or Government recognised that the external environment had a critical bearing on the development of the economies of the South Asian Region. They noted with deep concern that growth in the world economy had again slowed down with adverse consequences for South Asia and other developing countries, especially for the least developed and landlocked countries. They observed that equitable participation of the developing countries in international trading and economic systems and in arrangements for the coordination of global macro economic policies was essential for enhancing prospects and performance of the world economy.

7. The South Asian leaders noted that the world economy had long suffered from a structural disequilibrium. The pace of global economic expansion had further slowed down. The downward trend in commodity prices had continued. The net export earnings had fallen aggravating payment imbalances in developing countries. The terms of trade had further deteriorated with enormous losses to developing countries. At the same time, the diminishing financial flows to developing countries remained unchanged with contraction in new lendings and growing burden of debt servicing. In fact, there had been a reverse flow of resources from developing to developed countries. The trade conflicts had also sharpened with the rise

of protectionism thus further weakening the international trading system and eroding the principle of special and differential treatment in favour of developing countries.

8. The Heads of State or Government reiterated the urgent need for resumption of North-South Dialogue with a view to promoting coordinated actions by developed and developing countries to channel trade surpluses for development, revive growth in flagging economies, overcome debt difficulties, expand export access to the developing countries and stabilise commodity prices, regulate capital flows and exchange rates more closely, and provide emergency relief and assistance to the poorest countries. They called for an early convening of the International Conference on Money and Finance for Development. They also stressed the need for preserving and liberalizing the multilateral trading system with renewed efforts both within and outside the GATT Uruguay Round of Multilateral Trade Negotiations. They also underscored the importance of the developed countries folly respecting the commitments made in Punta del Este on "standstill and rollback" and called for the early and effective implementation of this commitment. The Heads of State or Government also reviewed the outcome of UNCTAD VII. They hoped that UNCTAD would play an increasingly effective role in promoting harmonious and equitable international economic relations.
9. The Heads of State or Government reaffirmed the need for special measures in favour of the least developed countries in order to strengthen their resource capabilities and structural transformation and urged the international community, in the light of recent decisions at UNCTAD VII, to speed-up tangible assistance including increased resource flows to these countries within the framework of the Substantial New Program of Action (SNPA) for the Least Developed Countries for 1980s.
10. The Heads of State or Government expressed concern at the deteriorating international political environment which was due to great power policies and practices of domination and intervention as well as the increased resort to threat or use of force, aggression, occupation, pressure, economic coercion

and interference in violation of the principles and purposes of the Charter of the United Nations. These destabilising measures were creating a climate detrimental to the policies of peace, goodwill, stability, prosperity and respect for each other.

11. The Heads of State or Government believed that the escalation in military expenditure was a major constraint on world development. In this regard they noted that the UN Conference on Disarmament and Development had clearly established a link between disarmament and development and had provided a valuable frame work for future action in this vital area.

12. They welcomed the understanding reached between the United States and the Soviet Union on Intermediate Nuclear Forces. This should be a precursor of further accords between them to reduce drastically their strategic nuclear missiles and to refrain from extending the arms race to Outer Space. They called for the early conclusion in the Geneva Conference on Disarmament of a Comprehensive Test ban Treaty and a Convention to ban Chemical Weapons. They declared their intention to continue their efforts to contribute to the realisation of the objective of halting the nuclear arms race and eliminating nuclear weapons. They declared their resolve to support every effort to conclude a treaty prohibiting vertical and horizontal proliferation of nuclear weapons.

13. The Heads of State or Government expressed their deep concern at the fast and continuing degradation of the environment, including extensive destruction of forests, in the South Asian region. They also noted that South Asia was afflicted with such natural disasters as floods, droughts, landslides, cyclones, tidal waves which have had a particularly severe impact recently, causing immense human suffering. At the same time they expressed concern over the danger posed by the global sea level rise and its effects on South Asian countries. These natural disasters and the degradation of the environment were severely undermining the development process and prospects of the member countries. They, therefore, decided to intensify regional cooperation with a view to strengthening their disaster management capabilities. They also decided to commission a

study for the protection and preservation of the environment and to the causes and consequences of natural disasters in a well-planned comprehensive framework. They entrusted the Secretary-General with this task.

14. The Heads of State or Government reaffirmed their conviction that the region being most populous in the world and having age-old socio-cultural links, rich and varied human and natural resources, offered immense scope and potential for regional cooperation and that the growing interaction among its people had added stimulus towards this end. They reiterated their determination to pursue their individual and collective efforts for the optimal utilisation of the vast human and untapped natural and other material resources.
15. The Heads of State or Government reviewed with satisfaction the progress made so far in the implementation of the SAARC Integrated Programme of Action and emphasised the need to further consolidate and streamline the process. They were conscious of the need to exercise greater discretion in the selection of activities in different sectors. They took note of the criteria and procedures relating to administrative structuring and financing of regional institutions endorsed by the SAARC Council of Ministers. They directed that the establishment of such regional institutions should proceed only after taking into account their viability and benefits to the member countries with due consideration to economy and efficiency.
16. The Heads of State or Government expressed satisfaction at the launching of the SAARC Audio Visual Exchange programme coinciding with the opening of the Third SAARC Summit in Kathmandu. While taking note of the dates for the institution of the SAARC Chairs, Fellowships and Scholarships and the commencement of Organised Tourism among SAARC member countries, they directed that the schemes for the SAARC Documentation Centre and the SAARC Youth Volunteer Programme be implemented at the earliest.
17. The Heads of State or Government noted with satisfaction the signing of the Agreement establishing a South Asian Food Security Reserve and expressed confidence that this will provide

a much-needed cushion against food shortages and scarcity situations in the region.

18. The Heads of State or Government expressed happiness at the signing of the SAARC Regional Convention on Suppression of Terrorism and considered it a historic step towards the prevention and elimination of terrorism from the region. In this regard, they also reiterated their unequivocal condemnation of all acts, methods and practice of terrorism as criminal and expressed their abhorrence of their impact on life and property, socio-economic development, political stability, regional peace and cooperation.
19. The Heads of State or Government reaffirmed their agreement to expand SAARC activities in other concrete areas of cooperation in order to ensure more tangible benefits from SAARC to the peoples of the region. They were convinced that regional cooperation could be consolidated and expanded on the basis of growing regional complementarities and interdependence. They believed that the SAARC long-term perspective should, therefore, focus on measures to expand and strengthen such areas of regional complementarities and interdependence not only through formulation and implementation of more concrete and action-oriented programmes, but also through coordination of national policies and approaches for finding common solutions to their common problems.
20. The Heads of State or Government welcomed the first annual review of the Situation of Children in the SAARC member countries. They reiterated their commitment made in the Bangalore Declaration to accord highest priority to the needs of children in national development planning and emphasised that more intensified action should be taken for the welfare and well-being of children. They further reiterated their call for an early conclusion and adoption of a United Nations Convention on the Rights of the Child.
21. The Heads of State or Government expressed their satisfaction at the establishment of the SAARC Secretariat in Kathmandu, strengthening further the process of regional cooperation in South Asia. They expressed their gratitude to His Majesty King

Birendra Bir Bikram Shah Dev for most graciously inaugurating the SAARC Secretariat.

22. The Heads of State or Government were conscious of the aspirations of the peoples of South Asia to communicate and cooperate with each other at the people-to-people level. They recognised that academics, researchers, non-governmental organizations and others have an important role to play in promoting the SAARC spirit and giving impetus to regional programmes and projects. They further observed that the interest and enthusiasm so far demonstrated by the increased interactions and exchange of information at the intergovernmental level should be capitalised and translated into tangible programmes and projects. They recognised the vast potential for the generation of friendship, goodwill and trust through interactions between the peoples which would foster harmonious relations in South Asia.
23. The Heads of State or Government expressed their deep conviction that the Kathmandu Summit has farther consolidated the gains of SAARC and given a renewed thrust and direction to the future course of regional cooperation. They were also convinced that the Kathmandu Summit has helped to create an atmosphere conducive to strengthening this process, besides generating further goodwill and friendship among the member countries in the larger interest of the region.
24. The Heads of State or Government were conscious that SAARC should be increasingly oriented to the people's needs and aspirations so that the masses of the region could be drawn to a greater extent into the mainstream of SAARC activities. This, they firmly held, would help bring about a qualitative improvement in the general atmosphere of the region contributing to peace, friendship and cooperation in the areas.
25. The Heads of State or Government reiterated their firm commitment to the spirit and objectives with which the South Asian Association for Regional Cooperation was launched and reaffirmed their determination to work, individually and collectively, towards the attainment of these objectives.
26. The Heads of State or Government of Bangladesh, Bhutan,

India, Maldives, Pakistan and Sri Lanka were deeply appreciative of the exemplary manner in which His Majesty the King of Nepal discharged his responsibilities as Chairman of the Meeting. They expressed their profound gratitude for the warm and gracious hospitality extended to them by His Majesty's Government and the people of Nepal and for the excellent arrangements made for the Meeting.

JOINT PRESS RELEASE

Joint Press Release Issued on November 4, 1987 at the End of the Third SAARC Summit, Kathmandu.

1. The President of Bangladesh, the King of Bhutan, the Prime Minister of India, the President of Maldives, the King of Nepal, the Prime Minister of Pakistan and President of Sri Lanka met in Kathmandu during November 2-4, 1987. Their meeting was marked by warmth, cordiality and mutual understanding.
2. They issued the Kathmandu Declaration providing a renewed thrust and direction to the future course of regional cooperation in South Asia.
3. They considered several issues of common concern, both regional and international, and assessed the overall progress in the context of SAARC objectives.
4. They expressed their happiness at the signing of the SAARC Regional Convention on Suppression of Terrorism and the Agreement establishing South Asian Food Reserve by the Foreign Ministers of the SAARC Member States in their presence, they firmly believed that the Convention and the Agreement constituted landmarks in their collective endeavours to eradicate terrorism and hunger from the region.
5. They declared their intention to initiate the process of dealing with the causes and consequences of natural disasters and decided to commission a study on natural disasters and the protection and preservation of the environment in a well planned and comprehensive framework. They entrusted the Secretary-General with this task.
6. They expressed their satisfaction with the progress achieved in the implementation of the Integrated Programme of Action in

the eleven agreed areas of cooperation and also with the concrete programmes related to the Five New Ideas identified at the last Summit for expanding and strengthening cooperative programmes under SAARC.

7. They also reaffirmed their view that measures for expanding regional cooperation should be progressively carried out within a broad framework of long-term perspective and stressed, in particular, the need for further consolidation and rationalization of the on-going activities pursued within SAARC framework.
8. The Heads of State or Government emphasized the need for strengthening inter-governmental efforts with increased people-to-people cooperation and called for greater participation of the Non-Governmental Organizations (NGOs), including professional bodies in the private sector, in the process of promoting socio-economic and cultural development of South Asia as envisaged in the SAARC Charter, under the auspices of the SAARC Secretariat.
9. They further welcomed the establishment of the SAARC Secretariat in Kathmandu as well as the assumption of office by the SAARC Secretary-General with effect from 16 January, 1987 and considered these as important events in strengthening the institutional framework of regional cooperation in South Asia. They expressed their appreciation to His Majesty's Government of Nepal at the cooperation and assistance extended and facilities provided to the SAARC Secretariat.
10. The Heads of State or Government took note of the Report submitted by the Council of Ministers relating, inter alia, to administrative structuring and financing of regional institutions and directed that for economy and efficiency all sectoral programmes should justify the establishment of such regional institutions.
11. They instructed that in its examination of the question of the admission of new members and the grant of observer/guest status in the Association, the Standing Committee should also include the aspect of the establishment of relations with similar organisations.
12. They gratefully accepted the offer of the President of Sri Lanka

to host the Fourth SAARC Summit in 1988 in Sri Lanka.

13. They also gratefully accepted the offer of the Prime Minister of the Islamic Republic of Pakistan to host the Fifth SAARC Summit in Pakistan in 1989.
14. The Heads of State or Government of Bangladesh, Bhutan, India, Maldives, Pakistan and Sri Lanka were deeply appreciative of the exemplary manner in which His Majesty the King of Nepal discharged his responsibilities as Chairman of the Meeting. They expressed their profound gratitude for the warm and gracious hospitality extended to them by His Majesty's Government and the people of Nepal and for the excellent arrangements made for the Meeting.

IV. ISLAMABAD SUMMIT

SOUTH ASIAN ASSOCIATION FOR REGIONAL COOPERATION DECLARATION

The Islamabad Declaration of the Heads of State or Government of the Member Countries of South Asian Association for Regional Cooperation issued on 31st December 1988.

INTRODUCTION

1. The President of Bangladesh, the King of Bhutan, the Prime Minister of India, the President of Maldives, the King of Nepal, the Prime Minister of Pakistan and the President of Sri Lanka met at the Fourth Summit of the South Asian Association for Regional Cooperation at Islamabad from 29-31 December, 1988.
2. The Heads of State of Government expressed their deep satisfaction at the progress achieved by the Association since the last Summit. They reiterated their commitment to the SAARC Charter and renewed their determination to cooperate in promoting the welfare of the peoples of South Asia and to improving their quality of life by eradicating poverty, hunger, disease, illiteracy, unemployment and environmental degradation.
3. They recalled that their countries were linked by cultural, social

and historical ties and they had at their disposal substantial human and natural resources. They recognised that these provided a sound basis as well as immense opportunities for regional cooperation. They therefore expressed their determination to make optimal use of their resources for the benefit of their people by working jointly to pursue their shared objectives. They were aware that by acting in concert they could realise the full potential for regional progress, taking into account complementarities and growing interdependence.

4. The leaders endorsed the decision of the Council of Ministers that any country in the region subscribing to the objectives and principles of the SAARC Charter may be admitted as a member of the Association by a unanimous decision of the Heads of State of Government.
5. The Heads of State of Government expressed satisfaction at the progress so far made in the implementation of the SAARC Integrated Programme of Action. They underlined the need for closer cooperation in the activities undertaken under this programme. They took note of the measures to streamline and re-orient various SAARC activities to make them more action-oriented so as to improve the quality of life of their peoples. They directed that the Secretary General may submit recommendation to the Standing Committee which should in turn decide how to streamline SAARC activities and make them more effective. They welcomed the establishment of the SAARC Agricultural Information Centre (SAIC), as well as the steps being taken for the establishment of other regional institutions.
6. The Heads of State of Government lauded the smooth functioning of the SAARC Audio Visual Exchange (SAVE) Programme which had proved to be a useful medium for promoting a South Asian consciousness amongst the peoples of the region. They decided that SAVE Programmes should also emphasise social, economic and technical themes. They also noted with satisfaction the successful launching of the Youth Volunteers Programme and the SAARC Chairs, Fellowships and Scholarships Scheme. They decided that Education may be included as an agreed area of cooperation.

7. The Heads of State of Government expressed satisfaction that the South Asian Food Security Reserve had become operational on 12 August 1988. The Reserve would serve as a cushion against food shortages and was a tangible manifestation of the spirit of cooperation in the region.
8. The Heads of State of Government noted with satisfaction that the SAARC Convention on Suppression of Terrorism had been ratified and had come into effect on 22 August 1988, thus reflecting the sincere desire on the part of the Member States to enter into meaningful cooperation to eliminate the scourge of terrorism from the South Asian region. They called for the adoption of enabling measures by Member States to implement the Convention at the earliest.
9. The Heads of State of Government expressed grave concern over the growing magnitude and the serious effects of drug abuse, particularly among young people, and drug trafficking. They recognised the need for urgent and effective measures to eradicate this evil and decided to declare the year 1989 as the "SAARC Year for Combating Drug Abuse and Drug Trafficking". They agreed to launch a concerted campaign, as suited to the situation in their respective countries, to significantly augment SAARC efforts to eliminate drug abuse and drug trafficking. These included closer cooperation in creating a greater awareness of the hazards of drug abuse, exchange of expertise, sharing of intelligence information, stringent measures to stop trafficking in drugs and introduction of more effective laws. They directed that the Technical Committee concerned should examine the possibility of a Regional Convention on Drug Control.
10. The Heads of State or Government expressed their deep sense of sorrow and profound sympathy at the loss of valuable lives and extensive damage to property suffered during the year by Bangladesh, India, Nepal and Pakistan as a result of unprecedented floods, cyclones and earthquakes. In this connection, they recalled their earlier decision at Kathmandu in November, 1987 to intensify regional cooperation with a view to strengthening their disaster management capabilities and

took note of the recommendations of the meeting of the SAARC Group of Experts on the Study on the Causes and Consequences of Natural Disasters and the Protection and Preservation of the Environment, that met in Kathmandu in July 1988. They expressed the conviction that identification of measures and programmes as envisaged by the Group of Experts would supplement national, bilateral, regional and global efforts to deal with the increasingly serious problems being faced by the region as a result of the recurrence of natural disasters and the continuing degradation of the environment. They urged that the study should be completed in the shortest period of time so that it could provide a basis for the member countries to draw up an action plan for meaningful cooperation amongst the Member States. They decided that a joint study be undertaken on the "Greenhouse Effect" and its impact on the region.

11. The Heads of State or Government noted with satisfaction that modalities for studies to be carried out for cooperation in the areas of trade, manufactures and services had been worked out by a Group of Experts, which met in Islamabad recently. They emphasised the need for the completion of the studies within the agreed time schedule. They directed that the Fourth Meeting of Planners should examine the possibility of cooperation in agreed areas of trade, manufactures and services, which would promote the objectives of meeting the basic needs of the peoples of the region. The report of the Planners should be considered at the next Council of Ministers meeting, with a view to making specific recommendations to the next Summit.

12. The Heads of State or Government reviewed the progress on the Situation of Children in SAARC countries. They reiterated their commitment made in the Bangalore Declaration to accord the highest priority to the needs of children in national development planning and stressed that the concept of Human Resource Development should lay particular emphasis on the welfare and well-being of children, especially in the literacy and health spheres. They called for the conclusion and adoption of the UN Convention on the Rights of the Child in 1989. They

decided to declare 1990 as the "SAARC Year of the Girl Child".

13. The Heads of State or Government noted with satisfaction the effective functioning of the SAARC Secretariat and its role in coordinating SAARC activities. They also noted that a Headquarters Agreement had been signed between the Secretariat and the host Government. They thanked His Majesty's Government of Nepal for the assistance and cooperation extended to the Secretariat.
14. The Heads of State or Government noted that the decision to involve regional NGOs or professional bodies in SAARC activities, taken at the Fifth Session of the Council of Ministers, pursuant to the direction given by the Kathmandu Declaration, was an important step towards the promotion of people-to-people contact which has always been emphasised by the Association.
15. The Heads of State or Government stressed the need for closer and more frequent contacts among the peoples of SAARC. As a beginning, they decided that Supreme Court Judges and Members of the National Parliaments of each member State would be entitled to a special SAARC travel document which would exempt them from visas. They further directed the Council of Ministers to examine what other categories of persons should be given this facility and to submit their recommendations.
16. They further noted with satisfaction the mandate given to the Secretary General by the Council of Ministers at its Fifth Session on the question of contacting organisations with similar aims and purposes.
17. The Heads of State or Government expressed their determination to give concrete shape to the objectives of SAARC. In this context they emphasised the need to progressively carry out SAARC activities within a broad framework of a long-term perspective and to harmonize their efforts to ensure tangible benefits to the peoples of South Asia as a whole. They were conscious of the fact that all South Asian countries faced problems in varying degrees in areas such as food, clothing, shelter, education, primary health care, population planning and

environmental protection. Towards this end they were of the view that all Member States should identity areas of core interest in their national perspective plans or prepare such plans and consolidate them into a regional plan to be called "SAARC-2000 : A Basic Needs Perspective", with specific targets to be met by the end of the century.

18. They recognised that Human Resource Development is one of the means of realizing these objectives. In this context they welcomed the offer of the Government of Pakistan to host a Centre for Human Resource Development and directed the Secretary-General to set up a Group of Experts from Member States to examine the proposal on the basis of a paper to be prepared by the Government of Pakistan and to submit its recommendations to the Standing Committee.

19. The Heads of State or Government reaffirmed their abiding commitment to the purposes and principles enshrined in the UN Charter, particularly those enjoining respect for the sovereign equality, territorial integrity and national independence, non-use or threat of use of force, non-interference in the internal affairs of other states and peaceful settlement of all disputes. They reiterated their faith in the United Nations as the most important forum for the maintenance of international peace and security and for the promotion of international cooperation aimed at the progress and prosperity of mankind.

20. The Heads of State or Government noted with satisfaction the relaxation of global tensions through intensified superpower dialogue on a broad range of international issues and welcomed the progress towards the resolution of protracted regional disputes and conflicts. They agreed that these developments had enhanced the prospects for disarmament, security, peace and progress for all peoples of the world. They appreciated the important role played by the United Nations in bringing about these positive changes in the international political environment. They also called upon all States to strengthen the capacity of the UN system in all respects to achieve the purpose of the UN Charter.

21. The Heads of State or Government reiterated their deep

commitment to the principles and objectives of the Non-aligned Movement as an important force for strengthening world peace and harmony as well as for promoting development with justice and equity. In this context they expressed satisfaction over the results of the Ministerial Conference of the Non-aligned Movement held in Cyprus in September 1988 and expressed the hope the decisions of the Conference would contribute to the reduction of tensions and to the promotion of development. They hoped that the current discussions on the improvement in the methodology of the Non-Aligned Movement would result in strengthening the movement and enable it to play its role with greater effectiveness.

22. The Heads of State or Government believed that the escalation in military expenditure was a major constraint on world development. In this regard they noted that the UN Conference on Disarmament and Development had clearly established a link between disarmament and development and had provided a valuable framework for future action in this vital area. They urged that resources saved through disarmament measures should be diverted in particular to developing countries for development.

23. They welcomed the agreement between the United States and the Soviet Union on Intermediate Nuclear Force. They hoped this would be a precursor to further accords to reduce strategic nuclear arsenals drastically and to prevent an arms race in Outer Space. They called for the early conclusion in the Geneva Conference on Disarmament of a Comprehensive Test Ban Treaty and a Convention to Ban Chemical Weapons. They declared their intention to continue their efforts to contribute to the realization of the objective of halting the nuclear arms race and eliminating nuclear weapons. They declared their resolve to support every effort to conclude a treaty prohibiting vertical and horizontal proliferation of nuclear weapons.

24. The Heads of State or Government noted with deep concern the continued structural disequilibrium from which the world economy had long suffered. This had resulted in slower growth in the developing countries, downward trends in commodity

prices, decline in the net export earnings of the developing countries and deterioration in their terms of trade. These developments combined with the overwhelming debt burdens, the reverse financial flows from the developing to the developed countries and the sharp rise of protectionism in the developed world had further aggravated the economic difficulties of the developing countries.

25. The Heads of State or Government emphasised the interdependent character of the economies of the developed and the developing countries. They called for the resumption of the North-South dialogue with a view to restructuring the international economic system and to establishing the New International Economic Order based on justice and equity. They called for coordinated actions by the developed and the developing countries to increase the net flow of developmental assistance, overcome debt difficulties, expand the access of the developing countries to the markets in developed countries, arrest the deterioration in terms of trade of the developing countries and stabilize commodity prices.

26. The Heads of State or Government reiterated the need for preserving and liberalizing the multilateral trading system with renewed efforts both within and outside the Uruguay Round of Multilateral Trade Negotiations. They also underscored the importance of the developed countries fully respecting and implementing the commitments made in Punta del Este on "standstill and rollback" arrangements. They expressed concern that on account of differences between major trading entities on the question of agricultural subsidies, the Montreal Meeting on the midterm review of the Uruguay round was inconclusive. They particularly regretted that there was no progress in the negotiations on issues of major interest to developing countries such as trade in textiles and a Safeguard System. They were disappointed that on some of the issues of interest to developing countries on which there was agreement, particularly tropical products, it would not be possible even to implement the decisions taken, from the beginning of 1989 as envisaged. They emphasised that the development dimension must be taken into

account in the negotiations on new issues, particularly services and intellectual property rights. They agreed to take concerted action to this end in the forthcoming negotiations.

27. The Heads of State or Government fully supported the call for the initiation of a comprehensive process for the preparation of an International Development Strategy for the Fourth United Nations Development Decade as well as the proposal of the Group of 77 for convening a Special Session of the General Assembly in 1990 to revive growth and development in the developing countries.
28. The Heads of State or Government reemphasized the need for increased resource flows and special measures in favour of the least developed countries within the Framework of the Substantial New Programme of Action (SNPA) for these countries. They supported the convening of a high level United Nations Conference on the least developed countries in 1990 to review progress and formulate national and international policies and measures for accelerating the development process in the least developed countries during the 1990s, especially in order to help them achieve their long term socio-economic objectives.
29. The Heads of State or Government of Bangladesh, Bhutan, India, Maldives, Nepal and Sri Lanka expressed their deep appreciation for the exemplary manner in which Prime Minister of Pakistan chaired the meeting. They expressed their profound gratitude for the excellent arrangements made for the meeting and for the warm and generous hospitality extended to them by the Government and the people of Pakistan.

JOINT PRESS RELEASE

Joint Press Release Issued on December 31, 1988 at the End of Fourth SAARC Summit, Islamabad.

1. The President of Bangladesh, the King of Bhutan, the Prime Minister of India, the President of Maldives, the King of Nepal, the Prime Minister of Pakistan and the President of Sri Lanka met at the Fourth Summit of the South Asian Association for Regional Cooperation at Islamabad from 29-31 December, 1988. The meeting was marked by an atmosphere of mutual

understanding and spirit of accommodation.

2. The Heads of State or Government reaffirmed their commitment to the principles and objectives of the Association enshrined in the SAARC Charter and renewed their determination to work collectively towards the attainment of these objectives. They issued the Islamabad Declaration.
3. The Heads of State or Government were deeply shocked at the armed attack on the Republic of Maldives on 3rd November, 1988 aimed at destabilising the Government and taking over the country. They strongly condemned these acts of violence which disrupted the peace and security of a Member State. They expressed full solidarity with the Government of Maldives.
4. The Heads of State or Government expressed concern at the high incidence of drug production, trafficking and abuse. They decided to declare 1989 as the "SAARC Year Against Drug Abuse" in order to focus attention on drug-related problems facing the region. They called upon Members States to prepare and implement national programmes in this regard.
5. They welcomed the launching of SAARC Chairs, Fellowships and Scholarships schemes and the Youth Volunteers programme. They recognised that Education was one of the principal areas requiring urgent attention in the region and decided to include Education among the agreed areas of cooperation. For this purpose they decided to set up a Technical Committee and accepted the offer of Bangladesh to chair the Committee.
6. The Heads of State or Government agreed to launch "SAARC-2000—A Basic Needs Perspective" which calls for a perspective regional plan with specific targets to be met by the end of the century in areas of core interest such as food, clothing, shelter, education, primary health care, population planning and environmental protection. In this context they welcomed the offer of the Government of Pakistan to host a Centre for Human Resource Development and directed the Secretary-General to convene an Expert Group Meeting of member countries to work out modalities for the realization of "SAARC 2000 - A Basic Needs Perspective".
7. The Heads of State or Government welcomed the idea of

holding South Asian Festivals from time to time and accepted the offer of India to host the first such festival.

8. The Heads of State or Government directed the Standing Committee to examine the desirability of establishing a regional body to promote cultural links among Member States.
9. They welcomed the coming into force of the SAARC Regional Convention on Suppression of Terrorism. They stressed the importance of the adoption of enabling measures at the national level that would be necessary in order to fully implement the provisions of the Convention.
10. They welcomed the Agreement regarding the establishment of a South Asian Food Security Reserve in August this year which marked a major breakthrough in the common endeavours of the Governments of member countries of SAARC to assist each other in food emergency situations.
11. The Heads of State or Government caressed their satisfaction at the progress achieved in the implementation of the Integrated Programme of Action (IPA). They recognised the need for focusing attention on more concrete and result-oriented activities within the SAARC framework.
12. They welcomed the establishment of the SAARC Agriculture Information Centre (SAIC) at Dhaka and were of the view that proposals for the setting up of regional institutions, focusing on problems of common concern in the region, should be given priority.
13. They reiterated their earlier commitment to accord priority to the needs of children in national development plans. They decided to declare 1990 as the "SAARC Year of the Girl Child" and directed that specific programmes and activities be undertaken to increase public awareness of the problems of the girl child.
14. They expressed satisfaction at the progress in the studies underway regarding the feasibility of cooperation in areas of trade, manufactures and services. In the meanwhile they directed the Secretary-General to convene a special meeting of the Group of Coordinators to identify any specific areas where cooperation may be feasible immediately. They directed that the

report of the Group should be presented to the next sessions of the Standing Committee and the Council of Ministers.

15. The Heads of State or Government expressed profound sorrow at the natural disasters suffered by Bangladesh, Nepal, India and Pakistan in 1988 and urged that the study on the Causes and Consequences of Natural Disasters and the Protection and Preservation of the Environment be completed in the shortest period of time so as to provide a rational basis for identifying areas keeping in view the potentials and possibilities of evolving a regional plan of action, particularly to strengthen disaster management capabilities and to protect and preserve the environment.
16. They expressed satisfaction at the concrete steps being taken for the implementation of the SAARC Audio Visual Exchange (SAVE) Programme. They directed that social, economic and technical themes should be given emphasis by the SAVE Programme.
17. Recalling the usefulness of the earlier Ministerial meeting on Women in Development held in India in 1986, the Heads of State or Government called for the holding of a second Ministerial level meeting and welcomed the offer of the Government of Pakistan to host the meeting.
18. They expressed satisfaction that pursuant to the direction given by the Kathmandu Declaration for enhancing people-to-people contact, concrete steps had been taken by including regional NGOs and professional bodies in SAARC activities.
19. They decided that any country in the region subscribing to the objectives and principles of the Charter may be admitted as a member of the Association by a unanimous decision of the Heads of State or Government.
20. The Heads of State or Government noted with satisfaction the effective functioning of the SAARC Secretariat and its role in coordinating SAARC activities. They appreciated the work of the SAARC Secretary-General in the discharge of his responsibilities and thanked His Majesty's Government of Nepal for the assistance and cooperation extended to the Secretariat.
21. The Heads of State or Government gratefully accepted the

offer of the Government of Sri Lanka to host the Fifth SAARC Summit in Colombo in 1989.

22. The Heads of State or Government expressed their deep appreciation for the outstanding manner in which the Prime Minister of Pakistan had conducted the meetings as the Chairperson of the Fourth SAARC Summit. They also expressed profound gratitude for the gracious hospitality extended to them by the Government and people of the Islamic Republic of Pakistan and for the excellent arrangements made for the conference.

V. MALE SUMMIT

SOUTH ASIAN ASSOCIATION FOR REGIONAL COOPERATION DECLARATION

The Male Declaration of the Heads of State or Government of the Member Countries of Asian Association for Regional Cooperation issued on 23rd November, 1990.

1. The President of the People's Republic of Bangladesh, His Excellency Mr. Hussain Muhammad Ershad, the King of Bhutan, His Majesty King Jigme Singye Wangchuck, the Prime Minister of the Republic of India, His Excellency Mr. Chandra Shekhar, the President of the Republic of Maldives, His Excellency Mr. Maumoon Abdul Gayoom, the Prime Minister of Nepal, The Right Honourable Krishna Prasad Bhattarai, the Prime Minister of the Islamic Republic of Pakistan, His Excellency Mr. Mohammad Nawaz Sharif and the Prime Minister of the Democratic Socialist Republic of Sri Lanka, His Excellency Mr. Dingiri Banda Wijetunga met at the Fifth Summit of the South Asian Association for Regional Cooperation at Male on 21-23 November, 1990.
2. The Heads of State or Government reiterated that cooperation among the countries of South Asia was necessary for improving the quality of life of the peoples of the region. They recalled their conviction that the objectives of peace and stability in South Asia could be best served by fostering mutual

understanding, cooperation and good neighbourly relations. They reaffirmed their commitment to the purposes and principles of the South Asian Association for Regional Cooperation and renewed their resolve to intensify cooperation under its aegis in pursuit of their common objectives.

3. The Heads of State or Government stressed their desire to promote peace, stability, amity and progress in the region through strict adherence to the principles of the United Nations Charter and the Nonaligned Movement, particularly respect for the principles of sovereign equality, territorial integrity, national independence, non-use of force, non-interference in the internal affairs of other States and peaceful settlement of disputes.
4. The Heads of State or Government expressed satisfaction that the launching of SAARC in 1985 and the initiatives under the Integrated Programme of Action for strengthening regional cooperation in South Asia had generated much enthusiasm and hope in their peoples, and that the South Asian consciousness necessary for the success of regional cooperation was gradually permeating the region. They reiterated their resolve to make optimal use of the positive forces of goodwill, trust and understanding existing among their peoples and to turn SAARC into a dynamic instrument for achieving its objectives and creating an order based on mutual respect, equity, cooperation and shared benefits.
5. The Heads of State or Government reviewed the status of children in South Asia and noted that the recent World Summit for Children had imparted a new impetus to the ongoing efforts in this field. They believed that relevant recommendations of the World Summit could be usefully incorporated into a Plan of Action in the South Asian context and its implementation should be reviewed annually. The guidelines for such Plan of Action could be prepared by a panel of experts to be appointed by the Secretary General and examined by the Technical Committee on Health and Population Activities. They also welcomed the adoption of the Convention on the Rights of the Child and its entry into force. They expressed the hope that those Member States, who have not already become party to the Convention,

would do so at an early date.

6. The Heads of State or Government endorsed the recommendations made by the Second SAARC Ministerial Meeting on Women in Development held in Islamabad in June 1990. They noted with satisfaction the enthusiastic response in all Member States to their collective call for the observance of 1990 as the "SAARC Year of the Girl Child". They decided that in order to maintain focus on the problems of the Girl Child, the years 1991-2000 A.D. should be observed as the "SAARC Decade of the Girl Child".
7. The Heads of State or Government noted with satisfaction the growing regional cooperation in combating the problems of drug trafficking and drug abuse. They expressed serious concern over the growing linkages between drug trafficking and international arms trade and terrorist activities. They agreed that observance of 1989 as the "SAARC Year for Combating Drug Abuse and Drug Trafficking" had had a profound impact in drawing attention to the menace and to the need for its elimination. They expressed satisfaction that following the decision of the Fourth SAARC Summit, the SAARC Convention on Narcotic Drugs and Psychotropic Substances had been signed at Male. They urged the Member States to take early measures to ratify the convention for its entry into force. They were convinced that the Convention would help in making SAARC efforts in this area more effective.
8. They endorsed the decision of the Council of Ministers in regard to the time-frame for completion of the Regional Study on the Causes and Consequences of Natural Disasters and the Protection and Preservation of the Environment. They noted with satisfaction that the methodology for undertaking the Study on the 'Greenhouse Effect' and its impact on the region was likely to be finalized in the near future and desired that the Study itself be completed for consideration at the Sixth Summit. In this context, they noted that the destruction of rain forests, the world over, was contributing significantly to adverse climatic changes and this aspect should also be covered in the proposed Study. They expressed the hope that these Studies would lead

to an action plan for meaningful cooperation in the field of Environment and Disaster Management.

9. Recognizing that environment had emerged as a major global concern, the Heads of State or Government noted with alarm the unprecedented climatic changes predicted by the Intergovernmental Panel on Climate Change (IPCC). They urged the international community to mobilize additional finances and to make available appropriate technologies to enable the developing countries to face the new challenges arising from climate changes and sea level rise. They agreed that Member Countries should coordinate their positions at international fora on this issue. They also decided to observe 1992 as the "SAARC Year of Environment".
10. The Heads of State or Government noted with satisfaction that the national studies on Trade, Manufactures and Services had been completed. They underlined the need for expeditious action for completing the Regional Study within the time-frame stipulated by the Council of Ministers. They expressed the hope that it would open new avenues of cooperation for the prosperity of the peoples of the region.
11. The Heads of State or Government approved the recommendations of the Council of Ministers regarding Special SAARC Travel Document and decided to launch the scheme.
12. The Heads of State or Government expressed concern that Member States were compelled to divert their scarce resources in combating terrorism. They called for expeditious enactment of enabling measures for the implementation of the SAARC Regional Convention on Suppression of Terrorism. They also urged Member States to continue to cooperate in accordance with the Convention.
13. The Heads of State or Government noted that as their countries stood on the threshold of the next millennium, the world was undergoing profound transformations characterised by popular upsurge for democracy, liberty and exercise of human rights, lowering of ideological barriers and the relaxation of global tensions and progress towards disarmament and the resolution of a number of regional and global conflicts. There was also a

welcome trend towards the opening up of the global economy and integration of national economies into the mainstream of the world economy. They further noted the trend of increasing integration of the pattern of global production, consumption and trade, growing multipolarity of the world economic structure and integration of the markets of the developed countries in order to maintain their technological lead and competitive edge. These changes presented new challenges and opened up new opportunities to the South Asian countries, as to the rest of the developing world. The Heads of State or Government were convinced that their mutual cooperation can be a critical factor in enabling them to pursue these objectives more effectively.

14. The Heads of State or Government, noting the vital importance of biotechnology for the long-term food security of developing countries as well as for medicinal purposes, decided that cooperation should be extended to this field and, in particular, to the exchange of expertise in genetic conservation and maintenance of germ-plasm banks. In this connection, they welcomed India's offer of training facilities and agreed that cooperation in the cataloguing of genetic resources stored in different SAARC countries would be mutually beneficial. Taking note of the proposal made by the Group of Fifteen Developing Countries (G 15) for the establishment of a gene bank for developing countries, they agreed to participate in this venture.

15. The Heads of State or Government welcomed the idea of setting up of a Fund for regional projects which could make available credit on easy terms for the identification and development of regional projects. They agreed that representatives of the national development banks of the Member Countries should get together to work out the precise modalities for the source of funds and the manner in which these could be related to joint venture projects. They accepted India's offer to host this meeting.

16. The Heads of State or Government regarded the recent developments in the Gulf as the most unfortunate aberration from the present trend of detente, cooperation and peaceful settlement of disputes. They reaffirmed their adherence to UN

Security Council Resolutions on this issue. While emphasizing the need for a peaceful solution of the issue, they called for immediate and unconditional withdrawal of Iraqi forces from Kuwait and the restoration of its legitimate Government. They stated that the Gulf crisis had dealt a severe blow to their economies. They needed massive international assistance to compensate the loss suffered by them due to a sharp decline in remittances, setback to their exports and severe strain on their balance of payments position imposed by increased oil prices. They recognized the potentiality of cooperation among themselves for mitigating the impact of these adverse consequences.

17. The Heads of State or Government noted with satisfaction that the initiative of the Government of the Maldives for the Protection and Security of Small States at the UN in 1989, which they all supported, had also received overwhelming support of the international community. They agreed that, because of their particular problems, small states merited special measures of support in safeguarding their independence and territorial integrity.

18. The Heads of State or Government expressed the hope that the talks between the two Super Powers on arms control would culminate in the conclusion of an agreement for substantial reduction in their nuclear arsenals leading to the total elimination of nuclear weapons. While welcoming the measures being considered for arms reduction at the global level, they were convinced that the objective could be best achieved through the promotion of mutual trust and confidence among the Member States. They underlined the inherent relationship between disarmament and development and called upon all countries, especially those possessing the largest nuclear and conventional arsenals, to rechannel additional financial resources, human energy and creativity into development. They expressed their support for the banning of chemical weapons and early conclusion of a Comprehensive Test Ban Treaty. In this context, they welcomed the convening of the UN Conference in January 1991 to consider amendments to the Partial Test Ban Treaty to

convert it into a Comprehensive Nuclear Test Ban Treaty.

19. The Heads of State or Government expressed concern that the international economic environment for the developing countries had been characterised by negative resource flows, high trade barriers, serious external debt problems and high interest rates. The need of SAARC countries for increased concessional resources and technology as well as access to markets for their exports could not, therefore, be under estimated. They called for collective efforts based on mutuality of interest and felt that regular North South consultations were essential for ensuring equitable management of global interdependence.
20. The Heads of State or Government recalled the usefulness of the First Ministerial Meeting on International Economic Issues held in Islamabad in 1986. They agreed that the second such Ministerial Meeting be held in India in 1991 to review the outcome of the Uruguay Round and to coordinate positions at international conferences including the U.N. Conference on Environment and Development, 1992.
21. Notwithstanding the continuing efforts on the international economic plane, the Heads of State or Government emphasised the pressing need for the Ministerial Meeting to address itself vigorously to the objective of self-reliance. They directed the Ministers to prepare a strategy for mobilising regional resources which would encourage and strengthen individual and collective self reliance in the region.
22. The Heads of State or Government expressed their support for the Paris Declaration (1990) and the Programme of Action adopted by the Second United Nations Conference on the Least Developed Countries. They called upon the international community to contribute to the successful implementation of the Programme of Action which is of special importance for the socio-economic development of the region.
23. The Heads of State or Government recognized the imperative need for providing a better habitat to the peoples of South Asia through optimum utilization of indigenous technology, know-how and material, and decided that 1991 be observed as the "SAARC Year of Shelter".

24. The Heads of State or Government noted that millions of disabled persons lived in the SAARC region and immediate action was required to reduce their sufferings and to improve their quality of life. They decided to observe 1993 as the "SAARC Year of Disabled Persons".
25. The Heads of State or Government were particularly happy that the Fifth SAARC Summit coincided with the Twenty Fifth Anniversary of the Independence of the Maldives which provided them with the opportunity to express their solidarity with the people and the Government of the Maldives. They expressed their conviction that the Male Summit had helped in consolidating the gains of regional cooperation and in strengthening the institutional base of SAARC.
26. The Heads of State or Government gratefully accepted the offer of the Government of Sri Lanka to host the Sixth SAARC Summit in 1991.
27. The Heads of State or Government of Bangladesh, Bhutan, India, Nepal, Pakistan and Sri Lanka expressed their deep appreciation for the exemplary manner in which the President of the Maldives had discharged his responsibilities as Chairman of the Meeting. They expressed their profound gratitude for the warm and gracious hospitality extended to them by the Government and the people of the Maldives and for the excellent arrangements made for the Meeting.

JOINT PRESS RELEASE

Joint Press Release issued on 23 November 1990 at the end of the Fifth SAARC Summit, Male.

1. The President of Bangladesh, the King of Bhutan, the Prime Minister of India, the President of the Maldives, the Prime Minister of Nepal, the Prime Minister of Pakistan and the Prime Minister of Sri Lanka met at the Fifth Summit of the South Asian Association for Regional Cooperation at Male from 21-23 November 1990. The Meeting was held in an atmosphere of warmth, cordiality and mutual understanding.
2. The Heads of State or Government reaffirmed their commitment to the principles and objectives of SAARC and reiterated their

resolve to intensify cooperation under its aegis. They issued the Male Declaration.

3. They welcomed the signing of the SAARC Convention on Narcotic Drugs and Psychotropic Substances by the Ministers at Male and undertook to take early measures to ratify the Convention.
4. The Heads of State or Government decided to launch the Special SAARC Travel Document which would exempt its holders from visas for travel within the region. They decided that Supreme Court Judges, Members of the National Parliaments, Heads of national academic institutions, their spouses and dependent children would be entitled to this Document.
5. The Heads of State or Government endorsed the decision of the Council of Ministers to launch the Scheme for the Promotion of Organised Tourism during the first half of 1991. They also welcomed the proposal for institutionalised cooperation among the tourist industries of the Member States with a view to attracting more tourists from outside the region.
6. They noted with satisfaction that all Member States had completed their national studies on Trade, Manufactures and Services. They underlined the need for completing the Regional Study within the stipulated time-frame.
7. They decided that measures for establishing joint ventures in the field of cottage industries and handicrafts should be taken up forthwith to set a stage for promoting collective self-reliance in the region. They directed the Secretary General to appoint a group of 23 Experts selected from within the region, to prepare a paper suggesting the modalities for the setting up of joint ventures, sources of funding and other necessary details for consideration at the next meeting of the Council of Ministers.
8. The Heads of State or Government noted the proposal for the establishment of a SAARC Regional Fund and directed the Standing Committee to submit its recommendations on the proposal for consideration at the next session of the Council of Ministers.
9. The Heads of State or Government emphasized the importance

of cooperation among the SAARC Member States in the field of mass media and directed the Secretary General to facilitate, under the auspices of SAARC, increased interaction among federations/associations of journalists, news agencies and mass media of the region.

10. The Heads of State or Government welcomed the decision authorizing the Secretariat to share information and exchange reports, studies and publications with the European Community (EC) and the Association of South East Asian Nations (ASEAN), to begin with, in the identified areas of cooperation.
11. The Heads of State or Government expressed satisfaction that the work was well under way for the setting up of a nucleus Centre for Human Resource Development in Pakistan. They were of the view that the Centre would contribute towards optimizing regional cooperation in this vital field.
12. They called for early completion of a regional plan "SAARC 2000 A Basic Needs Perspective" to facilitate activities within a broad framework of a long term perspective.
13. They directed that the theme of 'Poverty Alleviation' Strategies be discussed in depth by Planners for formulating suitable recommendations.
14. The Heads of State or Government decided that in order to maintain focus on the problems of the Girl Child the years 1991- 2000 A.D. would be observed as the "SAARC Decade of the Girl Child". They were deeply moved by the SAARC Girl Child's appeal for love and care for them and their right to childhood. They reiterated their resolve that the welfare of the child in general and the girl child in particular, would figure at the top of their list of priorities.
15. The Heads of State or Government emphasized the importance of regular exchange of views among the representatives of the SAARC Member Countries at international economic fora with a view to concerting positions, as far as possible, on matters of common concern. They decided to hold the Second Ministerial Meeting on International Economic Issues in India in 1991.
16. The Heads of State or Government underlined the imperative

need for providing a better habitat to the people of South Asia and decided that in order to focus attention on the problems of the Homeless, the Year 1991 be observed as the "SAARC Year of Shelter". They decided that each country would organise a series of events on this theme and share their experiences in order that the people of the region could derive practical benefit from the "SAARC Year of Shelter".

17. They directed that the Regional Study on the Causes and Consequences of Natural Disasters and the Protection and Preservation of the Environment and the Study on the 'Greenhouse Effect' and its impact on the region be finalized before the next Summit. They stressed that, pending the completion of the studies Member States should take necessary steps at national levels in this vital field. They decided to observe 1992 as the "SAARC Year of the Environment".

18. The Heads of State or Government stressed that immediate action was required to reduce the sufferings of the millions of disabled people who lived in the SAARC region. In order to focus attention on their problems and to improve their quality of life, they decided to observe 1993 as the "SAARC Year of Disabled Persons".

19. They decided that appropriate programmes should be worked out for observing the SAARC Year of the Shelter 1991, the SAARC Year of the Environment 1992, and the SAARC Year of Disabled Persons 1993. In order to derive the maximum benefit and to sensitize the peoples in the region in the above vital fields, they noted that Sri Lanka, the Maldives and Pakistan respectively will circulate the recommended Plans of Action for implementation at national level.

20. The Heads of State or Government noted that SAARC Agricultural Information Centre (SAIC) was already functioning at Dhaka. They decided that the SAARC Tuberculosis Centre and the SAARC Documentation Centre would be set up in Nepal and India respectively. They directed that necessary steps to establish the two Centres should be taken up urgently.

21. The Heads of State or Government stressed the need for adopting a more business like and functional approach in the conduct of meetings held under the aegis of SAARC. They requested the Chairman of the Fifth SAARC Summit and the President of Bangladesh to initiate consultations with the Member States in this regard.
22. The Heads of State or Government directed the Chairman of Council of Ministers to prepare recommendations on rationalizing SAARC activities with a view to promoting effective functioning of the Association.
23. The Heads of State or Government expressed appreciation for the pioneering work done by Ambassador Abul Ahsan, the first Secretary General, during the formative years of the Secretariat They welcomed his successor, Ambassador Kant Kishore Bhargava, and appreciated his valuable contribution to the ongoing activities of SAARC.
24. They expressed profound happiness that the Fifth SAARC Summit coincided with the Twenty Fifth Anniversary of the Independence of the Maldives which provided them with an opportunity to express personally their solidarity with the people and the Government of the Maldives.
25. The Heads of State or Government gratefully accepted the offer of the Government of Sri Lanka to host the Sixth SAARC Summit in Colombo in 1991.
26. The Heads of State or Government highly appreciated the exemplary manner in which the President of the Republic of Maldives conducted the meetings of the Association as the Chairman of the Fifth SAARC Summit. They also expressed their sincere gratitude for the gracious hospitality extended to them by the Government and the people of the Republic of Maldives and for the excellent arrangements made for the Conference.

VI. COLOMBO SUMMIT

SOUTH ASIAN ASSOCIATION FOR REGIONAL COOPERATION DECLARATION

The Colombo Declaration of the Heads of State or Government of the Member Countries of South Asian Association for Regional Cooperation issued on 21st December 1991.

INTRODUCTION

1. The Prime Minister of the People's Republic of Bangladesh, Her Excellency Begum Khaleda Zia; the King of Bhutan, His Majesty King Jigme Singye Wangchuck; the Prime Minister of the Republic of India, His Excellency Shri Narasimha Rao; the President of the Republic of Maldives, His Excellency Mr. Maumoon Abdul Gayoom; the Prime Minister of Nepal, the Rt. Hon. Girija Prasad Koirala; the Prime Minister of the Islamic Republic of Pakistan, His Excellency Mian Mohammed Nawaz Sharif and the President of the Democratic Socialist Republic of Sri Lanka, His Excellency Ranasinghe Premadasa met at the Sixth Summit of the South Asian Association for Regional Cooperation (SAARC) at Colombo, Sri Lanka on 21st December, 1991.
2. The Heads of State or Government reaffirmed their commitment to the principles and objectives enshrined in the Charter of SAARC. They resolved to promote regional cooperation for the benefit of their people, in a spirit of mutual accommodation, with full respect for the principles of sovereign equality, independence and territorial integrity of all States and in strict adherence to the principles of non-use of force, the peaceful settlement of disputes and non-interference in each other's internal affairs. They also reiterated their commitment to the principles of the United Nations Charter and the Nonaligned Movement.
3. The Heads of State or Government emphasised the vital importance of assessing the nature and extent of international economic interdependence and of the need for reviving the North/South dialogue. They noted the recent developments that

had radically transformed the international development relationship deeply affecting the prospects for the economies of the seven SAARC countries. The Heads of State or Government emphasised the need for vigorously promoting South-South economic cooperation to offset the negative consequences of international economic developments.

4. The Heads of State or Government also exchanged views on the priorities of their respective national economies. They identified, for the further development of their economies, the importance of securing less restrictive trading and marketing opportunities for their products, more extensive technology and resource transfers to South Asia, debt relief and access on favourable and on more concessional terms to resources from multilateral financial institutions. They agreed to keep an open dialogue on these aspects through mutual consultations.
5. The Heads of State or Government assessed current international developments in the political sphere particularly those that affected the lives of the people of South Asia. They noted the changing power structures in international relations and the reduction of confrontations and tensions, particularly among the Super Powers. These have contributed to the receding of the threat of nuclear confrontation and to agreements on disarmament measures. The Heads of State or Government: hoped that these developments would restrain the pursuit of military power in all areas of the world. They expressed the hope that the peace dividend would be used for promoting further development of developing countries. They welcomed the trend towards popularly based democratic governments in different parts of the world including in South Asia.
6. The Heads of State or Government observed however that some political issues in particular the Palestine question, the final elimination of Apartheid as well as other problems remained unresolved despite efforts towards their settlement.
7. In regard to human rights, the Heads of State or Government observed that civil and political rights, on the one hand and economic and social rights, on the other, are interdependent and of equal importance. Human rights issues should not therefore

be viewed in narrow and exclusively political terms. In this context they underlined the need to view the efforts of States to guarantee human rights in their full context, through the pursuit of development for all citizens in conditions of stability, which in turn guarantees the enjoyment of human rights of all persons.

8. The Heads of State or Government while reaffirming their commitment to democracy, human rights and the rule of law, emphasised the need to ensure that development remains at the centre of international attention.
9. The Heads of State or Government agreed to participate in the ongoing process of revitalising the United Nations as an effective universal instrument for addressing international issues on an equitable and democratic basis, taking full account of the interests and concerns of all states, including those in South Asia. Issues such as the protection and preservation of the environment and the equitable and sustainable management of global resources, economic development and the alleviation of poverty, the suppression of terrorism, drug trafficking and other international crimes required global responses and solutions calling for action by all states.
10. In the context of the SAARC Charter objective to strengthen cooperation among Member States in international fora, the Heads of State or Government resolved to encourage consultations among delegations of SAARC countries at all international fora and to promote articulation of joint positions where such action would be in the interests of all. They felt that the development of a collective position in international fora would accord them greater credibility and enhance the international profile of South Asia.
11. The Heads of State or Government welcomed the Report presented by the Chairman of the Fifth SAARC Summit, the President of Maldives, and the Head of Government of Bangladesh on the adoption of a more businesslike and functional approach in the conduct of SAARC meetings, as well as the Report submitted by the Chairman of the Ninth Session of the Council of Ministers, the Foreign Minister of Maldives, on

rationalizing SAARC activities. The Heads of State or Government also considered other proposals submitted by Member States and by the Secretariat to make the Association a more effective instrument for the realisation of the aspirations of the people of South Asia.

12. They decided that the Standing Committee should meet in special session in Colombo in April 1992 in order to collate and study all proposals and comments in this respect and to submit a report with its recommendations to the Eleventh Session of the Council of Ministers.
13. The Heads of State or Government reemphasised that regional self-reliance should be resolutely promoted through closer cooperation among countries of the Association and that this would help mitigate the adverse consequences of negative international developments operating against them.
14. The Heads of State or Government requested the Standing Committee at its Special Session to study the question of cooperation between SAARC and appropriate international and regional organizations taking into account the evolution of SAARC activities in the core economic areas and to report to the Eleventh Session of the Council of Ministers.
15. The Heads of State or Government noted the progress made by the Integrated Programme of Action (IPA) in expanding to cover a number of sectors crucial for the economic and social progress of the peoples of South Asia. They were of the view that the challenge facing the IPA was to achieve its identified targets within specific time periods. The Heads of State or Government welcomed the proposals made and the discussions proceeding in SAARC to heighten the effectiveness of the IPA.
16. The Heads of State or Government accorded the highest priority to the alleviation of poverty in all South Asian countries. They affirmed that South Asia's poor could constitute a huge and potential resource, provided their basic needs were met, and they were mobilized to create economic growth. This requires that the poor are empowered and are irreversibly linked to the mainstream of development. It was noted that each South Asian country has had significant success cases of this approach to poverty alleviation.

17. Recognising that a great majority of these people remain below the poverty line, they evinced keen interest in a "Daal-Bhaat", or assured nutritional standards approach towards the satisfaction of basic needs of the South Asian poor.
18. Deeply conscious that primary education is the cutting edge in the struggle against poverty and the promotion of development, the Heads of State or Government reaffirmed the importance of attaining the target of providing primary education to all children between the ages of 6 - 14 years by the year 2000. They agreed to share their respective experiences and technical expertise to achieve this goal.
19. The Heads of State or Government decided to establish an independent South Asian Commission on Poverty Alleviation consisting of eminent persons from each SAARC Member State to conduct an in-depth study of diverse experiences of the seven countries on poverty alleviation, and to report to the Seventh Summit, their recommendations on the alleviation of poverty in South Asia.
20. The Heads of State or Government were pleased to note the establishment of the Committee for Economic Cooperation as an important outcome of the Regional Study on Trade Manufactures and Services. They declared their commitment to the liberalization of trade in the region through a step by step approach in such a manner that all countries in the region share the benefits of trade expansion equitably.
21. The Heads of State or Government approved that the Inter Governmental Group (IGG) set up on the recommendation of the Committee on Economic Cooperation should formulate and seek agreement on an institutional framework under which specific measures for trade liberalisation among SAARC Member States could be furthered. It should also examine the Sri Lankan proposal to establish a SAARC Preferential Trade Arrangement (SAPTA) by 1997. They directed that the IGG should meet as early as possible and report to the Committee on Economic Cooperation. The Heads of State or Government accepted the offer of the Government of Sri Lanka to host the Second Meeting of the Committee on Economic Cooperation at Colombo

in June/July 1992 at which the report of the Inter Governmental Group would be considered.

22. The Heads of State or Government recognised that the degradation of the environment has emerged as a major global concern. While the protection of the environment is a common imperative for all humankind, the main responsibility in this regard rests on developed countries since most of the emission of pollutants originates in those countries and since they also have greater capacity for taking or facilitating corrective measures.
23. The Heads of State or Government called on the international community to address the question of unsustainable production and consumption patterns and life-styles which lead to environmental degradation. They were also of the view that environmental standards applicable to developed countries may have excessive and unwarranted economic or social costs if applied in developing countries.
24. Adequate new and additional resources are needed for developing countries to pursue an environmentally sensitive process of development that will banish the underlying causes of environmental degradation poverty, malnutrition and unemployment. Such resources should be transferred to developing countries on an assured basis together with environmentally sound technology at preferential and concessional terms.
25. The Heads of State or Government expressed their conviction that the framework could be laid for an equitable global partnership of all countries with a view to safeguarding the environment.
26. The Heads of State or Government noted that in preparation for the SAARC Year of the Environment, SAARC countries had taken various national as well as regional measures for the preservation of the environment.
27. The Heads of State or Government expressed their satisfaction at the completion of Regional Study on the Causes and Consequences of Natural Disasters and the Protection and Preservation of Environment. They urged the member countries

to promote cooperation amongst themselves for enhancing their respective disaster management capabilities and for undertaking specific work programmes for protection and preservation of the environment. They endorsed the decision of the Council of Ministers to establish a Committee on Environment to:

- examine the recommendations of the Regional Study
- identify measures for immediate action
- decide on modalities for their implementation and welcomed the offer of Bangladesh to hold the first meeting of the Committee in Dhaka.

28. The Heads of State or Government noted with satisfaction the decision of the Standing Committee concerning the time frame to finalise the regional study on the " 'Greenhouse Effect' and its Impact on the Region". They urged member countries to consult each other on key issues concerning climate change. Biodiversity and Biotechnology, a global consensus on forestry principles, transfer of environmentally sound technology, management of waste and other issues for discussion at Intergovernmental Negotiating Committee and the UNCED in 1992 so that the concerns of SAARC countries could be effectively articulated and projected, keeping in mind their respective national priorities.
29. The Government of India renewed its offer to host a Ministerial Meeting to harmonize the views of SAARC countries on these issues before UNCED 1992. The Heads of State or Government welcomed the offer.
30. The Heads of State or Government noted the useful activities conducted during 1991 which was observed as SAARC Year of Shelter. They decided to continue to work towards the global objective of "Shelter for All by the Year 2000."
31. The Heads of State or Government were of the view that Governments should play the critical role of facilitator and supporter of the initiatives of the people and non-governmental agencies in the field of shelter. In this role, they should be involved in the provision of affordable sites with secure tenure, making housing finance available on an affordable and sustainable

basis, providing infrastructure development such as water supply and sanitation, energy and waste disposal, increasing the supply of building materials at reasonable prices using indigenous resources, removing constraints to building activities, and creating maximum opportunities for public participation in decision making and management of shelter activities in the overall context of poverty alleviation. Such activities would be facilitated by the exchange of experience, personnel, research and information among the SAARC countries.

32. The Heads of State or Government welcomed the recommendation on the establishment of a shelter information network to be called "SHELTERNET".

33. The Heads of State or Government accorded the highest priority to the question of child survival, protection and development. They welcomed the adoption of a Plan of Action on Children for South Asia which incorporated relevant recommendations of the World Summit on Children.

34. The Heads of State or Government noted in this context that some member countries had completed their national Plans of Action and urged other member countries to complete their respective Plans. They also urged Member States to ensure coordinated follow-up action on their respective Plans.

35. The Heads of State or Government welcomed the offer of Sri Lanka to host a Conference on Children in South Asia in 1992 to consider implementation of the regional Plan of Action.

36. The Heads of State or Government welcomed the adoption of the Plan of Action for 1991-2000 A.D. as the SAARC Decade of the Girl Child. They requested the Council of Ministers to ensure an annual review of the status of implementation of the Plan of Action during the decade.

37. The Heads of State or Government expressed serious concern on the spread of terrorism in the region affecting the security and stability of all Member States and unequivocally condemned all acts, methods and practices of terrorism as criminal. They deplored all such acts for their impact on life, property, socio-economic development and political stability as well as on regional and international peace and cooperation.

38. They recognised that cooperation among SAARC States was vital if terrorism was to be prevented and eliminated from the region. In this regard they urged Member States to take all necessary measures to give full effect to their obligations under the SAARC Regional Convention on Suppression of Terrorism. They stressed in particular, the urgent need for the expeditious enactment of enabling legislation by those Member States which had not yet done so, for the implementation of the Convention and the need for a constant dialogue and interaction among the concerned agencies of Member States, including submission of periodic recommendations to the Council of Ministers.
39. The Heads of State or Government welcomed the initiative of the Government of the Republic of Maldives in drawing the attention of the international community to the protection and security of small states. They noted with satisfaction that the resolution submitted by the Maldives to the United Nations during the 46th Session of the General Assembly and cosponsored by 65 countries including all the members of SAARC was adopted without a vote. They agreed that small states may be particularly vulnerable to external threats and acts of interference in their internal affairs and that they merit special measures of support in safeguarding their sovereign independence, territorial integrity and the welfare of their people.
40. The Heads of State or Government noted with satisfaction the increasing regional cooperation in combating the problem of drug trafficking and drug abuse. They expressed serious concern over the growing linkages between drug trafficking, international arms trade and terrorist activities. While expressing satisfaction at the signing of the SAARC Convention on Narcotic Drugs and Psychotropic Substances at the Fifth SAARC Summit at Male, they urged Member States which had not yet done so to ratify the Convention for its entry into force. They also recognised the need for greater cooperation, including the submission of periodic recommendations to the Council of Ministers.
41. The Heads of State or Government recalled that important initiatives had been taken at the Bangalore and Kathmandu

Summits which had subsequently resulted in the increased involvement of the peoples of South Asia in the process of Regional Cooperation. They welcomed the steps being taken by business organisations/professional bodies, scholars, academics, National Cultural Councils and the media in South Asia to form regional entities/bodies. They called on the Standing Committee to expedite the formulation of guidelines for extending recognition to such groups and bodies.

42. The Heads of State or Government welcomed the setting up of a SAARC Fund for Regional Projects (SFRP) for identification and development of regional projects. They noted that the Fund would be managed by a Regional Council of Development Financing Institutions of the SAARC Member States and that the First Meeting of the Council would take place in India.
43. The Heads of State or Government requested the Secretary-General of SAARC to set up a panel of experts to examine the proposal of His Majesty the King of Bhutan to undertake a prefeasibility study for the establishment of a South Asian Development Fund, taking into account the views of all Member States.
44. The Heads of State or Government noted with satisfaction that the Scheme in regard to the entitled categories of Members of Parliament, Judges of the Supreme Court, Heads of national academic institutions and the accompanying spouses and dependent children will become operational from 1st March 1992. They called for expeditious action to implement the scheme as well as to consider other categories eligible for exemption.
45. The Heads of State or Government were conscious of the vast potential being afforded by current advances in scientific research for the application of science and technology towards the well-being of the peoples of South Asia. They agreed that for the South Asian region to derive the maximum benefit, scientific and technological cooperation should transcend national frontiers.
46. Recalling the decision of the Male Summit to institutionalize cooperation in the field of biotechnology, they welcomed the

proposal for the establishment of a networking arrangement between Research and Development Centres in the Member States as an important step in advancing such cooperation. They also welcomed the emphasis on organised study tours, workshops and seminars proposed in the identified areas of cooperation in the field of science and technology.

47. The Heads of State or Government gratefully accepted the offer of the Government of Bangladesh to host the Seventh SAARC Summit in 1992.

48. The Heads of State or Government of Bangladesh, Bhutan, India, Maldives, Nepal and Pakistan expressed their deep appreciation for the exemplary manner in which the President of Sri Lanka had discharged his responsibilities as Chairman of the Meeting, They expressed their profound gratitude for the warm and gracious hospitality extended to them by the Government and the people of Sri Lanka and for the excellent arrangements made for the Meeting.

VII. DHAKA SUMMIT

SOUTH ASIAN ASSOCIATION FOR REGIONAL COOPERATION
DECLARATION

The Declaration of the Seventh SAARC Summit of the Heads of State or Government of Member Countries of the South Asian Association for Regional Cooperation issued on 11th April 1993.

INTRODUCTION

1. The Prime Minister of the People's Republic of Bangladesh, Her Excellency Begum Khaleda Zia, the King of Bhutan, His Majesty Jigme Singye Wangchuck, the Prime Minister of the Republic of India, His Excellency Mr. P. V. Narasimha Rao, the President of the Republic of Maldives, His Excellency Mr. Maumoon Abdul Gayoom, the Prime Minister of Nepal, the Rt. Hon. Girija Prasad Koirala, the Prime Minister of the Islamic Republic of Pakistan, His Excellency Mr. Mohammed Nawaz Sharif and the President of the Democratic Socialist Republic of Sri Lanka,

His Excellency Mr. Ranasinghe Premadasa met at the Seventh Summit of the South Asian Association for Regional Cooperation (SAARC) at Dhaka, Bangladesh on 10-11 April, 1993.

REGIONAL COOPERATION

2. The Heads of State or Government reiterated their commitment to the principles and objectives of the South Asian Association for Regional Cooperation (SAARC), to the five principles of peaceful coexistence, the UN Charter and non-alignment. The Heads of State or Government noted the progress achieved in regional cooperation under the aegis of SAARC. They felt that time was now opportune for SAARC to provide a further dynamic impetus to activities in the core areas of economic, social and cultural cooperation in the SAARC region.

INTEGRATED PROGRAMME OF ACTION (IPA)

3. The Heads of State or Government welcomed the recent specific steps taken to consolidate and further streamline IRA-related SAARC activities. They also stressed the need for a progressive movement towards undertaking more well-defined, target-oriented and time-bound projects and programmes to ensure tangible benefits for the peoples of South Asia.

ACTIVITIES OUTSIDE IPA

4. The Leaders welcomed the recent decisions to institutionalize cooperation in the core areas.

MORE BUSINESS-LIKE AND FUNCTIONAL APPROACH IN THE CONDUCT OF SAARC MEETINGS

5. The Heads of State or Government approved the recommendations of the Eleventh Session of the Council of Ministers for adopting a more business-like and functional approach in the conduct of Summit meetings. They also noted with satisfaction the guidelines and procedures approved by the Eleventh Session of the Council in this respect relating to other SAARC meetings. They decided to meet informally whenever necessary, between Summits.

CONSENSUS ON ERADICATION OF POVERTY IN SOUTH ASIA

6. Conscious that the sheer magnitude and complexity of South Asian poverty constituted a major political and economic challenge, the Heads of State or Government reiterated their commitment to continue to accord a high priority to its eradication from the region in the shortest possible time.
7. They pledged to overcome this challenge through the implementation of appropriate pro-poor development strategies at micro and macro levels.
8. In this context, the Heads of State or Government welcomed the Report of the Independent South Asian Commission on Poverty Alleviation established at the Colombo Summit. The Report provided valuable insight and illustrative examples of successful poverty alleviation programmes in individual Member States.
9. Acknowledging that the abiding human qualities of dignity, creativity and productive potential are eroded by chronic poverty, the Heads of State or Government reiterated their commitment to empowering the poor for enhanced growth, consistent with human development and equity.
10. The Heads of State or Government committed their Governments unequivocally to the eradication of poverty in South Asia, preferably by the year 2002 A.D. through an Agenda of Action, which would, inter-alia, embody:
    - A strategy of social mobilization involving the building of organizations of the poor and their empowerment through appropriate national support mechanisms, with the assistance of respective Governments;
    - A policy of decentralized agricultural development and sharply focussed household level food security through universal provision of 'Daal-Bhaat' or basic nutritional needs;
    - A policy of decentralized small scale labour intensive industrialization, with the choice of efficient and cost-effective technology;

- A policy of human development, including the enhancement of the social role and status of poor women, the provision of universal primary education, skill development, primary health care, shelter for the poor and protection of children;
- A policy to support the above initiatives with adequate financial resources.

11. The Heads of State or Government stressed that within the overall conceptual approach of 'Daal-Bhaat', the right to work and the right to primary education should receive priority.
12. The Leaders also underscored the critical link between the success of national efforts aimed at poverty alleviation and the external factors affecting growth and development. They urged all major actors in the world economic scene, particularly the industrialized countries and multilateral and regional financial institutions, and Non-Govenunental Organizations to create an enabling international atmosphere that is supportive of poverty alleviation programmes in South Asia. This would require a new dialogue with donors.
13. The Heads of State or Government agreed to the follow-up action indicated below :
    - a national level pro-poor plan to be drawn up by each Member State. This plan is to be harmonized with the open economy and structural adjustment strategies;
    - to share during the next Summit, information regarding the progress achieved.

TRADE, MANUFACTURES AND SERVICES

14. The Heads of State or Government reaffirmed the need to liberalize trade as early as possible through a step by step approach. They underscored that this should be done in such a manner that all countries in the region could share the benefits of trade expansion equitably.
15. In this context, the Heads of State or Government welcomed the finalization of the framework Agreement on SAARC Preferential Trading Arrangement (SAPTA). They expressed their deep satisfaction over the signing of the framework Agreement. The Leaders stressed that all necessary steps should

be taken to begin the first round of trade negotiations to exchange trade preferences among Member States under the Arrangement.

16. The Heads of State or Government further underlined the critical importance of urgently promoting intra-regional cooperation, particularly in the area of manufactures in order to enhance the productive capacity of the Member Countries, and to promote sustained growth and development to prevent the marginalization of South Asia's trade interest in the larger global context.

ENVIRONMENT

17. The Heads of State or Government expressed their deep concern at the unabated degradation of the environment and recurrence of devastating natural disasters. They also underscored the risks and dangers involved in overlooking the challenge posed by these problems. They expressed their commitment to implementing at all levels—national, bilateral, regional and global - programmes for the protection and preservation of the environment and prevention of its degradation. The Heads of State or Government recognized that the completion of the Regional Study on the " 'Greenhouse Effect' and its Impact on the Region" was a significant step forward in promoting regional cooperation in this vital area. They also stressed the importance of continuing the ongoing SAARC activities in the field of environment.

18. The Heads of State or Government welcomed the outcome of the United Nations Conference on Environment and Development held in Rio de Janeiro in 1992 and underscored the imperative need to ensure the flow of resources to successfully implement the wide range of suggested initiatives and actions contained in Agenda 21. The Heads of State or Government noted that all international actions in the area of environment should be based on common but differential responsibilities, collective endeavours and a balanced perspective. Such actions, they stressed, must consider the protection of environment, economic growth and eradication of poverty as mutually reinforcing. All environmental

initiatives, they underscored, must preclude the imposition of arbitrary and one-sided pre-conditions and ensure a harmonious blending of environmental and development concerns. They further noted with satisfaction the establishment of the Commission on Sustainable Development. They urged that the Commission approach environmental problems of developed and developing countries in an equitable manner.

19. The Heads of State or Government expressed their satisfaction over the adoption of a common position by Member States prior to the United Nations Conference on Environment and Development. They expressed their determination to continue in future the practice of intra-SAARC consultations on matters of common concern.

POPULATION

20. Recognizing the sovereign right of all countries to promote, adopt and implement their population policies and mindful of their cultures, values and traditions, the Heads of State or Government stressed the need to integrate demographic objectives and population strategies in the formulation of the development strategies of Member Countries. In this context, they also noted the importance of adequate investment in the health and education sectors for the success of their population programmes. They agreed that cooperation among Member States should be strengthened, both through sharing experiences and in other practical ways, to enhance their capacity to deal with the population problem. The Leaders urged Governments of developed countries, as well as all concerned international and regional organizations, to strengthen their financial and technical support in the areas of health and education as part of their strategy of assistance to developing countries in their development efforts.

21. The Heads of State or Government welcomed the offer of Nepal to host a SAARC Ministerial Conference on Women and Family Health in Kathmandu in October/November 1993.

SHELTER

22. The Heads of State or Government reiterated that housing was

a basic right for all people and that Governments should act as facilitator and supporter of shelter programmes initiated by the people. They urged Member States to continue to work towards the global objective of "Shelter for All by the Year 2000".

CHILDREN

23. Reaffirming their commitment to accord the highest priority to child survival, protection and development, the Heads of State or Government noted with satisfaction that all Member States had completed their National Plans of Action on Children. They reiterated their call at the Colombo Summit to continue to ensure coordinated follow-up action by Member States on their respective plans.

24. The Heads of State or Government endorsed the "Colombo Resolution on Children" adopted by the Second SAARC Ministerial Conference on Children held at Colombo in September 1992 and urged Member States to implement programmes as appropriate in their respective national contexts, to achieve the illustrative goals embodied in the Resolution, and the goals of the SAARC Plan of Action on Children.

25. The Heads of State or Government noted, in particular, the need to take effective measures to protect children against all forms of neglect, cruelty and exploitation and agreed to promote cooperation among Member States in devising such measures.

YOUTH

26. Stressing that the youth of South Asia constituted a vital resource for national development and that mobilization of their latent power was imperative, the Heads of State or Government focussed special attention on the needs of the Youth in South Asia and their development.

27. The Leaders noted that the youth of South Asia faced a number of serious problems requiring urgent attention and remedial measures. They welcomed the offer of the Maldives to host a Ministerial Conference on Youth in South Asia in 1994 to address the problems of the Youth and focus on the broad theme of youth and development. They also agreed to designate

1994 as the "SAARC Year of the Youth".

PLAN OF ACTION FOR THE DISABLED PERSONS

28. The Heads of State or Government while recalling their decision at the Male Summit to observe 1993 as the "SAARC Year of Disabled Persons", adopted the Regional Plan of Action for the Disabled Persons. They urged Member States to take concrete steps to implement the Plan.
29. They welcomed the offer of Pakistan to host a Ministerial Conference on Disabled Persons in September 1993.

WOMEN IN DEVELOPMENT

30. While reviewing the situation of women in the region, it was noted with satisfaction that over a period of time, the content of regional cooperation which addresses the issue of development, gender and equality for women has steadily grown in SAARC. The Heads of State or Government hoped that the cooperation thus developed will enable Member States to achieve the ultimate goal of bringing women into the mainstream of development with independence and equality.
31. The Heads of State or Government recalled that in pursuance of their collective will expressed in the Male Summit to observe the 1990s as the "SAARC Decade of the Girl Child", Member States had undertaken to formulate National Plans of Action for the improvement of the condition of the Girl Child giving priority to her survival, protection and development. They expressed satisfaction that some Member States had already completed this task and others were expected to do so soon.

SCIENCE AND TECHNOLOGY

32. The Heads of State or Government emphasized that cooperation in the field of Science and Technology was of utmost importance in order to accelerate the process of development in South Asia.
33. They called for further intensification of efforts by Member States in this important area, particularly to facilitate research and exchange of information through networking arrangements in the field of bio-technology, genetic engineering, energy modelling techniques and other identified areas of cooperation.

TERRORISM

34. The Heads of State or Government reiterated their unequivocal condemnation of all acts, methods and practices of terrorism as criminal. They strongly deplored the adverse consequences of terrorism.
35. They noted with grave concern that the efforts to combat the growing threat of terrorism had resulted in the diversion of valuable scarce resources from urgent development programmes.
36. The Leaders reiterated the need to give high priority to the enactment of enabling legislation at the national level to give effect to the SAARC Regional Convention on Suppression of Terrorism, while urging the Member States which had not yet done so, to make every effort to finalize this matter before the Eighth SAARC Summit.
37. While recognizing that some progress had been achieved in the fields of consultation and exchange of information, they stressed the need for further enhancing cooperation in these fields as well as for coordinated action. They called for the expeditious implementation of the recommendations formulated for advancing cooperation in this regard in pursuance of their decision at the Colombo Summit.

DRUG TRAFFICKING AND DRUG ABUSE

38. The Heads of State or Government reiterated their grave concern at the growing menace of drug trafficking in the region and the aggravation of the problem of drug abuse among the South Asian population, particularly the youth.
39. They recognized the devastating impact of drug abuse on the very fabric of society and the serious threat to security and stability posed by drug trafficking through its growing linkages with organized crime, illicit arms trade and terrorism.
40. The Heads of State or Government were gratified to note the expanding cooperation among Member States to combat and eliminate the scourge of drug trafficking and drug abuse.
41. They reiterated the need for further strengthening cooperation

in this field and called for the expeditious implementation of the recommendations formulated for this purpose in pursuance of their decision at the Colombo Summit.

SECURITY OF SMALL STATES

42. The Heads of State or Government reaffirmed their commitment to pay special attention to the monitoring of the security of small States and underscored the need to consider special measures of support to preserve their sovereign independence, territorial integrity and the well-being of their people. They further noted that real protection of small and weaker States should be firmly rooted in the Rule of Law and strict adherence to universally accepted principles and norms relating to the sovereign rights and territorial integrity of all States - big or small. This, they stressed, should be ensured by all countries either severally or collectively through the pursuit of appropriate actions.

PEOPLE-TO-PEOPLE CONTACT

43. The Heads of State or Government stressed the need to further promote people-to-people contact in order to ensure increased involvement of peoples of South Asia in the process of regional cooperation. In this context, they noted that the formulation of guidelines and procedures for extending recognition to regional apex bodies would facilitate participation of these bodies in promoting regional cooperation at the people-to-people level.
44. The Leaders expressed the hope that the recent recognition of the SAARC Chamber of Commerce and Industry would contribute positively to enhancing cooperation in the crucial areas of trade and economic relations.
45. The Heads of State or Government expressed their appreciation to the Government and people of India for hosting the First South Asian Festival of SAARC Countries in 1992. The Festival provided the people of the region the opportunity to share in the rich cultural heritage of South Asia. The Heads of State or Government hoped that the South Asian Festival would become a regular feature.

ASSOCIATION OF SAARC SPEAKERS AND PARLIAMENTARIANS

46. The Heads of State or Government welcomed the initiative of the Speakers of Parliaments of SAARC Countries in forming an "Association of SAARC Speakers and Parliamentarians". They were of the view that the establishment of this Association would add another important dimension to the process of regional cooperation.

SOUTH ASIAN DEVELOPMENT FUND

47. The Heads of State or Government endorsed the recommendation of the Council of Ministers for the establishment of an Inter-Governmental Group (IGG) on South Asian Development Fund (SADF) on an ad-hoc basis. They directed that the IGG define in clear terms the size, structure, resources and operational modalities of the proposed Fund. They also directed the IGG to examine the complementarities between the SAARC Fund for Regional Projects (SFRP) and SADF, and their relationship, including the possibility of their merger. They welcomed the offer of the Maldives to host the meeting of IGG.

INTERNATIONAL POLITICAL DEVELOPMENTS

48. The Heads of State or Government had wide-ranging discussions on the current global political trends and future prospects, particularly those issues that affect South Asia. In this context, they reiterated their deep commitment to the purposes and principles of the UN Charter and reaffirmed their resolve to strengthen the United Nations as the central instrument for peace, security, disarmament, development and cooperation among the nations of the world. To this end, the Leaders supported all constructive initiatives aimed at strengthening the United Nations. They, however, underscored that any move to adapt or reform the United Nations must be undertaken with the sole objective of rendering the United Nations more democratic, efficient and effective and not to limit the focus of its attention to a narrow and isolated range of objectives.
49. The Heads of State or Government reiterated their firm

commitment to the principles and objectives of the Non-aligned Movement and underlined the continued validity and relevance of these principles and objectives in the contemporary global political and economic context. They recalled the important role the Movement had been playing in strengthening international peace, promoting development and establishing more equitable and just economic relations and enhancing international cooperation in all areas. They expressed their deep conviction that the Movement's innate strength uniquely equipped it to continue to play a most constructive role in laying the foundations and defining the characteristics of a new world order which should be based on the principles of justice, equity and democracy in international relations. In this context, the Heads of State or Government welcomed the success of the Jakarta Summit of the Non-aligned countries and called for the expeditious implementation of its decisions.

50. The Heads of State or Government noted that the end of the cold war presented new opportunities and challenges. They observed that despite many positive developments and recent successes in resolving some regional conflicts, the international political scene was still marred by strife and tension. They expressed their serious concern over the unfortunate and tragic consequences of ethnic conflict and violence afflicting people and communities in many parts of the world. They stressed that efforts must be intensified to find peaceful and viable solutions to conflicts of long standing nature and new problems through greater respect for international law and universally accepted humanitarian norms and standards.

51. The Heads of State or Government noted a number of recent positive developments in the area of nuclear, chemical and conventional disarmament including the agreements on bilateral arms reductions between the United States and the Russian Federation. They expressed their hope that the implementation of the farreaching arms reduction agreed in the Washington Agreement of June 1992 and START II signed in Moscow in January 1993 would be successfully carried out. The Leaders urged all Nuclear-Weapon States to collectively endeavour to

attain the ultimate goal of complete elimination of nuclear arsenals in the shortest possible time.

52. They also underscored the imperative to further broaden and deepen the dimensions to disarmament and to complement bilateral approaches to disarmament with effective multilateral approaches. While welcoming the recent progress in arms reduction at the global level, the Leaders were convinced that this objective could be best achieved through the promotion of mutual trust and confidence among Member States.

INTERNATIONAL ECONOMIC ISSUES

53. The Heads of State or Government noted that while it was important to build peace and create conditions of stability in the world, it was equally important to promote economic and social development. They underscored that international cooperation for development and eradication of poverty were inextricably linked with the preservation of international peace and security and hence needed to be treated on an equal footing and pursued with equal vigour. The Heads of State or Government expressed their grave concern over the continuing deterioration in economic situation in the majority of developing countries. The economies of developing countries, they observed, continued to suffer as a result of limited market access for their exports, dwindling resource flows, absence of adequate foreign investment, mounting external indebtedness, inadequate transfer of technology and the inequities in the global monetary, financial and trading systems. The Heads of State or Government noted that although the developing countries themselves had the primary responsibility for their economic development, the role of developed countries remained central to the revival of the growth of the world economy - in particular the economies of the developing countries.

54. The Heads of State or Government reiterated the vital importance of economic interdependence among nations and of the need for reviving North-South dialogue. They fully endorsed the view that there should be more equitable economic opportunities for all nations. These should include such important features as

the strengthening of a free, open and non-discriminatory multilateral trading system, effective macro-economic coordination and fiscal discipline to ensure stable conditions conducive to development in the global economy. They also reiterated their firm support for the broadening of the coordination of international macroeconomic policies to take into account concerns of all countries, specially the developing countries. Referring to the competing demands for capital and investment resources, the Heads of State or Government underscored the need to ensure the adequate flow of investment resources to the developing countries through increasing global savings and a more equitable utilization of the peace dividends. In this context the Heads of State or Government also underscored the need to fulfil the internationally agreed aid targets for the developing countries and the Least Developed Countries. They emphasized on the need for exceptional finance to facilitate implementation of economic reform programmes in SAARC Countries.

55. The Heads of State or Government also strongly underlined the need to continue efforts to seek a comprehensive, durable and growth-oriented solution to the external indebtedness of the developing countries. This, they stressed, was essential to accelerate the process of growth in these countries. A lasting solution to the debt crisis, the Heads of State or Government noted, must take into account the need to significantly reduce the stock and service of all types of debts of indebted developing countries to augment the concessional aid flows to SAARC Countries and work out anticipatory measures to prevent the recurrence and proliferation of the debt problem.

56. The Heads of State or Government also underlined the importance of a strengthened and liberalized international trading system. In this context, they noted that the successful conclusion of the Uruguay Round of Multilateral Trade Negotiations was a matter of great importance to the developing countries. Failure of the Round, the Leaders noted, would only further impair economic growth and encourage protectionist policy seriously weakening the multilateral trading system. The Heads of State or Government strongly urged the major partners in the

negotiations to demonstrate their political will and take positive steps to ensure without further delay a satisfactory conclusion of the Uruguay Round. They further stressed that although the main thrust of these negotiations in the recent past had been in respect of new issues, there was an imperative need to ensure that the Uruguay Round fully take into account the concerns and interests of developing countries. This, the Heads of State or Government stressed, was particularly important. The Leaders underscored the need to speedily conclude the current round of negotiations in a transparent, balanced and expeditious manner. They also stressed that before the conclusion of the Uruguay Round of Multilateral Trade Negotiations, an evaluation of results be held from the point of view of developing countries.

57. The Heads of State or Government expressed their concern over the increasing stock of anti-dumping and countervailing duty investigations against the exports of developing countries and the new threats to a liberal trading order in the form of measures taken in pursuit of the goals relating to workers' rights and the environment.

PROJECTION OF COLLECTIVE POSITIONS

58. The Heads of State or Government were of the view that greater consultations among the delegations of SAARC Countries in all international fora on the major issues of common concern to them would be in the interest of all their countries. They felt that the development of collective positions on such issues in the international fora would enhance the international profile of South Asia and would enable the countries in the region to articulate their position on them more effectively. They reiterated their common resolve to concert their position in all international fora and negotiations with a view to deriving maximum benefits from them in accordance with their needs and common priorities.

59. The Heads of State or Government underscored the vital importance attached by their countries to the forthcoming Second World Conference on Human Rights in 1993, the World Population Conference in 1994 and the 1995 World Conference on Women. They also supported the convening of a World

Summit for Social Development. The Heads of State or Government stressed the need to develop a common South Asian perspective on the issues to be discussed by these important international conferences. They also underscored the imperative to coordinate the position of SAARC countries in order to ensure a balanced equitable and action oriented outcome of these conferences.

OBSERVER STATUS

60. The Heads of State or Government decided that an Expert Group of the Member States will examine the various requests for observer status at SAARC/SAARC meetings in all its aspects on the basis of a working paper to be prepared by the Secretariat and make appropriate recommendations to the Nineteenth Session of the Standing Committee. In this respect, they welcomed the offer of Sri Lanka to host the Expert Group Meeting.

CONCLUSION

61. The Heads of State or Government expressed their deep satisfaction over the positive outcome of the Seventh SAARC Summit and expressed their conviction that this Summit would greatly contribute towards strengthening the policies and cooperative actions of the Member States in response to the challenges of the 1990s and beyond in areas where SAARC has a distinct contribution to make. They also reiterated once again their determination to strengthen and enrich SAARC as an instrument - endowing it with a clear set of forward looking goals and objectives as well as all the requisite institutional capacities - so that it can continue to work to enrich not only the lives of its own members but also promote peace, progress and stability in South Asia in a larger context.

DATE AND VENUE OF THE EIGHTH MEETING OF THE SAARC HEADS OF STATE OR GOVERNMENT

62. The Heads of State or Government gratefully accepted the offer of India to host the Eighth SAARC Summit in 1994.
63. The Heads of State or Government of Bhutan, India, the

Maldives, Nepal, Pakistan and Sri Lanka expressed their sincere appreciation for the exemplary manner in which the Prime Minister of Bangladesh had conducted the Meeting and guided its proceedings in her capacity as Chairperson. They expressed their deep gratitude for the warm and generous hospitality extended to them by the Government and people of Bangladesh and for the excellent arrangements made for the Meeting.

VIII. NEW DELHI SUMMIT

SOUTH ASIAN ASSOCIATION FOR REGIONAL COOPERATION DECLARATION

The Delhi Declaration of the Heads of State or Government of the Member Countries of South Asian Association for Regional Cooperation issued on 4th May 1995.

INTRODUCTION

1. The Prime Minister of the People's Republic of Bangladesh, Her Excellency Begum Khaleda Zia, the King of Bhutan, His Majesty Jigme Singye Wangchuck, the Prime Minister of the Republic of India, His Excellency Mr. P.V. Narasimha Rao, the President of the Republic of Maldives, His Excellency Mr, Maumoon Abdul Gayoom, the Prime Minister of Nepal, the Rt. Hon. Manmohan Adhikari, the President of the Islamic Republic of Pakistan, His Excellency Mr. Farooq Ahmad Khan Leghari and the President of the Democratic Socialist Republic of Sri Lanka, Her Excellency Mrs. Chandrika Bandaranaike Kumaratunga met at the Eighth Summit of the South Asian Association for Regional Cooperation (SAARC) at New Delhi, India on 2-4 May 1995.

SAARC DECADE

2. The Heads of State or Government expressed their satisfaction on the achievements of the First Decade of SAARC and resolved to celebrate its completion of the First Decade both in the individual Member States and collectively. They endorsed

the proposal of the Council of Ministers to convene a Commemorative Session of the Council on the theme "SAARC - Vision for the Second Decade" to identify the areas on which SAARC should focus in its Second Decade.

REGIONAL COOPERATION

3. The Heads of State or Government reaffirmed their resolve to intensify regional cooperation in order to accelerate the process of promoting the welfare and improving the quality of life of the peoples of South Asia. They reiterated their commitment to the principles and objectives enshrined in the SAARC Charter, particularly, to the principles of sovereign equality, territorial integrity, national independence, non-use of force and non-interference in each other's internal affairs. They recalled their conviction that in an increasingly interdependent world, regional cooperation was a dynamic instrument for promoting economic prosperity, mutual understanding and good neighbourly relations to achieve the objectives of peace and stability in South Asia. In this context, a climate of peace and stability would contribute to the economic growth.

ERADICATION OF POVERTY IN SOUTH ASIA

4. The Heads of State or Government reaffirmed their commitment to the eradication of poverty in South Asia, preferably by the year 2002 A.D. through an Agenda of Action.
5. The Leaders endorsed the recommendations of the Finance/ Planning Ministers' Meeting held in Dhaka in July 1994 which recommended that a mechanism should be set up which would act as a forum for exchange of information on poverty eradication programmes, in the context of the policies and strategies adopted, particularly exchange of information on technologies that are relevant to efforts at poverty eradication. They agreed that this process could be strengthened by sharing and exchanging relevant studies carried out by independent research institutions and experts. This mechanism would be in the form of a three-tier institutional structure as recommended in the Report and would meet once a year. They noted that such a

mechanism has been set up enabling the procedures of exchange of information to commence and welcomed the offer of India to host the first round of the three-tier mechanism.

6. The Heads of State or Government directed that the next meeting of Finance/Planning Ministers consider the efficacy of such mechanism towards eradicating poverty in the region and report on the progress achieved to the Ninth SAARC Summit, through the Council of Ministers.
7. In this context, they decided to declare 1995 as the "SAARC Year of Poverty Eradication".
8. Acknowledging that the abiding human qualities of dignity, creativity and productive potential are eroded by chronic poverty, the Heads of State or Government reiterated their commitment to empowering the poor for enhanced growth consistent with human development and equity.
9. Recognizing that poverty is a complex multi-dimensional problem with origins in both national and international domains, country-specific programmes to tackle poverty and international efforts supporting national efforts and the parallel process of creating a supportive international environment conducive to economic growth and social development of developing countries, are crucial for a solution to this problem. The World Summit for Social Development recognized the need for focusing the attention of the international community on and support the special needs of countries and regions in which there are substantial concentrations of people living in poverty, in particular those in South Asia and which face serious difficulties in achieving social and economic development. The Heads of State or Government reiterated their commitment to eradicate poverty and noted with appreciation the outcome of the World Summit for Social Development.
10. The Heads of State or Government committed themselves to addressing the fundamental causes of poverty and to provide for the basic needs of all. They reaffirmed their commitment to work for guaranteeing the realisation of the rights of all, in particular those of the poor, to food, work, shelter, health, education, resources and information.
11. The Heads of State or Government reaffirmed their commitment

to provide expanded opportunities to the poor to enhance their overall capacities and improve living conditions and to adequate economic and social protection during unemployment, disability and old age. While recognising the need to improve, expand and deregulate markets to promote sustained economic growth they felt it was essential to mitigate any negative features created by the market forces and make all efforts to make the markets friendly to the poor. The Heads of State or Government reaffirmed the necessity to ensure that financial systems and other public policies are geared towards poverty eradication and warned against increase in socially divisive disparities.

12. The Heads of State or Government agreed that the Governments of SAARC countries will have to play a lead role in promoting the support structures needed for poverty eradication, including people's institutions and nongovernmental organisations in the context of organising the people and fostering decentralisation and local self-governance and encouraging organisation of the poor, in the context of their social and economic interests.

SAARC PREFERENTIAL TRADING ARRANGEMENT (SAPTA)

13. The Heads of State or Government noted with satisfaction that subsequent to the signing of the Framework Agreement on SAARC Preferential Trading Arrangement (SAPTA) during their Seventh Summit in Dhaka in April 1993, the first round of trade negotiations to exchange trade concessions among Member States has been completed. They directed that all necessary steps should be taken to facilitate ratification by all Member States and operationalise SAPTA by the end of 1995 as mandated.
14. The Leaders reiterated their firm belief that the operationalisation of SAPTA will herald the beginning of a new and significant process of regional cooperation and would lend strength to SAARC as an institution for promoting the welfare of the peoples of South Asia.
15. In view of the fast changing international economic environment, creation of major trading and economic groupings, establishment of the World Trade Organisation subsequent to the successful conclusion of the Uruguay Round of Multilateral Trade

Negotiations and unilateral economic liberalisation measures being adopted by Member Countries, the Heads of State or Government emphasised the urgency of broadening and deepening cooperation within a specific and rapid time-frame in the core areas of trade and economic relations in the region. These developments call for added urgency to achieve more progress towards operationalisation of SAPTA and intensification of cooperation to expand regional trade. To that end, they decided that the "Components" and "Additional Measures" identified in Articles 4 and 6 respectively of the SAPTA Agreement should be implemented.

INTEGRATED PROGRAMME OF ACTION

16. The Heads of State or Government noted the progress made through the Integrated Programme of Action covering a number of crucial areas and activities.

REGIONAL CENTRES

17. The Leaders welcomed the establishment of the SAARC Documentation Centre (SDC) in New Delhi in May 1994 and the SAARC Meteorological Research Centre (SMRC) at Dhaka in January this year.

WOMEN IN DEVELOPMENT

18. Noting that increased political and social consciousness in the region had highlighted the issues of elimination of gender-disparity and empowerment of women which are essential for their socio-economic development, the Heads of State or Government underlined the urgency of addressing these issues through further affirmative action.

19. The Leaders endorsed the "Kathmandu Resolution on Women and Family Health", adopted by the Ministerial Conference on Women and Family Health in Kathmandu in November 1993, and expressed satisfaction that appropriate programmes were being undertaken to implement the Resolution at the national level by the Member States.

20. The Leaders noted the progress in the implementation of the

Plan of Action to mark 1991-2000 as the 'SAARC Decade of the Girl-Child', and requested the Council of Ministers to conduct a comprehensive mid-decade review for presentation to the Ninth SAARC Summit.

21. Recognising the serious threat faced by certain groups of Girl Children in Especially Difficult Circumstances (GCEDC) including those orphaned, disabled and exploited, the Leaders decided that an urgent appraisal of the situation of these children be undertaken by the Council of Ministers and specific recommendations be presented to the Ninth SAARC Summit.
22. Considering that the exploitation of the Girl Child is a direct reflection of the status of women in society, the Leaders reaffirmed their resolve to take necessary measures to eliminate all forms of discrimination against women and girl-children.

CHILDREN

23. The Heads of State or Government expressed satisfaction that the annual reviews of the situation of children in SAARC countries for the years 1993 and 1994 had been completed which indicated reduction in infant mortality and significant progress in the immunisation programme for children in the region.
24. Recalling the mid-decade goals of the World Summit for Children, the Heads of State or Government resolved to intensify their efforts both at the national and regional levels for attainment of these goals.
25. The Leaders welcomed that all Member States have become party to the Convention on the Rights of the Child. They felt that the recently held Cairo International Conference on Population and Development (ICPD) in September 1994 and the Copenhagen World Summit on Social Development in March 1995 had imparted fresh impetus to the on-going efforts for the survival, protection and development of children in South Asia.

YOUTH

26. The Heads of State or Government endorsed the Male Resolution on Youth adopted by the Ministerial Conference on Youth in South Asia held in the Maldives in May 1994 and noted that the Conference had, inter-alia, served to focus attention on the status of the youth and the challenges faced by them. The Leaders noted with satisfaction that the Agenda for Action incorporated in the Resolution is being implemented by Member States with a view to integrating the youth into the process of national development. They noted with satisfaction that the SAARC Youth Resolution had been adopted and the SAARC Youth Awards Scheme has been established.

27. The Leaders expressed satisfaction on the implementation of the Plan of Action to mark 1994 as the SAARC Year of the Youth in Member States and resolved to continue the momentum generated in Member States.

PERSONS WITH DISABILITY

28. The Heads of State or Government noted with satisfaction that the Ministerial Conference on Disabled Persons was held in Islamabad in December 1993. They endorsed the Islamabad Resolution on Disabled Persons and the recommendations of the Conference and noted that the Conference had further increased awareness among the peoples of South Asia regarding the needs and problems of the disabled persons. They welcomed the activities and programmes launched by the Member States in pursuance of the Resolution for the protection and promotion of persons with disability.

SHELTER

29. The Heads of State or Government, recognising that housing was a basic right for all people and that, in addition to governmental efforts, private initiatives of the people and non-governmental agencies should be supported, reaffirmed their commitment to work towards the global objective of "Shelter for All by the Year 2000."

LITERACY

30. The Heads of State or Government noted that illiteracy is one of the major causes of poverty, backwardness and social injustices and called on the Member States to initiate more concrete programmes aimed at eradicating illiteracy in the region preferably by the year 2000 A.D. They decided to observe 1996 as the "SAARC Year of Literacy".

ENVIRONMENT

31. Reaffirming the need for a concerted action for the protection and preservation of the environment, the Heads of State or Government expressed their satisfaction over the formulation of a common position by Member States prior to the World Conference on Natural Disaster Reduction and the presentation of the collective position at the Yokohama Conference. They recognised that international cooperation is vital for building up national capabilities, transfer of appropriate technology and promotion of multilateral projects and research efforts in natural disaster reduction.
32. The Heads of State or Government expressed their deep concern at the unabated degradation of the environment and recurrence of devastating natural disasters. They also underscored the risks and dangers involved in overlooking the challenge posed by these problems. They expressed their commitment to implementing at all levels - national, bilateral, regional and global - programmes for the protection and preservation of the environment and prevention of its degradation. The Heads of State or Government stressed the importance of continuing the on-going SAARC activities in the field of environment.
33. The Heads of State or Government noted that although some work has been carried out in the area of disseminating information on the problems of environmental degradation and their impact on the region, progress in the implementation of the recommendations of the SAARC Regional Study on the Causes and Consequences of Natural Disasters and the Protection and Preservation of the Environment and the Regional Study on Greenhouse Effect and its Impact on the Region, which were

completed in 1992, had been slow. They stressed the importance of effective and speedy implementation of the recommendations of the two Studies and requested Member States to take all necessary steps without further delay in vital areas such as sharing and developing scientific capabilities to protect and manage the environment. They further directed the Technical Committee on Environment to monitor the progress made in the implementation of the recommendations of the two Studies, and submit a report to the Ninth Summit through the Council of Ministers.

34. The Heads of State or Government recalled the decisions expressed in the Dhaka Declaration of April, 1993 on the outcome of the United Nations Conference on Environment and Development (UNCED) of June, 1992 and reiterated the urgent need to ensure the flow of new and additional resources that are adequate and predictable to successfully implement the programmes of Agenda 21. They also recalled the United Nations minimum target for developed countries of 0.7 per cent of GNP as Official Development Assistance, a target which is yet to be approximated by most developed countries. The Heads of State or Government also noted that international actions in the area of environment protection should be based on partnership and collective endeavours and should reflect the principle enunciated in the UNCED, of common but differentiated responsibilities. Integral to such actions is the promotion of economic growth in developing countries, that is both sustained and sustainable and direct action in eradicating poverty.

35. The Heads of State or Government also noted that the Commission on Sustainable Development set up to monitor the implementation of the Rio agreements has met thrice since their earlier meeting and expressed the hope that the Commission would be able to facilitate the necessary flow of resources and technology.

36. The Heads of State or Government also noted that the Convention on Biological Diversity and the United Nations Framework Convention on Climate Change have both come into force and the first meetings of the Conferences of Parties to each

Convention have been held. Welcoming these developments they urged that developing countries should be assisted in meeting their commitments under the Conventions. The establishment of the restructured Global Environment Facility (GEF) is a beginning in this direction. However, the Heads of State or Government urged that funds of a much larger order would be necessary if the needs of the Conventions are to be met.

TERRORISM

37. The Heads of State or Government expressed serious concern on the spread of terrorism in and outside the region and reiterated their unequivocal condemnation of all acts, methods and practices of terrorism as criminal. They deplored all such acts for their ruinous impact on life, property, socio-economic development and political stability as well as on regional and international peace and cooperation.
38. The Heads of State or Government once again emphasised that highest priority should be accorded to the enactment of enabling legislation at .the national level to give effect to the SAARC Regional Convention on Suppression of Terrorism. They urged Member States, which had not yet done so, to enact expeditiously enabling legislation at the national level to implement the convention and reiterated the need for a constant dialogue and interaction among the concerned agencies of Member States, including submission of periodic recommendations to the Council of Ministers.
39. They underlined that cooperation among SAARC Member States was vital if the scourge of terrorism was to be eliminated from the region.

DRUG TRAFFICKING

40. The Heads of State or Government recognised that drug abuse and drug trafficking with its linkages with organised crime, illicit arms trade and terrorism continues to pose a serious threat to the security and stability in the region.
41. While noting the efforts made by Member States as well as the

regional cooperation underway to combat this pernicious trade, the Leaders stressed the urgency of further strengthening the process of cooperation.

42. The Leaders welcomed the ratification of the SAARC Convention on Narcotic Drugs and Psychotropic Substances by all Member States and entry into force of the Convention in September 1993. They urged all Member States to take necessary follow-up action for effective implementation of the Convention.

SCIENCE AND TECHNOLOGY

43. The Heads of State or Government reiterated that cooperation in the area of Science and Technology should be accorded high priority. Noting that some progress had been made towards establishment of networking arrangements, inter-alia, in the fields of Bio-Technology, Genetic Engineering, Energy Modelling Techniques and Low-Cost Housing and Building Technologies, the Leaders called for further acceleration of this process.

PEOPLE-TO-PEOPLE CONTACT

44. Reiterating their earlier resolve to further promote people-to-people contact through increased involvement of the peoples of South Asia in the process of regional cooperation, the Heads of State or Government noted with satisfaction that such interaction has been taking place through various fora both within and outside the SAARC framework and has contributed to the promotion of mutual understanding in the region.

45. The Leaders noted that SAARC LAW (an association for persons of the legal communities of SAARC countries) had been accorded recognition by SAARC. The Leaders hoped that SAARC LAW would play an effective role in fostering closer cooperation among the legal communities in the region.

46. The Leaders noted with satisfaction that the SAARC Chamber of Commerce and Industry (SCCI) has been functioning satisfactorily. They expressed hope that the SAARC Chamber and its constituent units in the Member States will do their utmost to promote trade and economic cooperation in the SAARC region. The Leaders commended the SAARC Chamber

for disseminating information on the scope, content and potentials of SAARC Preferential Trading Arrangement (SAPTA) among the business community in the region.

47. The Heads of State or Government expressed satisfaction that the SAARC Visa Exemption Scheme is being implemented smoothly and has enhanced the scope of people-to-people contacts.

SOUTH ASIAN DEVELOPMENT FUND (SADF)

48. The Heads of State or Government endorsed the establishment of a three-window South Asian Development Fund with the merger of SAARC Fund for Regional Projects and the SAARC Regional Fund and a third window for social development and infrastructure development.

PROJECTION OF COLLECTIVE POSITIONS

49. The Heads of State or Government recalled their decision taken at the Seventh SAARC Summit regarding development of collective positions in international fora on such issues as would enhance the international profile of South Asia and would enable the Member States to articulate their position on them more effectively. They noted that Council of Ministers had formulated a procedure for projection of SAARC collective positions at such international fora.

50. They noted with satisfaction that pursuant to the decision at the Seventh SAARC Summit, collective positions were formulated by Member States which were presented at the World Conference on Natural Disaster Reduction and the World Summit for Social Development. The Leaders also noted with satisfaction that a SAARC collective position will also be presented at the Fourth World Conference on Women in Beijing in September 1995.

SECURITY OF SMALL STATES

51. The Heads of State or Government reaffirming their commitment to universally accepted principles and norms relating to the sovereign rights and territorial integrity of all States, recognised that small States, because of their particular problems, required special

measures of support for safeguarding their independence and territorial integrity. They reiterated that real protection of small and weaker States should be firmly rooted in the rule of law. This, they stressed should be ensured by all countries either severally or collectively through the pursuit of appropriate actions.

INTERNATIONAL POLITICAL DEVELOPMENTS

52. The Heads of State or Government noted that the end of the Cold War had resulted in fundamental changes in the political landscape. It was therefore important that a new idiom be found to address new concerns. The disappearance of the confrontation between the two power blocs presented an opportunity towards building a genuine consensus for a new international order.

53. The Heads of State or Government had wide ranging discussions on the current global political trends and future prospects, particularly those issues that concern South Asia. In this context, they reiterated their deep commitment to the purposes and principles of the UN Charter and reaffirmed their resolve to strengthen the United Nations as the central instrument for peace, security, disarmament, development and cooperation among the nations of the world. While pledging their support to all constructive initiatives aimed at strengthening the United Nations, the Leaders emphasised that such initiatives must be undertaken with the sole objective of rendering the United Nations and all its organs more democratic, efficient and effective and not to limit the focus of its attention to a narrow and isolated range of objectives.

54. Appreciating the role of some SAARC Member States in the UN Peace Keeping Operations in various parts of the world, the Heads of State or Government felt that such participation had contributed towards maintenance of peace and security in the world.

55. The Heads of State or Government reiterated their firm commitment to the principles and objectives of the Non-aligned Movement and underlined the continued validity and relevance of these principles and objectives in the contemporary world.

They recalled the stabilising role played by the Movement in global affairs since its inception. They expressed their deep conviction that the Movement's innate strength equipped it to continue to play a most constructive role in laying the foundations of a new world order based on the rule of law, non-discrimination, equity and cooperation.

56. The Heads of State or Government noted that while the international community had successfully created the norm against chemical and biological weapons, it had, unfortunately, been unable to do the same with regard to nuclear weapons. The Leaders were convinced that more needs to be done and at a far greater pace. Reiterating that the utmost priority was to be given to nuclear disarmament, given the danger posed by nuclear weapons, they urged the Conference on Disarmament to negotiate an international convention prohibiting the use or threat of use of nuclear weapons under any circumstances and undertake negotiations for the complete elimination of all nuclear weapons within a time bound framework.

57. The Heads of State or Government expressed their strong commitment to the promotion and protection of human rights. They agreed to take all necessary steps to achieve this objective.

INTERNATIONAL ECONOMIC AND SOCIAL ISSUES

58. The Heads of State or Government welcomed the successful conclusion of the Uruguay Round of multilateral trade negotiations and reaffirmed their commitment to implement fully and as scheduled, the Final Act of the Uruguay Round of multilateral trade negotiations. They also welcomed the coming into existence of the WTO and expressed the hope that it would help to expand international trade, particularly that of the developing countries. They reaffirmed the immediate need to elaborate policies to enable developing countries, to take advantage of expanded international trading opportunities, in the context of the full implementation of the Round. They called on all countries to refrain from any unilateral measure not in accordance with international law, the Charter of the United Nations and enlightened regionalism and globalism that creates

obstacles to trade relations among States and thereby impedes the full realisation of social and economic development.

59. Recognising that the promotion of mutually reinforcing broad-based sustained economic growth on a global scale, as well as a non-discriminatory, and multilateral rule-based international trading system, provided a basis for social development, the Heads of State or Government called for the establishment of an open, equitable, cooperative and mutually beneficial international economic environment. They also called for a reduction of trade barriers and promotion of expanded access to global markets.

60. The Heads of State or Government reaffirmed their commitment to safeguard the basic interests of workers. They called upon countries to refrain from erecting trade barriers in the guise of promotion and protection of workers' rights. They deplored the tendency to impose any conditionalities on international trade, whether as a "social clause" or as the "environmental clause", while reiterating their commitment to ensuring workers' rights as well as protection of the environment.

SPECIAL MEASURES FOR THE LEAST DEVELOPED AND LAND-LOCKED COUNTRIES

61. The Heads of State or Government noted with deep concern that economic growth in the Least Developed Countries and Land-Locked Countries is not satisfactory and emphasised the need to take special measures for accelerating the process of development. They reiterated the need to fulfil the internationally agreed aid targets for the developing countries and the Least Developed Countries. They emphasised on the need for exceptional finance to facilitate implementation of economic reform programmes in SAARC Countries.

DATES AND VENUE OF THE NINTH MEETING OF THE SAARC HEADS OF STATE OR GOVERNMENT

62. The Heads of State or Government gratefully accepted the offer of the Government of Maldives to host the Ninth SAARC Summit. The dates would be finalised in consultation with Member States.

63. The Heads of State or Government of Bangladesh, Bhutan, Maldives, Nepal, Pakistan and Sri Lanka expressed their deep appreciation for the exemplary manner in which the Prime Minister of India had discharged his responsibilities as Chairman of the Meeting. They expressed their profound gratitude for the warm and gracious hospitality extended to them by the Government and the people of the Republic of India and for the excellent arrangements made for the Meeting.

IX. MALE SUMMIT

SOUTH ASIAN ASSOCIATION FOR REGIONAL COOPERATION DECLARATION

The Male Declaration of the Heads of State or Government of the Member Countries of South Asian Association for Regional Cooperation issued on 14th May 1997.

INTRODUCTION

1. The Prime Minister of the People's Republic of Bangladesh, Her Excellency Sheikh Hasina; the King of Bhutan, His Majesty Jigme Singye Wangchuck; the Prime Minister of the Republic of India, His Excellency Mr. Inder Kumar Gujral; the President of the Republic of Maldives, His Excellency Mr. Maumoon Abdul Gayoom; the Prime Minister of Kingdom of Nepal, Rt. Hon. Mr. Lokendra Bahadur Chand; the Prime Minister of the Islamic Republic of Pakistan, His Excellency Mr. Mohammad Nawaz Sharif and the President of the Democratic Socialist Republic of Sri Lanka, Her Excellency Mrs. Chandrika Bandaranaike Kumaratunga met at the Ninth Summit of the South Asian Association for Regional Cooperation (SAARC) at Male, Maldives on 12-14 May 1997.

REGIONAL COOPERATION

2. The Heads of State or Government reiterated their commitment to SAARC and resolved to accelerate regional cooperation in order to realise the aims and objectives of the Association. They reaffirmed their commitment to the principles enshrined in the

SAARC Charter, especially to the principles of sovereign equality, territorial integrity, national independence, non-use of force and non-interference in each others' internal affairs. They were convinced that regional cooperation was indispensable in an interdependent world for the realisation of the full potential of the South Asian region.

3. The Heads of State or Government welcomed the holding of the Commemorative Session of the Council of Ministers in New Delhi in December 1995 to mark the First Decade, on the theme "SAARC - Vision for the Second Decade". They observed that over the past decade SAARC has matured as an institution and the scope and volume of cooperative activities have expanded. They expressed satisfaction that in addition to continued cooperation in agreed areas, SAARC has now moved into the core areas of economic cooperation.
4. The Heads of State or Government noted that, in the twelve years of its existence, SAARC has seen progress in various fields of its endeavour. They directed that a Group of Eminent Persons (GEP) be constituted, with distinguished backgrounds in activities pertaining to regional cooperation, comprising of one representative from each Member State, with the discretion of each Member State to appoint an additional representative. This Group, to which the SAARC Secretary-General will be invited, will undertake a comprehensive appraisal of SAARC, and identify measures including mechanisms to further vitalise and enhance the effectiveness of the Association in achieving its objectives. They further decided that the Group may develop a long-range vision and formulate a perspective plan of action including a SAARC Agenda for 2000 and Beyond which will spell out the target that can and must be achieved by the year 2020. The Group may report to the Heads of State or Government at the Tenth SAARC Summit.
5. With a view to enhancing the effectiveness of the role and functioning of the Secretariat, the Heads of State or Government agreed to amend Article V (1) of the Memorandum of Understanding on the Establishment of the Secretariat and decided that the tenure of the Secretary-General, with immediate

effect, shall be for a non-renewable term of three years.

6. The Heads of State or Government reiterated their determination to reinforce the unity and cohesion of SAARC. With the objective of enhancing regional solidarity and promoting overall development within SAARC, the Heads of State or Government encouraged, under the provisions of Articles VII and X of the Charter, the development of specific projects relevant to the special individual needs of three or more Member States.
7. They agreed that a climate of mutual accommodation and purposeful cooperation was needed to impart further impetus to the SAARC process during the second decade of SAARC in order to address the developmental challenges facing the region.

ENHANCING POLITICAL COOPERATION

8. The Heads of State or Government recalled their commitment to the promotion of mutual trust and understanding and, recognising that the aims of promoting peace, stability and amity and accelerated socio-economic cooperation may best be achieved by fostering good neighbourly relations, relieving tensions and building confidence, agreed that a process of informal political consultations would prove useful in this regard.

ERADICATION OF POVERTY IN SOUTH ASIA

9. The Heads of State or Government were unequivocal in their commitment to the eradication of poverty in South Asia at the earliest, preferably by the year 2002 A.D. through an Agenda of Action. They noted with satisfaction the establishment of a three-tier mechanism on poverty eradication and endorsed the recommendations of the two rounds of meetings under this mechanism hosted by India and Pakistan, respectively. They desired that the Ministers of Finance/ Planning should meet again in the near future to give further impetus to this process.
10. In considering the Report of the Ministers of Finance/Planning, the Heads of State or Government agreed that effective implementation of poverty eradication programmes required a focus on greater participation of target groups in the formulation and implementation of such programmes through social

mobilization. They, therefore, decided to designate 1997 as the "SAARC Year of Participatory Governance".

11. The Heads of State or Government welcomed the successful holding of the Micro-credit Summit in Washington, D.C. in February 1997 and its Declaration of support to launch a global campaign to reach 100 million of the world's poorest families, especially women, with credit for self-employment ,and other financial and business services, by the year 2005 A.D.

12. Recognising that micro-credit programmes have successfully demonstrated their usefulness toward achieving many goals of socio-economic upliftment, including the eradication of poverty and empowerment of women, the Leaders agreed to intensify endeavours in their respective countries so that the outreach of these programmes becomes widespread.

13. The Heads of State or Government were convinced that an enabling international environment to support poverty eradication efforts of the SAARC countries is an essential element in attaining success for these efforts. They urged all donor countries, international institutions and other bodies engaged in eradication of poverty to increase their support and assistance to these efforts.

ACCELERATION OF ECONOMIC COOPERATION

14. The Heads of State or Government noted with satisfaction the entry into force of the Agreement on SAARC Preferential Trading Arrangement (SAPTA) on 7 December 1995. They recognised the importance of achieving a free trade area by the year 2001 A.D. and reiterated that steps towards trade liberalisation must take into account the special needs of the smaller and the Least Developed Countries and that benefits must accrue equitably.

15. While expressing satisfaction at the conclusion of the two Rounds of Trade Negotiations under SAPTA, the Heads of State or Government welcomed the decision to launch the Third Round of Trade Negotiations shortly. They agreed that preferential tariff concessions should cover products which are being actively traded amongst Member States. They further

agreed that the Third Round should deepen tariff concessions along with the removal of non-tariff barriers and structural impediments in order to move speedily towards the goal of SAFTA.

16. The Leaders welcomed the holding of the First Meeting of the Commerce Ministers and the First SAARC Trade Fair in New Delhi in 1996 and noted the decision of the Commerce Ministers to meet annually. They further welcomed the offer of Pakistan to host the second SAARC Trade Fair to coincide with the SAARC Commerce Ministers' Meeting.
17. The Heads of State or Government agreed that the efforts to enhance trade and economic co-operation in the region would be further strengthened by initiating specific steps to promote and protect investment, increase complementaries in economic activities of Member States and other measures supportive of promotion of SAARC joint ventures. They also welcomed the offer of India to host a meeting on promotion and protection of investment and the offer of Pakistan to host a meeting on avoidance of double taxation. They also welcomed measures of cooperation in the areas of customs standardisation, arbitration and enhancing industrial economy and management.
18. The Heads of State or Government agreed that in intensifying economic cooperation the interests of smaller countries, especially the least developed among them, should be taken into account through the implementation of special measures in their favour.
19. The Heads of State or Government noted that inadequate communication facilities amongst the Member States were a major hindrance to closer economic co-operation. They stressed the importance of developing infrastructure and adequate communication networks among Member States to reinforce the process of economic co-operation. In this regard, they highlighted the need for the simplification of complex documentation procedures and transactional software to facilitate economic interaction across the region. They welcomed the offer of Sri Lanka to host a Meeting of the Communication Ministers of the Member States.

20. The Heads of State or Government reaffirmed their determination to encourage the private sector in the region to contribute increasingly to the strengthening of intra-SAARC links in key areas of trade, investment and finance. They welcomed the decision by the SCCI to convene annually an Economic Cooperation Conference in conjunction with the annual meeting of SAARC Commerce Ministers and SAARC Trade Fairs.

INTEGRATED PROGRAMME OF ACTION (IPA)

21. The Heads of State or Government emphasised the need to make the Integrated Programme of Action (IPA) more effective through the selection of target-oriented and time-bound activities within an overall framework of enhanced co-operation among Member States. In this context, they noted that the Secretary-General had been authorised by the Council of Ministers to constitute a Group of Experts to review the IPA.

REGIONAL CENTRES

22. The Heads of State or Government noted that Regional Centres have an important role to play in harnessing the resources and capabilities within the SAARC region in addressing specific and shared concerns of Member States. They welcomed the decision of the Council of Ministers to establish a Human Resource Development Centre in Pakistan.
23. They stressed that Regional Centres should implement action and result-oriented programmes and highlighted the importance of rationalising the functioning of these Centres.

WOMEN IN DEVELOPMENT

24. The Heads of State or Government recognised that increased social and political awareness in the region had brought positive contributions to the issues of gender equality and empowerment of women. They further emphasized the need for enhanced cooperation to achieve the desired objective of bringing women into the mainstream of socio-economic development in the region. In this context, they emphasised the urgency to effectively implement the recommendations of the "Dhaka

Resolution on Women", issued at the conclusion of the SAARC Ministerial Conference on Women and presented to the Fourth World Conference on Women.

25. Taking note of the mid-decade review of the SAARC Plan of Action on the Girl-Child, the Heads of State or Government expressed their determination to accelerate efforts at reduction of malnutrition and mortality rates, raising education and literacy rates, reduction of the proportion of early marriage among girls, and the postponement of the age of first pregnancy, thereby contributing to the increased welfare of the girl-child and reduction of population growth rates.
26. The Heads of State or Government reaffirmed their commitment to take urgent action to alleviate the situation of Girl Children in Especially Difficult Circumstances (GCEDC), including those orphaned, disabled and/or exploited. In this context, they endorsed the recommendations made by the Council of Ministers, aimed at the creation of a socio-economic environment in the SAARC region which would provide equal opportunities to children from all economic sections.
27. Expressing grave concern at the trafficking of women and children within and between countries, the Heads of State or Government pledged to coordinate their efforts and take effective measures to address this problem. They decided that existing legislation in Member States should be strengthened and strictly enforced. This should include simplification of repatriation procedures for victims of trafficking. They also decided that the feasibility of establishing a Regional Convention on Combating the Crime of Trafficking in Women and Children for Prostitution be examined by the relevant Technical Committee.

CHILDREN

28. The Heads of State or Government expressed satisfaction that the annual reviews of the situation of children in SAARC countries for the years 1995 and 1996 revealed significant progress in reducing infant mortality and in enhancing the coverage of immunisation in the region. They stressed that sustained efforts should be made by Member States to

consolidate the gains in these areas. In this regard, they welcomed the decision to designate Seventh December, 1997 and Eighteenth January, 1998 as "SAARC Polio Immunisation Days".

29. The Heads of State or Government resolved to implement appropriate policies at the national level to achieve the targets and objectives set out in the Rawalpindi Declaration issued at the end of the Third Ministerial Conference on the Children of South Asia held in August 1996, including the call to eliminate the evil of child-labour from the region by the year 2010 A.D. They called for stringent measures to protect children from all forms of exploitation. To this end, the Leaders agreed to set up a Study Group at an appropriate level to examine the social compulsions that create the problem.

30. They reaffirmed their commitment to improve the status of children in disadvantaged circumstances in the SAARC region. They recognised that the problems of these children are inextricably linked to the prevailing socio-economic conditions and problems of the region, and therefore, called for a holistic approach to address them. They expressed the need to formulate a Convention on Regional Arrangements on the Promotion of Child Welfare in South Asia in launching the SAARC Decade of the Rights of the Child, from the year 2001 A.D. to 2010 A.D.

NUTRITION

31. Noting that malnutrition, often severe, is a serious concern in South Asia, the Heads of State or Government agreed to launch an Initiative on Nutrition aimed at promotion of availability of food of essential nutritional value to individual household and evolving policies for supplementing and fortifying essential micro-nutrients, deficiencies of which have affected the well being of the most vulnerable sections of the population, particularly women and children.

32. The Heads of State or Government emphasised that the provision of a safe, secure and clean environment was an essential pre-requisite for the welfare of the most vulnerable sections of society in the region, particularly for the proper growth and development of children, and agreed on the need for launching

technology missions to develop low-cost, easily replicable technologies appropriate local conditions for sustainable harvesting of water, provision of clean drinking water and sanitation.

YOUTH

33. The Heads of State or Government welcomed the operationalization of the SAARC Youth Awards Scheme and noted that the Scheme will be reviewed in the near future with the purpose of expanding it. They also welcomed the initiative to organize Youth Camps in the region on various themes.

PERSONS WITH DISABILITY

34. Conscious of the continuing problems faced by disabled persons, the Heads of State or Government reaffirmed their resolve to continue the implementation of the recommendations of the Ministerial Conference on Disabled Persons held in Islamabad in December 1993.

SHELTER

35. The Heads of State or Government emphasized that housing was a basic right of all people and reiterated their determination to sustain efforts to improve the condition of human settlements in the region, with a view to achieving the global objective of "Shelter for All by the Year 2000".

LITERACY

36. The Heads of State or Government recognised that illiteracy is one of the major causes impeding the development of the vast human resource potential of the region and a major factor contributing to the region's economic backwardness and social imbalance. They noted that the Member States had observed "1996 as the SAARC Year of Literacy" and reiterated their commitment to continue endeavours to eradicate illiteracy from the region.
37. Recognising the resource, manpower and infrastructural constraints to the promotion of vocational and higher education

in the region, the Leaders agreed that new and innovative methods like Open Learning and Distance Education can play an effective role in meeting regional needs in a cost effective and flexible manner. Accordingly, they agreed that the institutional facilities in such education available in the region should be utilised on a regional scale. The possibility of the creation of a Consortium of Open Universities in the region should also be explored.

ENVIRONMENT

38. The Heads of State or Government expressed concern about the continuing degradation of the environment in different parts of the world including the SAARC region. While recognizing that collective initiatives were required urgently to address the challenge posed by such degradation, they noted that unsustainable consumption patterns in the developed countries and widespread poverty in the developing countries are major factors contributing to ecological degradation in different parts of the world. In this regard, they noted that although both developed and developing countries were required to undertake specific initiatives to face environmental concerns, stress should also be laid on the acceleration of development in developing countries to enable them to face environmental challenges.
39. Reviewing the work carried out in the area of disseminating information on the problems of environmental degradation and their impact on the region, the Heads of State or Government expressed the urgent need for the implementation of the recommendations of the SAARC Regional Study on the Greenhouse Effect and its Impact on the Region, and the Regional Study on the Causes and Consequences of Natural Disasters and the Protection and Preservation of the Environment. They welcomed the offer of the Maldives to host a meeting of the SAARC Environment Ministers to focus more directly on the Environment concerns of the region including the formulation of a Plan of Action for immediate implementation of recommendations contained in the two Studies, taking into account the recommendations made by the Meeting of the

Environment Ministers in New Delhi in April 1997. The Leaders felt that the meeting may also consider the feasibility of drawing up a Regional Treaty on Environment in the context of existing international Conventions on the subject. They reiterated their view that Member States should take all necessary steps in vital areas such as sharing and developing scientific capabilities to protect and manage the environment.

40. The Heads of State or Government agreed on the urgent need for cooperation through exchange of information, strategies and technologies for combating pollution of air and water and for evolving common minimum standards which could be applied region-wise in this regard. Recognising the wealth of bio-diversity in the South Asian region and expressing concern at the threat of its progressive depletion through degradation and fragmentation, they affirmed their commitment to take steps towards the protection and conservation of these genetic resources. They noted that many areas rich in bio-diversity in South Asia lay along shared borders and agreed to cooperate in the creation of contiguous protected areas where identified. They also agreed to cooperate in the prevention of illegal trafficking in flora and fauna and devise an appropriate mechanism for this purpose, including the possibility of concluding a Convention. They decided that the meeting of SAARC Environment Ministers should be institutionalised henceforth as an annual event.

41. While expressing concern at the slow progress in the implementation of the Agenda 21, the Heads of State or Government called for the urgent implementation of the commitments, recommendations and agreements reached at the United Nations Conference on Environment and Development held in Rio de Janeiro in June 1992. In particular, they also called for the early implementation of the United Nations Framework Convention on Climate Change and the adoption of a Protocol or another legal instrument for reduction of greenhouse gas emissions by developed countries within an early time-frame, but not later than the year 2005 A.D.

42. The Heads of State or Government underlined the importance of projecting an effective, and coordinated collective position of SAARC at the forthcoming Special Session of the United Nations General Assembly to Review and Appraise the Implementation of Agenda 21. In this regard, they fully endorsed the New Delhi Declaration issued at the end of the SAARC Ministerial Conference on Environment held from 2-3 April 1997, as amended at the Eighteenth Session of the Council of Ministers.

TERRORISM AND DRUG TRAFFICKING

43. Recognising that terrorism and drug trafficking pose a serious threat to security and stability of Member States, the Heads of State or Government reiterated their firm commitment to combat these activities in the region. They emphasised the urgent need to complete enabling legislation in order to implement the SAARC Regional Conventions on Suppression of Terrorism and on Narcotic Drugs and Psychotropic Substances.
44. The Heads of State or Government recalled the adoption of the 1996 UN Declaration on Measures to Eliminate International Terrorism and urged all Member States to work towards its implementation. They called for international action to prevent the abuse of Refugee Conventions and to halt activities which help terrorist groups to collect funds for their activities in South Asia.
45. The Heads of State or Government noted the establishment of the SAARC Terrorist Offences Monitoring Desk (STOMD) and the SAARC Drug Offences Monitoring Desk (SDOMD) in Colombo. They agreed on the need to maintain regular flow of relevant information to enable the Monitoring Desks to function effectively.
46. The Heads of State or Government noted with appreciation the convening of the First SAARC Conference on Cooperation in Police Matters in Colombo during July 1996. They endorsed the outcome of the Conference, particularly, the call for sharing of expertise with regard to the different areas of police investigation and investigation of organised crime and drug

related crimes. They welcomed the offer of the Maldives to host the second Conference in 1997.

SCIENCE AND TECHNOLOGY

47. Noting that cooperation in the field of Science and Technology was imperative in ensuring the acceleration of the process of development in the region and recognising the progress made in this field, the Heads of State or Government emphasised the need to continue cooperation in this area, especially in facilitating research and exchange of information in the fields of bio-technology, genetic engineering, energy modelling techniques and low-cost housing and building technologies.

TOURISM

48. Emphasising that tourism plays an important role in promoting people to people contact in the region, the Heads of State or Government stressed the importance of strengthening cooperation with the aim of realising its full potential in the region. They were convinced that greater cooperation in this area would contribute to the enhancement of people-to-people contact within the region as well as to the economic development of Member States.

49. The Heads of State or Government noted that organised tourism in South Asia has not yet achieved its full potential, and recommended that appropriate measures to promote tourism be given priority, and in this regard, welcomed the offer of Sri Lanka to host the SAARC Ministerial Meeting on Tourism in Colombo in 1997.

PEOPLE-TO-PEOPLE CONTACT

50. The Heads of State or Government reiterated their conviction that enhanced people-to-people contact would contribute to strengthening mutual understanding and goodwill among the people in the region. In this context, they noted the positive contribution made by SAARC Chamber of Commerce and Industry (SCCI) and SAARC LAW.

51. They observed that SAARC Chairs, Fellowships and Scholarships Scheme should be increasingly used to facilitate greater

interaction among students, scholars and academics in the region.

52. The Heads of State or Government noted with satisfaction the inclusion of new categories of persons from different walks of life in the SAARC Visa Exemption Scheme and believed that this would further promote people-to-people contact.
53. They noted the offer of Sri Lanka to host the First SAARC Film Festival in Colombo in 1998 to coincide with the 50th anniversary of the Independence of Sri Lanka.
54. The Heads of State or Government agreed that the SAARC countries possess enormous tourism potential that should be properly utilised for the benefit of the people of the region. In this context, they decided that the civil aviation authorities of Member States should meet in the very near future with a view to establishing direct air services between SAARC capitals which would promote people-to-people contact and encourage tourism. They welcomed the offer of Bangladesh to host the first meeting of the civil aviation authorities.

SOUTH ASIAN DEVELOPMENT FUND (SADF)

55. While expressing satisfaction that the South Asian Development Fund (SADF) had been established in June 1996 initially with its headquarters in Dhaka, Bangladesh, the Heads of State or Government recognised the need to make the Fund operational at the earliest.

PROJECTION OF COLLECTIVE POSITIONS

56. The Heads of State or Government reiterated their commitment to develop collective SAARC positions in international fora on issues of common concern, in order to enhance the international profile of South Asia as well as to enable Member States to articulate their position on such issues in a more effective manner. In this regard, they noted with satisfaction the collective SAARC positions finalised and presented prior to the Fourth World Conference on Women held in Beijing in September 1995, HABITAT II held in Istanbul in June 1996, and World Food Summit held in Rome in November 1996. They also

expressed satisfaction with the formulation of a SAARC common position before the forthcoming Special Session of the United Nations General Assembly to Review and Appraise the Implementation of Agenda 21.

SECURITY OF SMALL STATES

57. The Heads of State or Government recognised that small states, because of their particular vulnerabilities, require special measures of support from the international community for safeguarding their sovereign independence and territorial integrity. They further reaffirmed their view that such support should be firmly rooted in the scrupulous adherence to the UN Charter, the rule of law and strict adherence to universally accepted principles and norms related to sovereign rights and territorial integrity of all States irrespective of size. This, they emphasised, may be ensured by all countries either severally or collectively through the pursuit of appropriate action.

INTERNATIONAL POLITICAL DEVELOPMENTS

58. The Heads of State or Government had wide ranging discussions on current international issues, particularly those that affect South Asia. In this context, reiterating their deep commitment to the purposes and principles of the UN Charter, the Heads of State or Government recalled that the commemoration of the 50th anniversary of the founding of the United Nations in October 1995 had highlighted the need to strengthen, revitalize and reform the Organization. They reiterated their support to the on-going process of restructuring and revitalizing the Organization and reaffirmed their resolve to make it a more effective universal instrument for addressing international issues on an equitable and democratic basis, taking full account of the interests and concerns of all states.

59. Addressing the question of reform of the United Nations, the Heads of State or Government laid particular emphasis on the principle of sovereign equality of States and on equitable geographical representation in regard to the question of increase in the membership of the Security Council. They recognised

the need to make the Security Council more representative, democratic and transparent, so that it is better equipped to uphold its responsibility for the maintenance of international peace and security.

60. The Heads of State or Government reiterated their firm commitment to the principles and objectives of the Non-Aligned Movement (NAM) and underscored the continued validity and relevance of these principles and objectives in the contemporary world. They expressed their deep conviction that the Movement's innate strength equips it to continue to play a most constructive role in laying the foundations of a new world order based on the rule of law, non-interference, equity and cooperation.

61. The Heads of State or Government while expressing support to the continuation of the peace process in the Middle East, expressed concern at the setback to the peace process and unleashing of violence against Palestinian people in occupied territories and the resulting threat to the peace process due to policies of the Government of Israel in establishing and enlarging existing Jewish settlements in the occupied Palestinian territories. They were convinced that the peace process should be continued by honouring previous commitments made by all parties involved. They also called for the restoration of the inalienable rights of the Palestinian people, including the right of self determination and the establishment of a sovereign State under the leadership of PLO, their sole legitimate representative, which could co-exist with its neighbours in peace and harmony.

62. Noting that the end of the Cold War had created unprecedented opportunities in the field of disarmament, the Heads of State or Government recognised the need for the international community to pursue nuclear disarmament as a matter of highest priority. In this regard, they recognised the need to start negotiations through the Conference on Disarmament and to establish a phased programme for the complete elimination of nuclear weapons within a specified framework of time, including a Nuclear Weapons Convention.

63. While reiterating their commitment to the promotion and protection of human rights, the Heads of State or Government resolved to take all necessary steps to achieve this objective.

INTERNATIONAL ECONOMIC AND SOCIAL ISSUES

64. The Heads of State or Government noted that current trends of globalisation and liberalisation were imposing a heavy burden on developing economies, in particular, the least developed countries (LDCs) which are becoming marginalised from the mainstream of the world economy. They also expressed concern over trends to erect new protectionist barriers by linking imports from developing countries to politically motivated social and environmental values and concerns, such as human rights. They observed that the impact of these trends is compounded by new challenges relating to issues of access to markets, capital and new technologies. They also noted with regret the overall decline in the Official Development Assistance (ODA) over the years which has contributed to the aggravation of the condition of the LDCs.
65. The Heads of State or Government reaffirmed the promotion of a non-discriminatory and multilateral rule-based global system of economic relations in order to engage the developing countries constructively and on the basis of reciprocal shared benefits in the process of liberalisation, as well as to assist them integrate into the global economy.
66. The Heads of State or Government called on the developed countries to assist the developing countries through the creation of a favourable and supportive global economic environment, in particular, through domestic action in their countries for purposes of accelerating investment flows to developing countries thereby generating a positive impact on the developmental efforts of developing countries as well as assisting their integration into the multilateral trading system. They also called on the developed countries to substantially reduce tariff and non-tariff barriers and desist from restrictive trade practices, which would negatively affect the access of developing countries to global markets.

SPECIAL MEASURES FOR THE LEAST DEVELOPED AND LAND-LOCKED COUNTRIES

67. The Heads of State or Government emphasised the need for

priority action on various international development commitments, such as the Paris Declaration and the Programme of Action for LDCs for the 1990s.

68. While noting with deep concern that economic growth in the Least Developed and Land-Locked Countries is not progressing well, the Heads of State or Government stressed the need to take special measures for accelerating the process of development. They emphasized the need to fulfil the internationally agreed aid targets for ensuring accelerated and sustained economic growth in developing countries particularly in the Least Developed Countries. They stressed on the need for adequate resources to facilitate implementation of economic reform programmes in SAARC countries.

69. The Heads of State or Government emphasised that the review of the criteria for the determination of LDC status for consideration by the United Nations General Assembly this year, must take into account the special significance of the extent and magnitude of incidence of poverty in the poorest countries and the special vulnerabilities of small island states.

DATES AND VENUE OF THE TENTH MEETING OF THE HEADS OF STATE OR GOVERNMENT

70. The Heads of State or Government accepted with deep appreciation the offer of the Government of Sri Lanka to host the Tenth SAARC Summit. They further decided that the Eleventh and Twelfth Summits will be held in Nepal and Pakistan, respectively.

71. The Heads of State or Government of Bangladesh, Bhutan, India, Nepal, Pakistan and Sri Lanka expressed their sincere appreciation for the exemplary manner in which the President of the Republic of the Maldives had conducted the Meeting and guided its proceedings in his capacity as Chairman. They expressed their deep gratitude for the warm and generous hospitality extended to them by the Government and the people of the Maldives and for the excellent arrangements made for the Meeting.

X. COLOMBO SUMMIT

SOUTH ASIAN ASSOCIATION FOR REGIONAL COOPERATION DECLARATION

The Declaration of the Tenth SAARC Summit of the Heads of State or Government of the Member Countries of the South Asian Association for Regional Cooperation issued on 31 July 1998, in Colombo.

INTRODUCTION

1. The Prime Minister of the People's Republic of Bangladesh, Her Excellency Sheikh Hasina; Chairman, Council of Ministers and Head of Government of the Royal Government of Bhutan, His Excellency Lyonpo Jigmi Y. Thinley; the Prime Minister of the Republic of India, His Excellency Mr. Atal Behari Vajpayee; the President of the Republic of Maldives, His Excellency Mr. Maumoon Abdul Gayoom; the Prime Minister of the Kingdom of Nepal, Rt. Hon. Mr. Girija Prasad Koirala; the Prime Minister of the Islamic Republic of Pakistan, His Excellency Mr. Muhammad Nawaz Sharif; and the President of the Democratic Socialist Republic of Sri Lanka, Her Excellency Mrs. Chandrika Bandaranaike Kumaratunga met at the Tenth Summit of the South Asian Association for Regional Cooperation (SAARC) at Colombo from July 29 to 31,1998, in the year of the Golden Jubilee of the Independence of Sri Lanka.

REGIONAL COOPERATION

2. The Heads of State or Government reaffirmed their firm commitment to the objectives, principles and provisions of the Charter of the South Asian Association for Regional Cooperation (SAARC) and to the pursuit of regional cooperation on the basis of their acceptance of the principles of sovereign equality, territorial integrity of States, political independence, non-interference in each others internal affairs, non-use of force, the peaceful settlement of all disputes and mutuality of benefit.
3. The Heads of State or Government recognised that the rich potential for productive, equitable regional cooperation among the Governments and people of South Asia which accounts for

a fifth of humanity should be fully realised.

CULTURAL UNITY

4. The Heads of State or Government recognized that South Asia, while reflecting a rich, complex and varied plurality of cultural and religious traditions, was heir to a profound common civilizational continuum of great antiquity which constitutes a historical basis for sustaining harmonious relations among the people of the region. They acknowledged that the SAARC process could draw more deeply from the vitality and strength of South Asia's shared cultural heritage as a source influencing and enhancing creative energies in all fields.
5. The Heads of State or Government welcomed the offer of Sri Lanka to host a meeting of the Ministers of Cultural Affairs of SAARC to prepare a practical Action Plan to network the national institutes of cultural relations and to establish a South Asian Cultural Center to promote the distinctive arts of South Asia. They requested the Government of Sri Lanka to circulate a concept paper on the issues to be addressed by the meeting including financing arrangements for the proposed institute.

ENHANCING POLITICAL COOPERATION

6. The Heads of State or Government reiterated their commitment to the promotion of mutual trust and understanding and, recognising that the aims of promoting peace, stability and amity and accelerated socio-economic cooperation may best be achieved by fostering good neighbourly relations, relieving tensions and building confidence, agreed that a process of informal political consultations would prove useful in this regard. The Heads of State or Government further recognized that this process would contribute to the appreciation of each other's problems and perceptions as well as for decisive action in agreed areas of regional cooperation.

APPRAISAL OF SAARC ACTIVITIES

7. The Heads of State or Government continued their review of the nature, extent, and effectiveness of the cooperative activities

of SAARC. They considered the Report and Recommendations of the Group of Eminent Persons mandated by the Ninth Summit in Male to undertake a comprehensive appraisal of SAARC and to develop an Agenda for 2000 and beyond. They expressed appreciation for the Chairman of the Ninth Summit, His Excellency Mr. Maumoon Abdul Gayoom, the President of the Maldives for convening the Group of Eminent Persons (GEP) and encouraging them to complete their work within the time frame given to them by the Ninth SAARC Summit.

8. The Heads of State or Government directed the Council of Ministers to examine the Report of the Group of Eminent Persons in depth at their next Session, taking into consideration the views of Member States with regard to the viability of the recommendations and the method of their implementation.

SAARC IN THE CHANGING INTERNATIONAL ECONOMIC ENVIRONMENT

9. The Heads of State or Government assessed the implications of current global economic developments on the economies of South Asia and other developing countries. They noted the profundity of the widespread changes being effected in the economic, technological, social and information fields and their apparent unpredictability. They expressed serious concern over the severe distortions produced by the process of unrestrained globalisation as has been evidenced in the downturn of economies of several Asian States. The challenges and opportunities inherent in these fast evolving developments could best be met and the full potential of South Asia realized through effective practical regional and bilateral cooperation among Member States.

10. They noted that the benefits of the so described "liberalization" have been disappointingly asymmetrical with the process proceeding at a much slower pace in areas of special interest to developing countries. Increased opportunities in trade and investment have bypassed many developing countries. The Least Developed Countries have in particular been marginalised through a series of developments including the shrinking of ODA, concessional and other financial flows to these countries.

11. The Heads of State or Government noted the initiation of links between SAARC and economic unions and trading groups that were emerging in the wake of globalization and liberalization and considered how best relationships of mutual benefit could be established.
12. The Heads of State or Government observed that following the WTO Ministerial Conference in Geneva, a process has been initiated at the WTO where implementation issues, built in agenda issues, issues arising out of the WTO Ministerial Conference and other multilateral trade issues will be considered with a view to making recommendations to the next Ministerial Conference of the WTO in 1999. These issues and the decisions arising from this process will have farreaching consequences for our development strategies and prospects. The Heads of State or Government, therefore, resolved that SAARC countries would endeavour to coordinate their decisions on these issues in areas of common concern so as to protect and promote the interest of the developing countries. They expressed concern about the erection of protectionist barriers and the tendency to impose arbitrary "norms" relating to labour conditions, environmental regulations, governance and other extraneous issues to regulate trade exchanges, which would amount to additional non-tariff barriers, that would have the effect of restricting market access for developing countries including preferential access by Least Developed Countries (LDCs) into markets of developed countries. They agreed on the need for collective strategies to promote a rule-based, non-discriminatory and equitable international trading system in which the interests and concerns of developing countries would be fully safeguarded and served.
13. The Heads of State or Government noted that emerging issues relating to copyright, patents and marketing franchises including on foodgrains, plants and herbs indigenous to South Asia require firm collective responses to preserve these bio-resources from unregulated commercial exploitation by extra-regional interests. They emphasized in this regard, the principle of sustainable development of bio-resources and the provisions of the UN Convention on Bio-diversity which provided for regulated

access to such resources on terms and conditions to be agreed upon with the State in which such resources are located.

14. The Heads of State or Government cautioned that potential efforts to formulate a new Multilateral Investment Agreement should not overlook the need to ensure the continued independence of developing countries and Least Developed Countries (LDCs) to formulate specific investment policies appropriate to their stage of development.
15. While reviewing the beneficial effects of globalization, the Heads of State or Government stressed the fact that systemic crises are becoming unpredictable with increased globalization. They expressed their concern about the shortcomings of the international monetary and financial system, and its tardiness in anticipating impending financial market crises sufficiently in advance, so that pre-emptive remedial action be adopted. They noted that the problem is systemic, and not unique to Asia, nor confined to emerging economies, and that it can have global ramifications, unless more fundamental reforms are put in place.
16. They recognized the risk that ad-hoc approaches, however prompt, once crises supervene, may lead to excessive social costs in the attempt to restore financial discipline. More effective social safety nets would, therefore, need to be devised for protecting vulnerable groups and a more appropriate balance between financing and adjustment found in a reformed international system or architecture, if both the economic and social aspirations of SAARC countries are to be realized. They acknowledged the need to strengthen the individual financial systems of SAARC countries through enhancing institutional capacity, surveillance mechanisms as well as through closer consultations on, and coordination of macroeconomic policies where appropriate.
17. The Heads of State or Government recognized that not with standing all national and regional endeavours for economic development and financial stability, the pervasive global economic environment continued to exert a major, sometimes negative influence on the outcome of these endeavours.

18. Against this background of the need to address systemic issues, they agreed on the vital imperative for strengthened cooperation among SAARC Members to identify, analyze and effectively contend with the complex multi-faceted challenges inherent in the global economic environment that is changing so radically, particularly in this last decade preceding the new millennium. They acknowledged the need to enhance the collective capacity of SAARC in respect of policy analysis, with a specific emphasis on international financial, monetary, trade and investment issues and their domestic ramifications.
19. The Heads of State or Government also expressed their abhorrence over the practice of imposition of unilateral coercive economic measures as an instrument of policy against developing countries. They called for their immediate cessation.
20. They stressed the need for more efficient capacity building to enable informed decision-making in these areas to enable innovative collective intervention to safeguard South Asian interests in international negotiations, as wall as to develop some edge for effective leverage in such negotiations. The Heads of State or Government agreed on the urgent need for harnessing the rich intellectual and resource capacity of South Asia for this purpose.
21. The Heads of State or Government requested Sri Lanka, as Chairperson of the 10th Summit, to conduct consultations with Member States for the convening of a network of researchers comprising members of the Private Sector, Central Banks, Planning Ministries, Research Institutes and eminent economists nominated by Governments to identify, analyse and help SAARC faced up to current global, financial and economic developments affecting the region. They requested Sri Lanka to coordinate on necessary practical measures while keeping Member States informed in the matter. Heads of State or Government welcomed the offer of Sri Lanka to host a meeting in Colombo of representatives of SAARC, nominated by their Governments to study the matter further and report with practical recommendations on the matter in advance of the 21st Session of the Council of Ministers to facilitate early decisions.

ACCELERATION OF ECONOMIC COOPERATION

22. The Heads of State or Government assessed progress made in the two rounds of negotiations already undertaken under SAPTA. They decided that the third round should be concluded well before the Twenty-first Session of the Council of Ministers. The Heads of State or Government decided that to accelerate progress in the next round of SAPTA negotiations, deeper preferential tariff concessions should be extended to products which are being actively traded, or are likely to be traded, among Members; that discriminatory practices and non-tariff barriers should be simultaneously removed on items in respect of which tariff concessions are granted or have been granted earlier. Measures to remove structural impediments should also be taken in order to move speedily towards the goal of South Asian Free Trade Area (SAFTA). They also directed that domestic content requirements under SAPTA Rules of Origin should be reduced and that the SAPTA Committee of Participants should meet by mid-October '98 in Colombo to finalise the extent of reduction in keeping with the decision of the Second SAARC Commerce Ministers' Meeting. The Heads of State or Government reaffirmed that measures to enable smaller and Least Developed Countries to benefit equitably from economic liberalization were specially important.
23. The Heads of State or Government reiterated the importance of achieving SAPTA as mandated by the Ninth SMRC Summit. To this end they decided that a Committee of Experts, in consultation with Member States, be constituted with specific Terms of Reference (TOR) to work on drafting a comprehensive treaty regime for creating a free trade area. The Heads of State or Government expressed the view that such a treaty must incorporate, among other things, binding time-frames for freeing trade, measures to facilitate trade, and provisions to ensure an equitable distribution of benefits of trade to all states, especially for smaller and least developed countries, including mechanisms for compensation of revenue loss. They emphasised the importance of finalising the text of the regulatory framework by the year 2001.

24. The Heads of State or Government agreed that the benefits of economic liberalization would be more extensive and better balanced through the promotion of trade- creating joint ventures, investment and trade in services such as tourism.
25. The Heads of State or Government noted with satisfaction the outcome of the Second Meeting of the SAARC Commerce Ministers in Islamabad and welcomed their decision to coordinate SAARC's position on issues of common concern at the WTO. They welcomed in this connection the Declaration issued by the SAARC Commerce Ministers on the eve of the Second WTO Ministerial Meeting in Geneva, setting out a SAARC approach on these issues. Recognizing that critical issues would be decided at the Third WTO Ministerial Conference in the USA in 1999, the Heads of State or Government urged SAARC Commerce Ministers to work closely with a view to evolving better co-ordinated positions on all issues. They directed the Consultative Group of SAARC Permanent Representatives to the WTO at Geneva to consult closely with like-minded countries to advance the interests of developing countries at all WTO Conferences.
26. The Heads of State or Government noted the progress made in preparations for the Second SAARC Trade Fair to be held in Sri Lanka from September 8-15, 1998. The Heads of State or Government welcomed the offer of Bangladesh to host the Third Meeting of SAARC Commerce Ministers in 1999 and the offer of Pakistan to stage the Third SAARC Trade Fair in 1999.

PEOPLE-TO-PEOPLE CONTACT

27. The Heads of State or Government noted arrangements being finalized by Sri Lanka to host the First SAARC Film Festival in Colombo in 1998 in commemoration of the 50th Anniversary of the Independence of Sri Lanka.
28. The Heads of State or Government stressed that more convenient travel connections between SAARC countries were essential to facilitate fruitful interaction among people in the region, in

particular, professional groups, creative artistes, pilgrims and journalists.

29. The Heads of State or Government considered means of encouraging more productive cooperation and collaboration between governments and the private sectors, including in the commissioning of studies relating to regional economic interaction.

30. They welcomed the contribution made by the SAARC Chamber of Commerce and Industry in facilitating the engagement of the private sector in regional economic interaction as well as initiating linkages with other regions for the purpose of promoting SAARC exports. The Heads of State or Government noted that a document entitled "Road Map to SAFTA" was presented by the President of the SAARC Chamber of Commerce and Industry (SCCI) to the Chairperson of the Twentieth Session of the Council of Ministers.

LINKS WITH OTHER INTERNATIONAL AND REGIONAL ORGANIZATIONS

31. The Heads of State or Government noted links initiated between SAARC and other international and regional organizations. They considered the prospects for the development of SAARC projects and programmes in association with such organizations with which SAARC has cooperative arrangements as well as through other forms of cooperation. The Heads of State or Government were of the view that priority needs to be given in establishing contact with those regional groupings which have experience in economic cooperation and functional regional cooperation.

32. The Heads of State or Government also noted proposals for developing cooperation between SAARC and individual States outside the region. They requested the Council of Ministers to consider such proposals with a view to developing such contacts on the basis of mutual benefit and for the advancement of SAARC objectives.

PROJECTION OF COMMON POSITIONS

33. The Heads of State or Government reiterated their resolve to

promote the articulation of joint positions at the United Nations and other fora where such action would be in the clear interest of all members of the Association.

SUB-REGIONAL COOPERATION

34. With the objective of enhancing regional solidarity and promoting overall development within SAARC, the Heads of State or Government encouraged the development of specific projects relevant to the individual needs of three or more Member States under the provisions of Articles VII and X of the Charter.

SECURITY OF SMALL STATES

35. The Heads of State or Government recognized that due to their particular vulnerability, small States require special measures of support from the international community for the safeguarding of their sovereign independence and territorial integrity. They reiterated that real protection of small States should be firmly rooted in scrupulous adherence to the UN Charter, the rule of law and strict adherence to universally accepted principles and norms related to sovereign rights and territorial integrity of all States irrespective of size. This, they stressed should be ensured by all the countries either severally or collectively through the pursuit of appropriate action.

SPECIAL MEASURES FOR LEAST DEVELOPED AND LAND-LOCKED COUNTRIES

36. The Heads of State or Government emphasised the need for priority action on various international development commitments, such as the Paris Declaration and the Programme of Action for LDCs for the 1990s.

37. While noting with deep concern that economic growth in the Least Developed and Land-Locked Countries is not progressing well, the Heads of State or Government stressed the need to take special measures for accelerating the process of development. They emphasised the need to fulfil the internationally agreed aid targets for ensuring accelerated and sustained economic growth in developing countries particularly

in the Least Developed Countries. They stressed on the need for adequate resources to facilitate implementation of economic reform programmes in SAARC countries.

38. The Heads of State or Government emphasised that the review of the criteria for the determination of LDC status for consideration by the United Nations General Assembly this year, must take into account the special significance of the extent and magnitude of incidence of poverty in the poorest countries and the special vulnerabilities of small island states.

EDUCATION AND LITERACY

39. The Heads of State or Government were in agreement that illiteracy was a major impediment to economic development and social emancipation and that the eradication of illiteracy in the Region including through co-operative endeavours within SAARC must continue to be pursued resolutely.

40. The Heads of State or Government noted that the concepts of Open Learning and Distance Education could help substantially towards equal opportunities and access to knowledge. The Heads of State or Government directed that SAARC should build on the substantial expertise already existing in the Region in the field of open education, by establishing a SAARC Forum of Vice Chancellors of Open Universities. This Forum, consisting of regional leaders in the field, should strengthen cooperation in areas such as the sharing and joint development of programmes, credit transfers for specific programmes and the translation of existing programmes.

41. The Heads of State or Government urged the Forum, to spearhead the development of distance education outside the Open University System as well, drawing on the advances in Information Technology, to reach out to the remote and under-privileged sections. They welcomed the offer of Sri Lanka to host a meeting of Vice-Chancellors of SAARC Open Universities during the last quarter of 1998 to discuss the modalities for the establishment of the Forum and to draw up a programme to achieve the objectives identified by the Heads of State or Government. The Heads of State or Government requested the

Forum to report to the Standing Committee on a continuous basis on its programmes.

ERADICATION OF POVERTY IN SOUTH ASIA

42. The Heads of State or Government reiterated the commitment of SAARC to the eradication of poverty in the Region at the earliest possible, preferably by the year 2002. They emphasised the need to encourage maximum participation by target groups in the formulation and implementation of poverty eradication programmes. The Heads of State or Government were of the view that such participation is essential for success of efforts in this field. They stressed the need for effective utilisation of the SAARC Three-Tier Mechanism on Poverty Eradication and in that context welcomed the offer of the Government of Pakistan to host the next meeting of the SAARC Finance/ Planning Ministers under the Mechanism in October 1998.
43. The Heads of State or Government noted that the South Asian countries have provided leadership in developing and implementing Micro Credit Programmes, which have immense potential to contribute to the eradication of poverty. They were of the view that their respective programmes in this regard have proven to be effective and Member States would benefit by sharing experiences and exchanging information and expertise in this important area.
44. The Heads of State or Government noted that Human Resource Development is a key element in any poverty eradication programme. The Heads of State or Government, therefore, agreed that once the SAARC Centre for Human Resource Development in Islamabad is established, it could look in to the possibility of its contributing to the strengthening of the human resource development components of the regional poverty eradication programmes.

SOCIAL CHARTER

45. The Heads of State or Government reviewed the progress made in the social sector by SAARC and determined that, in order to increase effectiveness, it would be necessary to develop, beyond

national plans of action, a regional dimension of action including a specific role for SAARC. In this context, they agreed that it would be necessary for SAARC to develop a Social Charter, which would focus on drawing up targets with a broad range to be achieved across the region in the areas of poverty eradication, population stabilisation, the empowerment of women, youth mobilisation, human resource development, the promotion of health and nutrition and the protection of children. The Heads of State or Government further directed the Council of Ministers to initiate work on drawing up a Social Charter.

COMMUNICATIONS

46. The Heads of State or Government welcomed the results of the First Conference of SAARC Communication Ministers held in Colombo in May, 1998. They noted that technological advances were making telecommunications an important medium for socio-economic development and developing commercial and business relations as well as promotion of people-to-people contact. They called for the speedy implementation of the Plan of Action adopted by the First Meeting of the SAARC Communication Ministers.

TOURISM

47. The Heads of State or Government recognized that further efforts were required for South Asia to effectively tap the economic potential afforded by the global tourist industry as well as to encourage intra-SAARC tourism. They welcomed the convening of the First SAARC Tourism Ministers' Meeting in Colombo as a step towards this end and called for the effective implementation of its decisions, including the encouragement of active private sector participation in the promotion of tourism, both intra-regionally and internationally, simplification of visa-procedures for tourists and pilgrims, more convenient air and other travel links among SAARC countries including special regional fares and the coordination of activities of tour operators.

48. The Heads of State or Government identified the need to

strengthen the existing air services between their respective Capitals, with a view to both facilitating tourism as well as people to people contacts. They called in this regard, for an early meeting of the Chairpersons/Chief Executive Officers of the national air lines.

SCIENCE AND TECHNOLOGY

49. The Heads of State or Government noted that the development of a regional self-reliance capability for South Asia in scientific research and development was essential, given a global context in which barriers to the free flow of technology still remained in place. The Heads of State or Government appreciated the efforts to foster under the SAARC umbrella, collective cooperation in this field.

50. The Heads of State or Government welcomed the offer by the Government of India to hold a Special Meeting of SAARC Science and Technology Ministers to consider a SAARC Technology Initiative to Identify and implement specific regional projects in rural areas which would have the direct impact in improving the day-to-day life of people there. Such an initiative could include rural telecommunications, drinking water and sanitation and improvement of life standards.

51. The Heads of State or Government reiterated their earlier call for the effective and rapid institutionalization of SAARC cooperation in the field of bio-technology. They pointed out that South Asia with its vast reservoir of bio-diversity and tropical climate, has substantial potential for bio-industry development on a sustainable basis. Many of the food and nutritional needs of the SAARC region could be met by the application of biotechnology. Contemporary developments in intellectual property and patent law, moreover, heightened the need for vigilance against encroachment on the regional bio-diversity heritage by external entities.

52. The Heads of State or Government accordingly requested the Standing Committee, with assistance of the SAARC Secretariat, to report to the forthcoming Twenty-First Session of the Council of Ministers on practical and cost effective measures

towards rapidly operationalising SAARC cooperation in biotechnology.

ENVIRONMENT

53. The Heads of State or Government expressed their deep satisfaction at the positive outcome of the Environment Ministers' Conference held in Male in October 1997, and called for the effective and early implementation of the SAARC Environment Action Plan. In this context, they welcomed the offer of Maldives to prepare a feasibility study on the establishment of a Coastal Zone Management Centre. The Heads of State or Government also committed their governments to prepare National Environment Action Plans and State of the Environment Reports before the end of 1998.
54. The Heads of State or Government expressed their satisfaction over the adoption of a common position by Member States prior to the Third Session of the Conference of the Parties to the United Nations Framework Convention on Climate Change, held in Kyoto, Japan and welcomed the adoption of the Kyoto Protocol to the United Nations Framework Convention on Climate Change in December 1997, and underscored the importance of the Protocol for the protection of the climate system. They urged all industrial countries to ratify the Protocol and to undertake urgent and effective steps to implement the commitments undertaken by them to reduce their emissions of greenhouse gases.
55. The Heads of State or Government also emphasised the need for complementary action by organisations and institutions in the region in their efforts to protect the environment and achieve sustainable development in the region.
56. The Heads of State or Government noted that the SAARC Environment Ministers would be meeting in Sri Lanka in late 1998. They urged that the Ministers should at this forthcoming meeting also mandate any specific measures required for SAARC to further strengthen cooperation on environment issues, with other international or regional organizations engaged in the same field.

YOUTH

57. The Heads of State or Government affirmed the importance they attached to providing adequate opportunities to youth in South Asia to participate productively in national development and underscored the need for developing programmes in this regard at the national and regional levels.

CHILDREN

58. Recalling targets and objectives set out in the Rawalpindi Declaration of 1996, the Heads of State or Government noted that the 1997 Review of the Situation of Children in South Asia had revealed progress in the reduction of infant mortality and increased coverage of immunization programmes. They stressed, however, that continued efforts required to be sustained in these areas. Serious efforts were also required in respect of education for all children and the reduction of gender disparities. In addition to national programmes, the Heads of State or Government called for the identification of practical regional programmes which could benefit from cooperation with relevant regional and international organisations with which SAARC has cooperative arrangements for the promotion of the welfare of children.
59. The Heads of State or Government condemned the exploitation of children by terrorist groups in hostilities and called for special measures for the psychological, physical and social rehabilitation of child victims. In this respect, the Heads of State or Government noted the initiative taken by Maldives in pursuance of their directive at the Ninth SAARC Summit in drafting the Convention on Regional Arrangements for the Promotion of Child Welfare in South Asia. They welcomed the offer of Maldives to hold an Expert Group Meeting to finalise the draft Convention for its adoption at the Eleventh SAARC Summit.

SITUATION OF WOMEN AND THE GIRL CHILD

60. The Heads of State or Government noted that many groups of women and girl children in South Asia continue to be in

disadvantaged positions and lack equal opportunities for economic and social development. They were of the view that sustained efforts and practical affirmative action was required to offset the effects of discriminatory, social and psychological perceptions and to empower women through affirmative action, including where necessary, legislative measures. The Heads of State or Government condemned in particular violence against women and acts of discrimination and humiliation which tend to depress the status of women. They also expressed concern over the plight of women and girl children in situations of conflict. Equal opportunities in education, health facilities and nutrition were vital for the integration of women in the mainstream of national development. They agreed to work in close association, where possible, with professional and other women's groups in the region to ameliorate their conditions.

61. The Heads of State or Government recalled that the Ninth SAARC Summit expressed concern at the trafficking of women and children within and between countries and pledged to coordinate efforts of Member States to take effective measures to address this problem. In this context, they welcomed the finalisation of the draft text on the Regional Convention on Combating the Crime of Trafficking in Women and Children for Prostitution and noted that this would be a vital instrument in dealing with this problem. They approved that the Convention be signed at the Eleventh SAARC Summit

62. The Heads of State or Government also recommended that the feasibility of establishing a Regional Fund for Rehabilitation of Victims of Trafficking in Women and Children for Prostitution on a voluntary basis may be explored.

63. The Heads of State or Government were also of the view that the scope of the Convention should be broadened to cover purposes other than prostitution.

64. The Heads of State or Government noted that a gender disaggregated data-base on the basis of data provided by Member States would be a valuable means of assisting the formulation of national and regional policies and programmes in respect of women and the girl child.

HEALTH

65. The Heads of State or Government noted the rich heritage of traditional systems of medicine (TSM) in the region. They observed that regional cooperation in this area would be worthwhile and relevant for meeting basic health needs. They welcomed the offer of India to host the First Health Ministers Conference to evolve proposals for cooperation in this field.
66. The Heads of State or Government urged that the regional pharmaceutical industries should strengthen cooperation. They were further of the view that the Member States could establish Action Committees in terms of Article VII of the SAARC Charter for such cooperation, if required.

DISABLED PERSONS

67. The Heads of State or Government recalled the Islamabad Resolution on Disabled Persons and underscored the importance of having a very definite humanistic approach to ensuring the welfare of the 100 million disabled persons of this region. In this respect, the Heads of State or Government accepted the proposal of the Prime Minister of Bangladesh for the establishment of a SAARC Voluntary Fund for Disabled Persons.

INFORMATION

68. The Heads of State or Government welcomed the recommendations of the First Meeting of SAARC Information Ministers held in Dhaka in April, 1998 and the offer of Pakistan to host the Second Meeting of Information Ministers of SAARC Countries.
69. The Heads of State or Government called for concerted endeavours for the promotion of practical programmes among South Asian countries, including through professional organizations, in the field of information and media exchanges benefiting from technological advances. Such action would help promote deeper understanding of issues common to the region, as well as to project a more balanced view of developments in the region. They welcomed the offer of India

to host the First Meeting of SAARC Editors and Journalists.

TERRORISM AND DRUG TRAFFICKING

70. The Heads of State or Government recognized that the Member States and peoples of South Asia continue to face the serious threat of terrorism in all its forms and manifestations and drug trafficking. They reiterated their firm commitment to combat these activities in the region. They emphasized the urgent need to complete enabling legislation in order to implement the SAARC Regional Conventions on Suppression of Terrorism and on Narcotic Drugs and Psychotropic Substances.
71. The Heads of State or Government urged all Member States to enhance cooperation against terrorism, wherever, by whomever, against whoever it occurs and to fully observe and implement the SAARC Regional Convention on Terrorism.
72. The Heads of State or Government affirmed that criminal acts intended to provoke a state of terror in the general public, a group of persons or particular persons, for whatever purposes, are unjustifiable in any circumstances.
73. The Heads of State or Government recalled the adoption of the 1996 UN Declaration on Measures to Eliminate International Terrorism and urged all Member States to work towards its implementation. They called for international action to prevent the abuse of Refugee Conventions and to halt activities which help terrorist groups to collect funds for their activities in South Asia.
74. The Heads of State or Government noted that two SAARC Conferences on Cooperation in Police Matters had been held since 1996. They called for the continued sharing of expertise with regard to the different areas of police investigation, and investigation of organized crime and drug related crimes.

UNIVERSAL DECLARATION OF HUMAN RIGHTS

75. The Heads of State or Government taking note of the 50th Anniversary of the Universal Declaration of Human Rights, reaffirmed their commitment to the further promotion of human rights and fundamental freedoms by strengthening the respective national institutions in South Asia in this field. The Leaders agreed that tolerance and mutual accommodation, combined

with the strengthening of participatory governance, constituted the foundation for the sustainable economic and social development of the SAARC region.

INTERNATIONAL POLITICAL DEVELOPMENTS

76. The Heads of State or Government consulted informally on a range of international issues, particularly those which have a bearing on South Asia. They reaffirmed their strong commitment to the purposes and principles of the UN Charter and agreed that their delegations would work closely in the ongoing negotiations for the reform and strengthening of the UN system, so that the Organisation could be more democratic, efficient and financially viable and responsive to the interests of its membership, especially developing countries.
77. The Heads of State or Government also underscored the importance of the role of the Non-Aligned Movement in promoting a just and equitable global order and called for the further enhancing of the efforts of the Movement to influence positively contemporary international relations. In this context, they expressed full confidence that the Twelfth Summit of the Movement scheduled to take place in South Africa would contribute towards augmenting the Movement's effectiveness.
78. The Heads of State or Government were of the view that stability, peace and security in South Asia could not be considered in isolation of the global security environment. Although great power rivalry which the NAM had consistently opposed, no longer posed a serious threat and the danger of a global nuclear conflagration had abated, yet some States had sought to maintain huge arsenals of nuclear weapons. The NPT and the CTBT, to which some SAARC members were signatories, had not led to any progress towards nuclear disarmament nor prevented proliferation. They underscored their commitment to the complete elimination of nuclear weapons and the need for promoting nuclear disarmament on a universal basis, under effective international control. They recognised that global non-proliferation goals cannot be achieved in the absence of progress towards nuclear disarmament and in this context called upon all nuclear weapon states, whether party

or non-party to the NPT to engage constructively through a transparent and credible process of negotiations at the Conference on Disarmament.

79. The Heads of State or Government therefore urged the Conference on Disarmament to commence negotiations on a comprehensive, universal and non-discriminatory international instrument prohibiting the use or the threat of nuclear weapons as well as eliminating such weapons in existing arsenals.

80. The Heads of State or Government noted the outcome of the recent UN Diplomatic Conference on the establishment of an International Criminal Court and the fact that the Conference had not addressed such issues as the crime of drug trafficking and the crime of terrorism with its use of indiscriminate violence aimed at innocent civilians and use of weapons of mass destruction. They emphasised the need to ensure that the proposed Court should respect the sovereignty of States consistent with the principle of complementarity with national jurisdiction on which the Statute of the Court is based.

81. The Heads of State or Government welcomed the enhanced status accorded to Palestine at UN fora. They however expressed growing concern at numerous setbacks affecting the peace process in the Middle East, including illegal attempts to change the jurisdiction and borders of Jerusalem. They reaffirmed their support for the achievement of a just, lasting and comprehensive peace based on Security Council Resolution 242 (1967) and Resolution 338 (1973) to restore the inalienable national rights of the Palestinian people.

82. The Heads of State or Government called for intensification of efforts for promoting peace and stability at the global and regional levels for realising universal progress and prosperity.

DATES AND VENUE OF THE ELEVENTH MEETING OF THE HEADS OF STATE OR GOVERNMENT

83. The Heads of State or Government accepted with deep appreciation the offer of His Majesty's Government of Nepal to host the Eleventh SAARC Summit in the second half of 1999.

84. The Heads of State or Government of Bangladesh, Bhutan,

India, the Maldives, Nepal and Pakistan expressed their appreciation for the skilful manner in which the President of the Democratic Socialist Republic of Sri Lanka had conducted the meeting and guided its deliberations, in her capacity as Chairperson. They also expressed their deep gratitude for the warm and generous hospitality extended to them by the Government and the people of Sri Lanka and the excellent arrangements made for the Summit and the meetings preceding it.

XI. KATHMANDU SUMMIT

SOUTH ASIAN ASSOCIATION FOR REGIONAL COOPERATION DECLARATION

The Eleventh SAARC Summit was convened in Kathmandu on 4-6 January 2002. Attached below is the Declaration adopted by the Heads of State or Government.

- The 22nd Session of the Council of Ministers,
- 27th Session of the Standing Committee, and
- 22nd Session of the Programming Committee convened.

THE COUNCIL OF MINISTERS

The 22nd Session of the Council of Ministers was held in Kathmandu on 2-3 January, 2002. Among other things, the Council of Ministers deliberated on the report of the Group of Eminent Persons (GEP) which was submitted to the Tenth Summit in Colombo. The GEP was constituted by the Ninth Summit in Male with a view to reappraise the activities of SAARC and suggest a long-range vision for 2000 and beyond. After deliberating on the subject, the Council made a set of recommendations for the consideration of the Eleventh Summit. The recommendations cover a broad area of regional cooperation including an economic vision, social mobilization in respect of poverty alleviation and other institutional issues.

Other recommendations to the Eleventh Summit, include the appointment of Mr. Q.A.M.A. Rahim as the Secretary-General effective from 11 January 2002; reconstitution of the Independent South Asian Commission on Poverty Alleviation for reviewing the progress made in cooperation on poverty alleviation and for suggesting appropriate and effective measures; and to finalise the text of the Draft Treaty Framework by end of 2002 in order to move quickly towards a South Asian Free Trade Area.

THE STANDING COMMITTEE

The 27th Session of the Standing Committee was held in Kathmandu from 30 December 2001 to 1 January 2002. Among other things, the Committee identified eight Ministerial meetings to be held during the year 2002. These are on the areas of information, communications, culture, poverty alleviation, science and technology, environment, health and traditional medicine, and commerce. The Committee also recommended the calendar of activities for the year 2002. In addition, the Standing Committee approved the elevation of the South Asian Federation of Accountants (SAFA) from the status of SAARC recognised body to that of SAARC Apex Body. Six other regional associations were accorded the status of SAARC Recognised Body.

THE PROGRAMMING COMMITTEE

The 22nd Session of the Programming Committee was held in Kathmandu on 28-29 December, 2001. Among other things, the Committee examined the status of agreed activities and finalized recommendations on activities to be held under the SAARC Integrated Programme of Action during the year 2002 for endorsement by the Standing Committee. The Committee also considered the Reports of the Governing Boards and Budgets of the SAARC Regional Centres, as well as noted the performance audit of the Centres being undertaken by the Secretary-General of SAARC. In addition, the Committee recommended to the Standing Committee for approval, activities for funding under the SAARC-Japan Special fund for the year 2002.

An Expert Group on Institutional Matters, which will meet at the SAARC Secretariat early this year will review the functioning of the Regional Centres and evolve a Common Agreement on the Establishment and Operation of Regional Centres.

Memorandum of Understanding Signed between SAARC and UNIFEM

A Memorandum of Understanding was signed between SAARC and the United Nations Fund for Women on December 30, 2001. Nihal Rodrigo, Secretary-General of SAARC, and Chandni Joshi, Regional Programme Director of UNIFEM represented their respective organizations at the signing ceremony, which preceded the opening of the 27th session of the SAARC Standing Committee in Kathmandu. Under the MoU, SAARC and UNIFEM have agreed to help the Member States to strive towards the goals of Gender Equality based upon the empowerment approach in terms of the Beijing Platform for Action (BPFA) and the Beijing Plus Five Outcome Document as well as to promote mutual learning and cross fertilization among developing countries for effectively tackling the challenges relating to gender discrimination, women's human rights and women's participation.

SAARC Convention on Preventing and Combating the Trafficking in Women and Children for Prostitution and SAARC Convention on Regional Arrangements for the Promotion of Child Welfare in South Asia signed during the Eleventh Summit

SAARC Convention on Preventing and Combating the Trafficking in Women and Children for Prostitution and SAARC Convention on Regional Arrangements for the Promotion of Child Welfare in South Asia were signed on January 5, 2002 at the inauguration of the Eleventh Summit. The Foreign Ministers of SAARC countries signed these Conventions, as witnessed by the Heads of State or Government.

The scope of the Convention on the Preventing and Combating the Trafficking in Women and Children for Prostitution is to promote cooperation amongst Member States to effectively deal with various aspects of prevention, interdiction and suppression of trafficking in women and children; repatriation and rehabilitation of victims of trafficking and preventing the use of women and children in international prostitution networks, particularly where the SAARC Member Countries are the countries of origin, transit and destination. The purposes and objectives of the Convention on Regional Arrangements for the Promotion of Child Welfare in South Asia are to unite the SAARC Member Countries in their determination of redeeming the promises made by them to the South Asian Child at the

World Summit for Children and various other national, regional and international conferences and successive SAARC Summits; to facilitate and help in the development and protection of the full potential of the South Asian child, promote understanding and awareness of the rights, duties and responsibilities of the children and others; and to set up appropriate regional arrangements to assist the Member States in fulfilling the rights of the child, taking into account the changing needs of the child.

DECLARATION OF THE ELEVENTH SAARC SUMMIT

The Prime Minister of the People's Republic of Bangladesh, Her Excellency Begum Khaleda Zia; the Prime Minister of the Royal Government of Bhutan, His Excellency Lyonpo Khandu Wangchuk; the Prime Minister of the Republic of India, His Excellency Mr. Atal Behari Vajpayee; the President of the Republic of Maldives, His Excellency Mr. Maumoon Abdul Gayoom; the Prime Minister of the Kingdom of Nepal, Right Honourable Mr. Sher Bahadur Deuba; the President of the Islamic Republic of Pakistan, His Excellency General Pervez Musharraf; and the President of the Democratic Socialist Republic of Sri Lanka, Her Excellency Mrs. Chandrika Bandaranaike Kumaratunga met at the Eleventh Summit meeting of the South Asian Association for Regional Cooperation (SAARC) in Kathmandu, Nepal from 4 to 6 January 2002.

REGIONAL COOPERATION

1. The Heads of State or Government reaffirmed their commitment to regional cooperation through SAARC and underscored the importance of annual Summit meetings in charting common strategies for the realization of the objectives and principles set out in the Charter of the Association. Meeting for the first time at the dawn of the new millennium, they solemnly renewed their pledge to strengthen the Association and make it more cohesive, result oriented, and forward looking, by adopting clearly defined programs and effective implementation strategies in line with popular expectations. To give effect to the shared aspirations for a more prosperous South Asia, the Leaders agreed to the vision of a phased and planned process eventually leading to a South Asian Economic Union.

2. The Heads of State or Government stressed that equitable sharing of the benefits of regional cooperation is essential to achieve and maintain a minimum acceptable level of economic and social development in each Member State. To this end, they expressed their commitment to a speedier process of harmonizing their policies and practices and imbibing regional goals and strategies in their national development programs.
3. The Heads of State or Government expressed their firm determination to fully benefit from the wealth of traditional wisdom, creativity and enterprise in the region. They also pledged to enhance transparency and accountability in governance and to encourage effective participation of the peoples and civil societies in the formulation as well as implementation of the programs of cooperation.
4. Reiterating their resolve to promote South Asian regional identity and to strengthen cooperation at the international level, the Heads of State or Government also reemphasized the need to evolve common positions on. issues of shared interest at the international fora.

COOPERATION IN THE ECONOMIC SECTOR

5. The Heads of State or Government agreed to accelerate cooperation in the core areas of trade, finance and investment to realize the goal of an integrated South Asian economy in a step-by-step manner. They expressed their determination to make full use of regional synergy to maximize the benefits of globalisation and liberalization and to minimize their negative impacts on the region. While recognizing that trade and economic expansion is closely inter-linked, the Leaders made a commitment to widen and deepen the scope of regional networks of activities in trade and financial matters.
6. The Heads of State or Government noted with satisfaction the outcomes of the successive meetings of the SAARC Commerce Ministers aimed at enlarging the scope of cooperation in the core areas. They recognised the importance of achieving a free trade area and reaffirmed that the treaty regime for creating a free trade area must incorporate, inter alia, binding time-frames

for freeing trade, measures to facilitate trade and provisions to ensure an equitable distribution of benefits of trade to all states, especially for small and least developed countries, including mechanisms for compensation of revenue loss.

7. Recognising the need to move quickly towards a South Asian Free Trade Area, the Heads of State or Government directed the Council of Ministers to finalize the text of the Draft Treaty Framework by the end of 2002. They also directed that in moving towards the goal of SAFTA, the Member States expedite action to remove tariff and non-tariff barriers and structural impediments to free trade. They also instructed to conclude the meeting of the Inter Governmental Group on Trade Liberalization for the Fourth Round of Trade Negotiations under SAPTA as early as possible as per the decision of the Tenth SAARC Summit in Colombo.
8. The Heads of State or Government renewed their commitment to encourage the participation of the private sector and assured their full support for their socially responsible economic initiatives. While welcoming the practice of holding trade fairs in cooperation with the private sector at the regional level, they appreciated the efforts of the SAARC Chamber of Commerce and Industry to promote regional economic cooperation in the spirit of public and private sector partnership.
9. The Heads of State or Government also decided to instruct the Secretary-General to facilitate the early finalization of a regionally agreed investment framework to meet investment needs of the SAARC Member States.
10. The Heads of State or Government recognized the immense tourism potential of South Asia and underlined the need to take measures to promote South Asia as a common tourist destination through joint efforts in areas such as upgrading of infrastructure, air linkages, simplification and harmonization of administrative procedures and training and joint marketing.

POVERTY ALLEVIATION

11. The Heads of State or Government acknowledged that investment in poverty alleviation programs contributes to social

stability, economic progress and overall prosperity. They were of the view that widespread and debilitating poverty continued to be the most formidable developmental challenge for the region. Conscious of the magnitude of poverty in the region, and recalling also the decision of the UN Millennium Summit 2000 to reduce world poverty to half by 2015, and also recalling the commitments made at the five year review of the World Summit for Social Development to reduce poverty through enhanced social mobilization, the Heads of State or Government made a review of the SAARC activities aimed at poverty alleviation and decided to reinvigorate them in the context of the regional and global commitments to poverty reduction.

12. The Heads of State or Government expressed their firm resolve to combat the problem of poverty with a new sense of urgency by actively promoting the synergetic partnership among national governments, international agencies, the private sector, and the civil society. They reaffirmed their pledge to undertake effective and sustained poverty alleviation programs through pro-poor growth strategies and social as well as other policy interventions with specific sectoral targets. The Leaders also agreed to take immediate steps for the effective implementation of the programs for social mobilization and decentralization, and for strengthening institution building and support mechanisms to ensure participation of the poor, both as stakeholder and beneficiary, in governance and the development process.

13. The Heads of State or Government decided to undertake sustained measures to extend rural micro-credit programs with focus on women and the disadvantaged sections of society. They also stressed the need for widening the opportunities for gainful employment. While highlighting the importance of promoting agriculture, indigenous skills and small scale and cottage industries to address the incidence of rural poverty, they decided to enhance cooperation in agricultural research, extension and adoption. They specifically instructed that the Technical Committees should identify programmes and activities that impact on poverty alleviation. They urged the need to create gainful employment and promote cooperation in vocational training.

14. The Heads of State or Government emphasized the need to promote sharing of the best practices and experiences among the Member States and to this end, instructed the Secretary-General to disseminate such information to the Member States on a regular basis. They directed the Council of Ministers to review, on a continuous basis, the regional poverty profile to be prepared by the Secretary-General with the assistance of the related UN agencies, nodal agencies and independent research institutions specialized in the field.
15. In order to ensure social stability and to protect the vulnerable sections of population from the adverse impacts of globalisation and liberalization, the Heads of State or Government stressed the need to enhance cooperation to create and maintain appropriate safety nets.
16. The Heads of State or Government agreed that a Special Session on poverty alleviation at the Ministerial level should undertake a comprehensive review and evaluation of the status of implementation of poverty eradication policies and programs carried out so far, and to recommend further concrete measures to enhance effective cooperation at the regional level to the Twelfth SAARC Summit. They also directed the Council of Ministers to take necessary steps to fully activate the existing three-tier mechanism for poverty alleviation.
17. The Leaders directed the Council of Ministers to coordinate efforts to integrate poverty alleviation programs into the development strategies of Member States. In this context, they agreed to reconstitute the Independent South Asian Commission on Poverty Alleviation, with Nepal as its Convener and Bangladesh as Co-convenor, for reviewing the progress made in cooperation on poverty alleviation and for suggesting appropriate and effective measures. They instructed the Chairman of the Council of Ministers to seek two nominations from each Member State by end of January 2002 to enable the convening of its first meeting before the proposed Ministerial Meeting on Poverty Alleviation in Pakistan in April 2002.
18. Expressing concern at the region's special vulnerability in the slowdown in world economy and its negative impact on the

poor and the marginalized, the Heads of State or Government called for a supportive international environment and an enhanced level of assistance by the international community for poverty alleviation programs in South Asia.

COOPERATION IN THE SOCIAL AND CULTURAL SECTOR

19. The Heads of State or Government reiterated the need for an early finalisation of the SAARC Social Charter and instructed the Inter Governmental Expert Group to expedite their work on the basis of the draft to be submitted by the Secretary-General, as a working paper for its consideration and to complete the draft framework of the Charter as early as possible for consideration at the next meeting of the Council of Ministers. In drawing up the Charter, they also directed the Council of Ministers to include the important areas of poverty eradication, population stabilization, the empowerment of women, youth mobilization, human resources development, the promotion of health and nutrition and the protection of children as decided at the Tenth Summit.
20. The Leaders recognized the debilitating and widespread impact of the HIV/AIDS, TB and other deadly communicable diseases on the population of South Asia and stressed the need for evolving a regional strategy to combat these diseases. The strategy should include, inter alia, culturally appropriate preventive measures, an affordable treatment regime and should specially target the vulnerable groups. In this regard, they felt that SAARC should collaborate with the international organizations and civil society. They also emphasized that the SAARC Tuberculosis Centre in Kathmandu should play a coordinating role in the related areas.
21. In accordance with the Colombo Declaration, the Heads of State or Government decided to mandate the Meeting of Ministers of Cultural Affairs in Sri Lanka to finalise the details relating to the establishment of the SAARC Cultural Centre including its financing and to submit its report to the next session of the Council of Ministers.

WOMEN AND CHILDREN

22. The Heads of State or Government welcomed the signing of the SAARC Convention on Preventing and Combating the Trafficking in Women and Children for Prostitution and expressed their collective resolve to treat the trafficking in women and children for commercial sexual exploitation as a criminal offence of a serious nature. They also welcomed the signing of the SAARC Convention on Regional Arrangements for the Promotion of Child Welfare in South Asia and observed that the Convention reflected their commitment to place the child first in the national and regional programs of the Member States. They instructed the Secretary-General, in consultation with Member States and other specialised agencies, to present a report on measures for the effective implementation of the Conventions to the next meeting of the Council of Ministers.
23. The Heads of State or Government agreed to establish, on the basis of recommendations of the Regional Task Force responsible for the implementation of the provisions of the SAARC Convention on Preventing and Combating Trafficking in Women and Children for Prostitution, a voluntary fund with contributions from Member States, individuals, and donor countries and agencies for the rehabilitation and reintegration of the victims of trafficking.
24. The Leaders recognized the need to form an autonomous advocacy group of prominent women personalities from the Member States with a view to making recommendations to the SAARC bodies on a broad spectrum of gender related issues. They directed the Council of Ministers to take necessary steps to prepare and present, for consideration at their next meeting, the Terms of Reference for the purpose.
25. The Heads of State or Government recognized the need to actively pursue and promote social development through empowerment of women and to achieve their full participation in decision making at all levels. They reaffirmed their commitment to uplift the social status of the people, women and children in particular, in the region and expressed their common resolve to accord the highest priority to promoting social development

through specific and targeted programs. The Leaders directed the Council of Ministers to take necessary measures to ensure the enjoyment by women and girl children of their inherent potential. They also directed the Council of Ministers to constitute a Task Force to review the status of implementation of past decisions related to the social sector and to suggest guidelines for their effective implementation in the future.

26. The Leaders directed the Council of Ministers to take concrete steps to give priority to investing in children as an effective means for poverty reduction in the long run. Reaffirming their commitment to the Colombo Plan of Action and the Rawalpindi Declaration and recalling the declaration of 2001 to 2010 as the SAARC Decade of the Rights of the Child, the Heads of State or Government noted with appreciation the South Asia High-level Meeting on Children held in Kathmandu in May 2001. They reaffirmed their conviction that the children in South Asia deserve urgent and focused attention to enhance the long-term and overall progress of the countries of the region.

27. The Heads of State or Government agreed to mobilize the necessary resources and intensify broad based actions to achieve a set of priority goals related to improving the status of children, such as polio eradication by 2005, protection of children from mother-to-child transmission of HIV/AIDS, and quality basic education to the children within a time-bound period.

EDUCATION

28. The Heads of State or Government instructed the concerned Ministries of Governments to devise appropriate strategies for raising the quality of education through the exchange of information among the universities in the region. While emphasizing the importance of mutual recognition of the educational institutions, they agreed to give the necessary impetus to realize the goal of a common regional educational standard through uniform methods of instruction and teaching aids. They were unanimous in recognizing the benefit of introducing SAARC in the national curricula at appropriate levels of study in order to enhance the awareness about

Association's goals and objectives.

29. The Heads of State or Government recognized that access to quality education was an important element for the empowerment of all segments of society, and undertook to develop or strengthen national strategies and action plans to ensure that all children particularly the girl child have access to quality primary education by 2015; and to improve levels of adult literacy by fifty per cent by eliminating gender disparities in access to education as envisaged in the Dakar Framework for Action on Education for All adopted by the World Education Forum held at Dakar in April 2000.

INTERNATIONAL POLITICAL AND ECONOMIC ENVIRONMENT

30. The Heads of State or Government reiterated their firm support for the principles and purposes of the United Nations in order to create a just, balanced and equitable world order. They reaffirmed their commitment to continue working with the NAM and other like-minded countries for the reform and democratisation of the United Nations System with a view to making it an effective and more democratic institution for international peace, security, progress and cooperation.
31. The Heads of State or Government were of the view that stability, peace and security in South Asia should be promoted together with efforts to improve the global security environment. They underscored their commitment to general and complete disarmament including nuclear disarmament on a universal basis, under effective international control. They agreed that global non-proliferation goals could not be achieved in the absence of progress towards nuclear disarmament and in this context called upon all nuclear weapon states, whether party or non-party to the NPT, to engage constructively through a transparent and credible process of negotiations at the Conference on Disarmament. The Leaders also recognized the linkage between disarmament and development.
32. The Leaders emphasized the need to take appropriate measures to make international financial institutions and the global trading

regime more responsive to the needs and concerns of the developing countries. They reiterated the call for genuine partnership among the developed and developing countries in international trade and finance and for the reform of the global financial architecture with an enhanced level of resources.

33. The Leaders also called upon the developed countries to facilitate and ensure an unimpeded and enhanced level of market access to products from the developing, the least developed and the land-locked countries.

34. Recognizing the important role that trade can play in advancing the overall development of a country, thus contributing to an equitable and sustainable world order, the Heads of State or Government also called for an early realization of a rule-based and non-discriminatory world trade regime. In this context, they appreciated the positive elements of the Fourth WTO Ministerial Conference held in Doha and called upon the developed countries to fulfill their commitments to address the particular concerns and needs of the developing and the least developed countries. The Leaders also instructed the forthcoming meeting of the Committee on Economic Cooperation to devote at least half a day for discussions on the evaluation of the decisions of the recently concluded Doha conference in order to evolve better co-ordinated positions among the Member States on all WTO issues. They further stressed the need to intensify coordination among the SAARC missions in Geneva and begin the necessary preparation to advance the common interest of the region in the Fifth WTO Ministerial conference.

35. The Heads of State or Government noted with serious concern the adverse impact of the shrinking Official Development Assistance (ODA) and other concessional financial flows on developing countries in general, and the least developed among them in particular. They further noted with concern the current trend of the global economic slowdown and its adverse effects on these economies. Taking into account the interdependent nature of the global economy, the Leaders urged the developed countries to enhance the level of ODA flows to meet the internationally agreed targets.

36. Recalling the recommendations of the Third United Nations Conference on the Least Developed Countries held in Brussels in May 2001 and the decisions of the Zanzibar Declaration of July 2001, the Leaders urged the developed countries to adopt more liberal trade and aid policies responsive to the particular needs of the least developed countries. Referring to the forthcoming International Conference on Financing for Development to be held in Mexico in March 2002, the Leaders urged the international community to strengthen cooperation for development by addressing international and systemic issues related to financing for development in the developing and the least developed countries in a holistic manner.
37. The Heads of State or Government welcomed the initiative of the donor countries to relieve the external debt burden of the Highly Indebted Poor Countries. They urged the international donor community and financial institutions to widen the scope and extent of debt relief initiatives to cover all those developing and the least developed countries, which are facing developmental difficulties particularly due to the current global recession. In the context of growing global interdependence, they underlined the importance of forging cooperative partnership between the developed and the developing countries to ensure equitable benefits to all.
38. The Heads of State or Government expressed concern over the continued violence and bloodshed in the Middle East, and the set backs suffered by the peace process. They reaffirmed their support for the achievement of a just, lasting and comprehensive peace based on Security Council Resolution 242 (1967) and Resolution 338 (1973) and the establishment of a sovereign Palestine State under the leadership of PLO, which could coexist with its neighbours in peace, security and harmony.

SECURITY OF SMALL STATES

39. The Heads of State or Government recognized that due to their particular vulnerability, small states require special measures for support from the international community for the safeguarding of their sovereign independence and territorial

integrity. They reiterated that the real protection of small states should be firmly rooted in the scrupulous adherence to the UN Charter, the rule of law and the strict adherence to universally accepted principles and norms related to sovereign rights and territorial integrity of all states, irrespective of size. This, they stressed, should be ensured by all the countries, either severally or collectively through the pursuit of appropriate action.

TERRORISM

40. The Heads of State or Government were convinced that terrorism, in all its forms and manifestations, is a challenge to all states and to all of humanity, and cannot be justified on ideological, political, religious or on any other ground. The Leaders agreed that terrorism violates the fundamental values of the United Nations and the SAARC Charter and constitutes one of the most serious threats to international peace and security in the Twenty-first century.
41. The Heads of State or Government emphasized the need for the urgent conclusion of a Comprehensive Convention on Combating International Terrorism. They also emphasized that international co-operation to combat terrorism should be conducted in conformity with the UN Charter, international law and relevant international conventions.
42. The Heads of State or Government reiterated their support to the United Nations Security Council Resolution 1373 of September 28, 2001 and affirmed their determination to redouble efforts, collectively as well as individually, to prevent and suppress terrorism in all its forms and manifestations, including by increased cooperation and full implementation of the relevant international Conventions relating to terrorism to which they are parties. In this context, they called on all states to prevent and suppress the financing of terrorist acts by criminalizing the collection of funds for such acts and refraining from organizing, instigating, assisting or participating in terrorist acts in states or acquiescing in organized activities within its territory directed towards the commission of such acts. The Leaders reaffirmed that the fight against terrorism in all its forms and manifestations

has to be comprehensive and sustained.

43. The Heads of State or Government were unanimous in recognizing the distinct ominous link between terrorism, drug-trafficking, money laundering and other trans-national crimes and emphasized the need to coordinate efforts at the national and regional levels to strengthen the global response to this serious challenge and threat to international security. They called upon the international community to assist Member States of SAARC to deal effectively with the adverse economic effects of terrorism, in general and to meet the rising insurance and security related costs in particular.

44. The Heads of State or Government reaffirmed their commitment to SAARC Regional Convention on Suppression of Terrorism, which, among others, recognizes the seriousness of the problem of terrorism as it affects the security, stability, and development of the region. They also reiterated their firm resolve to accelerate the enactment of enabling legislation within a definite time-frame for the full implementation of the Convention, together with strengthening of SAARC Terrorist Offences Monitoring Desk and the SAARC Drug Offences Monitoring Desk in an effective manner.

REPORT OF THE GROUP OF EMINENT PERSONS

45. The Leaders noted with appreciation that the Report of the Group of Eminent Persons (GEP) was an important contribution in the on-going process of introspection into the functioning of the Association as well as in setting out a perspective plan of action for that purpose. They endorsed the report of the Council of Ministers on the implementation of the recommendations of the GEP Report, and directed the Council of Ministers to undertake a review of progress in this regard.

ENHANCING POLITICAL COOPERATION

46. The Heads of State or Government reaffirmed their commitment to the promotion of mutual trust and understanding and, recognizing that the aims of promoting peace, stability and amity and accelerated socio-economic cooperation may best be achieved by fostering good neighbourly relations, relieving tensions and

building confidence, agreed that a process of informal consultations would prove useful in this regard. The Leaders further recognized that this process would contribute to the appreciation of each other's problems and perceptions as well as for decisive action in agreed areas of regional cooperation. They underlined the importance of informal political consultations in promoting mutual understanding and reinforcing the confidence building process among the Member States.

SUB-REGIONAL COOPERATION

47. The Heads of State or Government reaffirmed the validity of the idea of encouraging the development of specific projects relevant to the individual needs of three or more Member States under the provisions of Articles VII and X of the SAARC Charter.

SOUTH ASIAN DEVELOPMENT FUND (SADF)

48. The Heads of State or Government underlined the urgent need to make the South Asian Development Fund operational by making utilization of the existing funds. They also instructed the Secretary-General to submit a proposal for seeking possible assistance from regional and international sources for the implementation of specific regional poverty alleviation priority projects.

ENVIRONMENT

49. The Heads of State or Government noted with satisfaction the growing public awareness on the need for protecting the environment within the framework of regional cooperation. They reiterated their call for the early and effective implementation of the SAARC Environment Plan of Action as endorsed by the SAARC Environment Ministers. They directed their Environment Ministers to take this into account and come up with an agreed position in their forthcoming meeting.
50. The Heads of State or Government also felt a strong need to devise a mechanism for cooperation in the field of the early warning on as well as preparedness and management of natural disasters, alongwith programs to promote conservation of land and water resources.

51. The Heads of State or Government also stressed the need to develop a cooperative mechanism for the protection, enrichment and utilization of bio-diversity as provided for in the UN Convention on Biological Diversity and to establish a regional bio-diversity database with a view to providing equitable benefits to all Member States. They also underscored the importance of protecting associated knowledge and other indigenous intellectual manifestations for the advancement of the region. They also directed the Council of Ministers to explore the possibility of establishing a SAARC Seed Security Reserve to strengthen cooperation in the field of agriculture and to protect IPRs of the seeds of the Reserve.

PEOPLE-TO-PEOPLE CONTACT

52. The Heads of State or Government were unanimous in recognizing the need for further promoting a sense of regional identity amongst the peoples of the region. The Leaders lauded the roles played by intellectuals, professionals and eminent persons in promoting people-to-people contacts within the region and agreed to encourage such endeavours as a healthy sign of regional cohesion and fraternity. In this context, they took note of the activities of the SAARC LAW including other recognized bodies. They also took note of the First Meeting of the Chief Election Commissioners of SAARC Countries held in Kathmandu in February 1999 and appreciated the initiative on free and fair elections. The Leaders instructed the Secretary-General to collect on a regular basis study reports and other relevant documents and information from the civil society on matters relating to regional cooperation for dissemination to Member States.

RATIONALIZATION AND INSTITUTIONAL ISSUES

53. The Heads of State or Government were in agreement that the Summit and all other meetings of SAARC needed to be made more business-like and result-oriented with focus on programs and activities supported by informed regional inputs from the cross-sections of the society. They directed the Chairman of

the Council of Ministers to undertake a review of the functioning and operation of SAARC Secretariat, and to make recommendations to advance the process of rationalization and to make SAARC more functional and business-like, to the next meeting of the Council of Ministers.

SAARC AWARD

54. The Heads of State or Government noted with appreciation the proposal made by Nepal to institute a SAARC Award to honour the outstanding work of individuals and organizations within the region in the fields of peace, development, poverty alleviation and regional cooperation, and requested His Majesty's Government of Nepal to submit a concept paper for consideration by the next session of the Council of Ministers.

DATE AND VENUE OF THE TWELFTH SUMMIT

55. The Heads of State or Government welcomed with appreciation the offer of the Government of the Islamic Republic of Pakistan to host the Twelfth Summit Meeting of the Heads of State or Government of the South Asian Association for the Regional Cooperation (SAARC) in Pakistan in early 2003.
56. The Heads of State or Government of Bangladesh, Bhutan, India, Maldives, Pakistan and Sri Lanka expressed their deep appreciation for the exemplary manner in which the Right Honourable Prime Minister of Nepal conducted the proceedings of the Eleventh SAARC Summit in his capacity as Chairperson. They also expressed their deep gratitude for the generous hospitality extended to them by His Majesty's Government and people of Nepal, and for the excellent arrangements made for the Summit.

XII ISLAMABAD SUMMIT

The XIIth SAARC Summit is slated to be held at Islamabad in Pakistan in 2003. Expectedly, this summit would pave the way for an area of further mutual coopration and prove to be a historic one. Indian Prime Minister Atal Bihari Vajpayee has already expressed his willing to attend the meet.

PART 3

Record Sheet

EIGHT

Documents

MEMORANDUM OF UNDERSTANDING ON THE ESTABLISHMENT OF THE SECRETARIAT

I

ESTABLISHMENT OF THE SECRETARIAT

In pursuance of Article VIII of the SAARC Charter the Governments of Bangladesh, Bhutan, India, the Maldives, Nepal, Pakistan and Sri Lanka have agreed on the following arrangements with regard to the establishment of the SAARC Secretariat.

II

LOCATION

The Secretariat shall be located in Kathmandu, Nepal.

III

ROLE OF THE SECRETARIAT

The role of the Secretariat shall be to co-ordinate and monitor the implementation of SAARC activities and to service the meetings of the Association.

IV

STRUCTURE

The Secretariat shall comprise a Secretary General, and Professional and General Service Staff, and contain an appropriate number of functional units to be called divisions.

V

APPOINTMENT OF SECRETARY GENERAL

1. The Secretary General shall be appointed by the Council of Ministers upon nomination by the Member State on the basis of the principle of rotation in alphabetical order. The appointment of the

Secretary General shall be for a non-renewable tenure of two years. He shall hold the rank and status of Ambassador.

2.* In the event of the Secretary General being unable to serve his full term, the unexpired portion of his term shall be filled in by the nominee of the Government of the country from which the Secretary General comes upon the approval of the Council of Ministers. Until this arrangement is made the Director from the country next in alphabetical order shall be the Officer-in-Charge.

* As amended by the Fourth Session of the Council of Ministers, para 2 now reads as follows:
Director of the highest rank will act as the officer-in-charge of the SAARC Secretariat, in the absence of the Secretary-General, by rotation in alphabetical order of the member countries.

VI
APPOINTMENT OF PROFESSIONAL STAFF

1. The Professional Staff of the Secretariat shall be appointed by the Secretary General upon nomination by Member States.

2. Each Member State shall nominate one officer at the level of Director who, on appointment shall take charge of a Division/ Divisions to be assigned by the Secretary General.

3. The appointment of the Director shall be for three years. In special circumstances the Secretary General may, in consultation with the Member State concerned, extend the tenure for a period not exceeding another full term.

4. A Director shall be of the rank of Counsellor.

VII
APPOINTMENT OF GENERAL SERVICE STAFF

1. The Secretary General shall employ such General Services Staff as are necessary for the normal functioning of the Secretariat.

2. The General Services Staff shall be nationals of the member states recruited through competition after advertisement, and shall be appointed by the Secretary General.

3. The General Service Staff on satisfactory completion of one year's probation shall be confirmed in their appointments.

4. The appointment of the General Services Staff shall be subject to the proviso that no objection is raised by their respective Government.

VIII

FUNCTIONS AND POWERS OF THE SECRETARY GENERAL

The Secretary General, as head of the SAARC Secretariat, shall:

1. Be responsible for conducting the work of the Secretariat including co-ordination and monitoring of SAARC activities.
2. Submit Staff Rules and Financial Regulations to the Standing Committee for approval of the Council of Ministers;
3. Act as the channel of communication and linkage, when so empowered by the Standing Committee, between SAARC and other international organizations on matters of mutual interest. In doing so, the Secretary General shall be guided by the decision of the Council of Ministers that initiatives for collaboration with external agencies should stem from SAARC itself based on it own determination of priorities and keeping in mind the relevant provisions of the SAARC Charter.
4. Assist in organization and preparation of SAARC meetings at the levels of Standing Committee, Council of Ministers and the Summit and such other meetings as directed by the Standing Committee. The Secretary-General shall attend those meetings or nominate a member of his Professional Staff to do so;
5. Submit the Annual Budget of the Secretariat to the Standing Committee for approval of the Council of Ministers;
6. Act as the custodian of all SAARC documents and publications;
7. Report periodically to the Standing Committee;
8. Perform such other functions as the Standing Committee and Council of Ministers may assign.

IX

FUNCTIONS OF THE DIRECTORS

The Directors shall perform such functions as may be assigned to them by the Secretary General.

X
LANGUAGE

English shall be the working language of the Secretariat.

XI
FOUNDING AND BUDGET

1. Nepal as the host country shall provide the following facilities for the Secretariat:

(i) Accommodation with initial decoration and furnishing and provision of basic utilities and services including power, water, gas, air-conditioning, telephone, telex and major maintenance of the same; and

(ii) Machines, equipment and vehicles for the initial stage.

2. The Annual Budget of the Secretariat shall contain two main components:

(i) Capital Expenditure, including all capital costs on such items as procurement of machines, equipment and vehicles; and

(ii) Recurrent expenditure, including all expenses associated with the running of the Secretariat during the Budget Year including payment of salaries, allowances and perquisites of all Secretariat personnel, utility charges, office requisites and stationery, minor maintenance and any other regular expenses.

3. The Annual Budget of the Secretariat shall be shared by member states on the basis of a formula agreed upon by the Council of Ministers.

XII
SALARIES AND ALLOWANCES

The salaries and allowances of the Secretary General and Professional and General Services Staff of the Secretariat shall be determined by the Council of Ministers.

XIII
PRIVILEGES AND IMMUNITIES

1. The Secretariat, the Secretary General and members of the Professional Staff of the Secretariat shall enjoy such privileges and immunities as are admissible to diplomatic missions/envoys and as

detailed in the headquarters Agreement to be reached between the Secretariat and the host country.

2. Other SAARC States will take steps to accord immunities and privileges to the Secretary General and other members of the Professional Staff when visiting their territories on official duties, consistent with local laws and practices.

XIV
AUDIT AND ACCOUNTS

The accounts of the Secretariat shall be audited annually by a Panel of Auditors comprising three qualified members nominated by three member states by rotation and appointed every year for a contract period of three weeks by the Standing Committee. The Report of the Panel of Auditors along with the annual accounts shall be submitted to the Standing Committee for approval of the Council of Ministers.

XV
AMENDMENT

An amendment to this Memorandum will require approval of the Council of Ministers.

XVI
GENERAL

1. The Secretariat shall commence functioning from a date to be determined by the Council of Ministers.

2. Signed this Seventeenth Day of November of the Year One Thousand Nine Hundred and Eighty-Six at Banglaore, India.

HUMAYUN RASHEED CHOUDHURY
Minister of Foreign Affairs
People's Republic of Bangladesh

DAWA TSERING
Minister of Foreign Affairs
Kingdom of Bhutan

NARAYAN DATT TIWARI
Minister of External Affairs
Republic of India

FATHULLA JAMEEL
Minister of Foreign Affairs
Republic of Maldives

SHAILENDRA KUMAR UPADHYAYA
Minister of Foreign Affairs & Land Reforms
His Majesty's Government of Nepal

SAHABZADA YAQUB KHAN
Minister of Foreign Affairs
Islamic Republic of Pakistan

A.C. SHAHUL HAMEED
Minister of Foreign Affairs
Democratic Socialist Republic of Sri Lanka

Charter of the South Asian Association for Regional Cooperation

We, the Heads of State or Government of BANGLADESH, BHUTAN, INDIA, MALDIVES, NEPAL, PAKISTAN and SRI LANKA;

1. *Desirous* of promoting peace, stability, amity and progress in the region through strict adherence to the principles of the UNITED NATIONS CHARTER and NON-ALIGNMENT, particularly respect for the principles of sovereign equality, territorial integrity, national independence, non-use of force and non-interference in the internal affairs of other States and peaceful settlement of all disputes;

2. *Conscious* that in an increasingly interdependent world, the objectives of peace, freedom, social justice and economic prosperity are best achieved in the SOUTH ASIAN region by fostering mutual understanding, good neighbourly relations and meaningful cooperation among the Member States which are bound by ties of history and culture;

3. *Aware* of the common problems, interests and aspirations of the peoples of SOUTH ASIA and the need for joint action and enhanced cooperation within their respective political and economic systems and cultural traditions;

4. *Convinced* that regional cooperation among the countries of SOUTH ASIA is mutually beneficial, desirable and necessary for promoting the welfare and improving the quality of life of the peoples of the region;

5. *Convinced* further that economic, social and technical cooperation among the countries of SOUTH ASIA would contribute significantly to national and collective self-reliance;

6. *Recognising* that increased cooperation, contacts and exchanges among the countries of the region will contribute to the promotion of friendship and understanding among their peoples;

7. *Recalling* the DECLARATION signed by their Foreign Ministers in NEW DELHI on August 2, 1983 and noting the progress achieved in regional cooperation;

8. *Reaffirming* their determination to promote such cooperation within an institutional framework;

DO HEREBY

AGREE to establish an organisation to be known as SOUTH ASIAN ASSOCIATION FOR REGIONAL COOPERATION hereinafter referred to as the ASSOCIATION, with the following objectives, principles, institutional and financial arrangements:

ARTICLE I

OBJECTIVES

The objectives of the ASSOCIATION shall be:

(a) to promote the welfare of the peoples of SOUTH ASIA and to improve their quality of life;

(b) to accelerate economic growth, social progress and cultural development in the region and to provide all individuals the opportunity to live in dignity and to realise their full potential;

(c) to promote and strengthen collective self-reliance among the countries of SOUTH ASIA;

(d) to contribute to mutual trust, understanding and appreciation of one another's problems;

(e) to promote active collaboration and mutual assistance in the economic, social, cultural, technical and scientific fields;

(f) to strengthen cooperation with other developing countries;

(g) to strengthen cooperation among themselves in international forums on matters of common interests; and

(h) to cooperate with international and regional organisations with similar aims and purposes.

ARTICLE II

PRINCIPLES

Cooperation within the framework of ASSOCIATION shall be based on respect for the principle of sovereign equality, territorial integrity, political independence, non-interference in the internal affairs of other States and mutual benefit.

2. Such cooperation shall not be a substitute for bilateral and multilateral cooperation but shall complement them.

3. Such cooperation shall not be inconsistent with bilateral and multilateral obligations.

ARTICLE III

MEETINGS OF THE HEADS OF STATE OR GOVERNMENT

The Heads of State or Government shall meet once a year or more often as and when considered necessary by the Member States.

ARTICLE IV

COUNCIL OF MINISTERS

A Council of Ministers consisting of the Foreign Ministers of the Member States shall be established with the following functions:

(a) formulation of the policies of the ASSOCIATION;

(b) review of the progress of cooperation under the ASSOCIATION;

(c) decision on new areas of cooperation;

(d) establishment of additional mechanism under the ASSOCIATION as deemed necessary;

(e) decision on other matters of general interest to the ASSOCIATION.

2. The Council of Ministers shall meet twice a year. Extraordinary session of the Council may be held by agreement among the Member States.

ARTICLE V

STANDING COMMITTEE

The Standing Committee comprising the Foreign Secretaries shall have the following function:

(a) overall monitoring and coordination of programme of cooperation;

(b) approval of projects and programmes, and the modalities of their financing;

(c) determination of inter-sectoral priorities;

(d) mobilisation of regional and external resources;

(e) identification of new areas of cooperation based on appropriate studies.

2. The Standing Committee shall meet as often as deemed necessary.

3. The Standing Committee shall submit periodic reports to the Council of Ministers and make reference to it as and when necessary for decisions on policy matters.

ARTICLE VI

TECHNICAL COMMITTEES

Technical Committees comprising representatives of Member States shall be responsible for the implementation, coordination and monitoring of the programmes in their respective areas of cooperation.

2. They shall have the following terms of reference:

(a) determination of the potential and the scope of regional cooperation in agreed areas;

(b) formulation of programmes and preparation of projects;

(c) determination of financial implications of sectoral programmes;

(d) formulation of recommendations regarding apportionment of costs;

(e) implementation and coordination of sectoral programmes;

(f) monitoring of progress in implementation.

3. The Technical Committees shall submit periodic reports to the Standing Committee.

4. The Chairmanship of the Technical Committees shall normally rotate among Member States in alphabetical order every two years.

5. The Technical Committee may, *inter-alia,* use the following mechanisms and modalities, if and when considered necessary:

(a) meetings of heads of national technical agencies;

(b) meetings of experts in specific fields;

(c) contact amongst recognised centres of excellence in the region.

ARTICLE VII

ACTION COMMITTEES

The Standing Committee may set up Action Committees comprising Member States concerned with implementation of projects involving more than two but not all Member States.

ARTICLE VIII

SECRETARIAT

There shall be a Secretariat of the ASSOCIATION.

ARTICLE IX

FINANCIAL ARRANGEMENTS

The contribution of each Member State towards financing of the activities of the ASSOCIATION shall be voluntary.

2. Each Technical Committee shall make recommendations for the apportionment of costs of implementing the programmes proposed by it.

3. In case sufficient financial resources cannot be mobilised within the region for funding activities of the ASSOCIATION, external financing from appropriate sources may be mobilised with the approval of or by the Standing Committee.

ARTICLE X

GENERAL PROVISIONS

Decisions at all levels shall be taken on the basis of unanimity.

2. Bilateral and contentious issues shall be excluded from the deliberations.

IN FAITH WHEREOF We have Set Our Hands Seals Hereunto.

DONE in DHAKA, BANGLADESH, On This The Eighth Day Of December Of The Year One Thousand Nine Hundred Eighty Five.

HUSSAIN MUHAMMAD ERSHAD
President of the Peoples
Republic of Bangladesh

JIGME SINGYE WANGCHUCK
King of Bhutan

RAJIV GANDHI
Prime Minister of the Republic
of India

JUNIUS RICHARD JAYEWARDENE
President of Democratic Socialist
Republic of Sri Lanka

MAUMOON ABDUL GAYOOM
President of the Republic of
Maldives

BIRENDRA BIR BIKRAM SHAH DEV
King of Nepal

MUHAMMAD ZIA-UL-HAQ
President of the Islamic Republic
of Pakistan

SAARC Youth Resolution

PREAMBLE

Whereas the right of the youth for a healthy and balanced development in an environment of equity, harmonious family relationship and social peace is recognized,

Whereas social and economic opportunities like education, marketable skill acquisition, gainful employment, sound health and healthy recreation for youth create an appropriate atmosphere for peace, growth of democratic ethos and achievement of social justice,

Whereas inadequate provision of such social and economic opportunities to the youth necessary for their participation in self and national-development process not only hurts their aspirations but also results in anomie, violence, gender insensitivity, drug abuse, health hazards and social degeneration,

Whereas the youth have to be developed both as a productive human resource and harbingers of ethical, spiritual and cultural values to facilitate their active involvement in the development process,

Whereas cooperation in the region is promoted by the cultural exchanges and friendly contacts between the youth of SAARC member nations,

Now, therefore,

We,

the Member Nations

proclaim this SAARC Youth Resolution incorporating the rights, privileges and obligations of the youth and the commitment of society to the overall development of youth.

RIGHTS

1. All youth irrespective of their socio-economic position, creed, religion, gender and race have equal rights to education, health employment and healthy creation.

2. All youth persons have the right to cherish and express their idealism through their participation in national life.

3. The youth have the right to opportunities for market-responsive professional training and skill development so as to be able to overcome difficulties in securing gainful wage or self-employment.

4. The youth have the right to be safeguarded against rapid population growth, which results in shrinking opportunities, especially in areas of employment, health and education.

5. The youth have the right to a secure future through policies ensuring sustainable development.

6. All young women have the right to equality of opportunities for their overall development and protection against gender biases leading to their exploitation, which affect their lives adversely.

7. The youth have the right to be sheltered against drug abuse and consumption of alcohol and tobacco, which endanger their health and well-being.

8. The youth have the right to moral and health education, as they are most susceptible to the scourge of HIV/AIDS.

9. The youth have the right to healthy recreation, sports and entertainment opportunities and facilities.

10. The youth have the right to adequate, clean and hygienic housing and civic environment.

11. The youth have the right of access to their cultural heritage for a balanced development of their personality.

12. The youth have the right to privacy in and control over their personal lives.

13. The youth shall be protected against crimes and social evils like abduction, rape, incest, prostitution, pornography and drug trafficking.

14. The youth of the member countries have the right of access to information and sharing of experiences of mutual benefit.

15. The youth have the right to participate in the decision-making process and involve actively in planning and implementation of projects having any bearing on their lives and careers.

16. The member countries shall strive to recognize the dreams and aspirations of the youth and encourage fulfilment of the same.

RESPONSIBILITIES AND OBLIGATIONS

1. The youth shall have the responsibility to pursue self-development through creative endeavours and spirit of innovation.

2. The youth shall have the duty to contribute meaningfully to community, national and regional development.

3. The youth shall make concerted efforts to reduce and eliminate social injustice and economic exploitation, and promote social harmony, national unity and regional cooperation.

4. The youth shall have the responsibility to foster the spirit of peaceful co-existence among communities within the country and also among member countries.

5. The youth shall be actively involved in the spread of humanism, scientific temper and rationality.

6. The youth shall have the obligation to promote inter-generational understanding, where the wisdom of the elderly and enthusiasm of the young shall be mutually complementary.

7. The youth shall work for promoting the rights of the disadvantaged sections of the society.

8. The youth shall endeavour to value and preserve cultural heritage.

9. The youth shall strive to prevent environmental degradation and promote sustainable development.

10. The youth shall strive for excellence in all spheres of human endeavour.

11. The youth shall involve themselves through participatory approach in socio-economic upliftment of their region.

These rights and obligations of youth will be exercised in accordance with the spirit and principles of the SAARC.

Agreement on SAARC Preferential Trading Arrangement (SAPTA)

PREAMBLE

The Government of the People's Republic of Bangladesh, the Kingdom of Bhutan, the Republic of India, the Republic of Maldives, the Kingdom of Nepal, the Islamic Republic of Pakistan and the Democratic Socialist Republic of Sri Lanka hereinafter referred to as "Contracting States".

Motivated by the commitment to promote regional cooperation for the benefit of their peoples, in a spirit of mutual accommodation, with full respect for the principles of sovereign equality, independence and territorial integrity of all States;

Aware that the expansion of trade could act as a powerful stimulus to the development of their national economies, by expanding investment and production, thus providing greater opportunities of employment and help securing higher living standards for their population;

Convinced of the need to establish and promote regional preferential trading arrangements for strengthening intra-regional economic cooperation and the development of national economies;

Bearing in mind the urgent need to promote the intra-regional trade which presently constitutes a negligible share in the total volume of the South Asian trade;

Recalling the direction given at the Fourth SAARC Summit meeting held in Islamabad in December 1988 that specific areas be identified where economic cooperation might be feasible immediately;

Guided by the declared commitment of the Heads of State or Government of the Member Countries at the Sixth SAARC Summit held in Colombo in December 1991 to the liberalisation of trade in the region through a step by step approach in such a manner that countries in the region share the benefits of trade expansion equitably;

Cognizant of the mandate given by the Sixth SAARC Summit in Colombo to formulate and seek agreement on an institutional framework under which specific measures for trade liberalisation among SAARC Member States could be furthered and to examine the Sri Lankan proposal to establish the SAARC Preferential Trading Arrangement (SAPTA) by 1997;

Recognising that a preferential trading arrangement is the first step towards higher levels of trade and economic cooperation in the region,

Have agreed as follows:

ARTICLE 1

DEFINITIONS

For the Purpose of this Agreement:

(1) "Least Developed Country" means a country designated as such by the United Nations.

(2) "Contracting State" means any Member State of the South Asian Association for Regional Cooperation (SAARC) which has entered into this Agreement.

(3) "Serious injury" means significant damage to domestic producers, of like or similar products resulting from a substantial increase of preferential imports in situations which cause substantial losses in terms of earnings, production or employment unsustainable in the short terms. The examination of the impact on the domestic industry concerned shall also include an evaluation of other relevant economic factors and indices having a bearing on the state of the domestic industry of that product.

(4) 'Threat of serious injury" means a situation in which a substantial increase of preferential imports is of a nature to cause "serious injury" to domestic producers, and that such injury, although not yet existing, is clearly imminent. A determination of threat of serious injury shall be based on facts and not on mere allegation, conjecture, or remote or hypothetical possibility.

(5) "Critical circumstances" means the emergence of an exceptional situation where massive preferential imports are causing or threatening to cause "serious injury" difficult to repair and which calls for immediate action.

(6) "Sectoral basis" means agreements amongst Contracting States regarding the removal or reduction of tariff, non-tariff and para-tariff barriers as well as other trade promotion or cooperative measures for specified products or groups of products closely related in end-use or in production.

(7) "Direct trade measures" means measures conducive to promoting mutual trade of Contracting States such as long and medium-term contracts containing import and supply commitments in respect of specific products, buy-back arrangements, state trading operations, and government and public procurement.

(8) "Tariffs" means customs duties included in the national tariff schedules of the Contracting States.

(9) "Para-tariffs" means border charges and fees, other than "tariffs", on foreign trade transactions of a tariff-like effect which are levied solely on imports, but not those indirect taxes and charges, which are levied in the same manner on like domestic products. Import charges corresponding to specific services rendered are not considered as para-tariff measures.

(10) "Non-tariffs" means any measure, regulation, or practice, other than "tariffs" and "para-tariffs", the effect of which is to restrict imports, or to significantly distort trade.

(11) "Products" means all products including manufactures and commodities in their raw, semi-processed and processed forms.

ARTICLE 2
ESTABLISHMENT AND AIMS

1. By the present Agreement, the Contracting States establish the SAARC Preferential Trading Arrangement (SAPTA) to promote and sustain mutual trade and the economic cooperation among the

Contracting States, through exchanging concessions in accordance with this Agreement.

2. SAPTA will be governed by the provisions of this Agreement and also by the rules, regulations, decisions, understandings and protocols to be agreed upon within its framework by the Contracting States.

ARTICLE 3
PRINCIPLES

SAPTA shall be governed in accordance with the following principles:

(a) SAPTA shall be based and applied on the principles of overall reciprocity and mutuality of advantages in such a way as to benefit equitably all Contracting States, taking into account their respective levels of economic and industrial development, the pattern of their external trade, trade and tariff policies and systems;

(b) SAPTA shall be negotiated step by step, improved and extended in successive stages with periodic reviews;

(c) The special needs of the Least Developed Contracting States shall be clearly recognised and concrete preferential measures in their favour should be agreed upon;

(d) SAPTA shall include all products, manufactures and commodities in their raw, semi-processed and processed forms.

ARTICLE 4
COMPONENTS

SAPTA may, *inter-alia,* consist of arrangements relating to:

(a) tariffs;

(b) Para-tariffs;

(c) non-tariff measures;

(d) direct trade measures.

ARTICLE 5
NEGOTIATIONS

1. The Contracting States may conduct their negotiations for trade liberalisation in accordance with any or a combination of the following approaches and procedures:

(a) Product-by-product basis;
(b) Across-the-board tariff reductions;
(c) Sectoral basis;
(d) Direct trade measures.

2. Contracting States agreed to negotiate tariff preferences initially on a product-by-product basis.

3. The Contracting States shall enter into negotiations from time to time with a view to further expanding SAPTA and the fuller attainment of its aims.

ARTICLE 6
ADDITIONAL MEASURES

1. Contracting States agree to consider, in addition to the measures set out in Article 4, the adoption of trade facilitation and other measures to support and complement SAPTA to mutual benefit.

2. Special consideration shall be given by Contracting States to requests from Least Developed Contracting States for technical assistance and cooperation arrangements designed to assist them in expanding their trade with other Contracting States and in taking advantage of the potential benefits of SAPTA. The possible areas for such technical assistance and cooperation are listed in Annex-I.

ARTICLE 7
SCHEDULES OF CONCESSIONS

The tariff, para-tariff and non-tariff concessions negotiated and exchanged amongst Contracting States shall be incorporated in the National Schedules of Concessions. The initial concessions agreed to by the Contracting States are attached as Annex-II.

ARTICLE 8
EXTENSION OF NEGOTIATED CONCESSIONS

The concessions agreed to under SAPTA, except those made exclusively to the Least Developed Contracting States in pursuance of Article 10 of this Agreement, shall be extended unconditionally to all Contracting States.

ARTICLE 9
COMMITTEE OF PARTICIPANTS

A Committee of Participants, hereinafter referred to as the Committee, consisting of representatives of Contracting States, is hereby established. The Committee shall meet at least once a year to review the progress made in the implementation of this Agreement and to ensure benefits of trade expansion emanating from this Agreement accrue to all Contracting States equitably. The Committee shall also accord adequate opportunities for consultation on representations made by any Contracting State with respect to any matter affecting the implementation of the Agreement. The Committee shall adopt appropriate measures for settling such representations. The Committee shall determine its own rules of procedures.

ARTICLE 10
SPECIAL TREATMENT FOR THE LEAST DEVELOPED CONTRACTING STATES

1. In addition to other provisions of this Agreement, all Contracting States shall provide, wherever possible, special and more favourable treatment exclusively to the Least Developed Contracting States as set out in the following sub-paragraphs:

(a) Duty-free access, exclusive tariff preferences or deeper tariff preferences for the export products,
(b) The removal of non-tariff barriers,
(c) The removal, where appropriate, of para-tariff barriers,
(d) The negotiations of long-terms contracts with a view to assisting Least Developed Contracting States to achieve reasonable levels of sustainable exports of their products,
(e) Special consideration of exports from Least Developed Contracting States in the application of safeguard measures,
(f) Greater flexibility in the introduction and continuance of quantitative or other restrictions provisionally and without discrimination in critical circumstances by the Least Developed Contracting States on imports from other Contracting States.

ARTICLE 11
NON-APPLICATION

Notwithstanding the measures as set out in Articles 4 and 6, the provisions of this Agreement shall not apply in relation to preferences already granted or to be granted by any Contracting State to other Contracting States outside the framework of this Agreement, and to third countries through bilateral, plurilateral and multilateral trade agreements, and similar arrangements. The Contracting States shall also not be obliged to grant preferences in SAPTA which impair the concession extended under those agreements.

ARTICLE 12
COMMUNICATION, TRANSPORT AND TRANSIT

Contracting States agree to undertake appropriate steps and measures for developing and improving communication system, transport infrastructure and transit facilities for accelerating the growth of trade within the region.

ARTICLE 13
BALANCE-OF-PAYMENTS MEASURES

1. Notwithstanding the provisions of this Agreement, any Contracting State facing serious economic problems including balance of payments difficulties may suspend provisionally the concessions as to the quantity and value of merchandise permitted to be imported under the Agreement. When such action has taken place, the Contracting State which initiates such action, shall simultaneously notify the other Contracting States and the Committee.

2. Any Contracting State which takes action according to paragraph 1 of this Article shall afford, upon request from any other Contracting State, adequate opportunities for consultations with a view to preserving the stability of the concessions negotiated under the SAPTA. If no satisfactory adjustment is effected between the Contracting States concerned within 90 days of such notification, the matter may be referred to the Committee for review.

ARTICLE 14
SAFEGUARD MEASURES

If any product, which is a subject of a concession with respect to a preference under this Agreement, is imported into the territory of a Contracting State in such a manner or in such quantities as to cause or threaten to cause, serious injury in the importing Contracting State, the importing Contracting State concerned may, with prior consultations, except in critical circumstances, suspend provisionally without discrimination, the concession accorded under the Agreement. When such action has taken place the Contracting State which initiates such action shall simultaneously notify the other Contracting State(s) concerned and the Committee shall enter into consulations with the concerned Contracting State and endeavour to reach mutually acceptable agreement to remedy the situation. In the event of the failure of the Contracting States to resolve the issue within 90 days of the receipt of original notification, the Committee of Participants shall meet within 30 days to review the situation and try to settle the issue amicably. Should the consultations in the Committee of Participants fail to resolve the issue within 60 days, the parties affected by such action shall have the right to withdraw equivalent concession(s) or other obligation(s) which the Committee does not disapprove of.

ARTICLE 15
MAINTENANCE OF THE VALUE OF CONCESSIONS

Any of the concessions agreed upon under this Agreement shall not be diminished or nullified, by the application of any measures restricting trade by the Contracting States except under the provisions as spelt out in other Articles of this Agreement.

ARTICLE 16
RULES OF ORIGIN

Products contained in the National Schedules of Concessions annexed to this Agreement shall be eligible for preferential treatment if they satisfy the rules of origin, including special rules of origin, in respect of the Least Developed Contracting States, which are set out in Annex-III.

ARTICLE 17
MODIFICATION AND WITHDRAWAL OF CONCESSIONS

1. Any Contracting State may, after a period of three years from the day the concession was extended, notify the Committee of its intention to modify or withdraw any concession included in its appropriate schedule.

2. The Contracting State intending to withdraw or modify a concession shall enter into consultation and/or negotiations, with a view to reaching agreement on any necessary and appropriate compensation, with Contracting States with which such concession was initially negotiated and with any other Contracting States that have a principal or substantial supplying interest as may be determined by the Committee.

3. Should no agreement be reached between the Contracting States concerned within six months of the receipt of notification and should the notifying Contracting State proceed with its modification or withdrawal of such concessions, the affected Contracting States as determined by the Committee may withdraw or modify equivalent concessions in their appropriate schedules. Any such modification or withdrawal shall be notified to the Committee.

ARTICLE 18
WITHHOLDING OR WITHDRAWAL OF CONCESSION

A Contracting State shall at any time be free to withhold or to withdraw in whole or in part any item in its schedule of concessions in respect of which it determines that it was initially negotiated with State which has ceased to be a Contracting State in this Agreement. A Contracting State taking such action shall notify the Committee, and upon request, consult with Contracting States that have a substantial interest in the product concerned.

ARTICLE 19
CONSULTATIONS

1. Each Contracting State shall accord sympathetic consideration to and shall afford adequate opportunity for consultations regarding such representations as may be made by another Contracting State with respect to any matter affecting the operation of this Agreement.

2. The Committee may, at the request of a Contracting State, consult with any Contracting State in respect of any matter for which it has not been possible to find a satisfactory solution through such consultation under paragraph 1 above.

ARTICLE 20
SETTLEMENT OF DISPUTES

Any dispute that may arise among the Contracting States regarding the interpretation and application of the provisions of this Agreement or any instrument adopted within its framework shall be amicably settled by agreement between the parties concerned. In the event of failure to settle a dispute, it may be referred to the Committee by a party to the dispute. The Committee shall review the matter and make a recommendation thereon within 120 days from the date on which the dispute was submitted to it. The committee shall adopt appropriate rules for this purpose.

ARTICLE 21
WITHDRAWAL FROM SAPTA

1. Any Contracting State may withdraw from this Agreement at any time after its entry into force. Such withdrawal shall be effective six months from the day on which written notice thereof is received by the SAARC Secretariat, the depositary of this Agreement. That Contracting State shall simultaneously inform the Committee of the action it has taken.

2. The rights and obligations of a Contracting State which has withdrawn from this Agreement shall cease to apply as of that effective date.

3. Following the withdrawal by any Contracting State, the Committee shall meet within 30 days to consider action subsequent to withdrawal.

ARTICLE 22
ENTRY INTO FORCE

This Agreement shall enter into force on the thirtieth day after the notification issued by the SAARC Secretariat regarding completion of the formalities by all Contracting States.

ARTICLE 23
RESERVATIONS

This Agreement may not be signed with reservations nor shall reservations be admitted at the time of notification to the SAARC Secretariat of the completion of formalities.

ARTICLE 24
AMENDMENTS

This Agreement may be modified through amendments to this Agreement. All amendments shall become effective upon acceptance by all Contracting States.

ARTICLE 25
DEPOSITARY

This Agreement shall be deposited with the Secretary General of SAARC who shall promptly furnish a certified copy thereof to each Contracting State.

IN WITNESS WHEREOF the undersigned being duly authorized thereto by their respective Governments have signed this Agreement on the SAARC Preferential Trading Arrangement.

Done at DHAKA this ELEVENTH day of APRIL One Thousand Nine Hundred Ninety Three in eight originals in the English Language.

A.S.M. MOSTAFIZUR RAHMAN
Minister of Foreign Affairs
People's Republic of Bangladesh

DAWA TSERING
Minister of Foreign Affairs
Kingdom of Bhutan

DINESH SINGH
Minister of External Affairs
Republic of India

FATHULLA JAMEEL
Minister of Foreign Affairs
Republic of Maldives

MAHESH ACHARYA KHANKANJU
State Minister of Finance
His Majesty's Government of Nepal

MOHAMMAD SIDDIQUE
Minister of State for Foreign Affairs
Islamic Republic of Pakistan

HAROLD HERAT
Minister of Foreign Affairs.
Democratic Socialist Republic of Sri Lanka

Agreement on Establishing the SAARC Food Security Reserve

PREAMBLE

The Governments of Bangladesh, Bhutan, India, the Maldives, Nepal, Pakistan and Sri Lanka.

Recalling the Declaration on South Asian Regional Cooperation signed in New Delhi in August 1983 which called for cooperative action with a view to promoting economic and social development in South Asia.

Reaffirming their commitment to the realisation of this objective by joining together in the establishment of the South Asian Association for Regional Cooperation and adopting a Charter in Dhaka in December 1985.

Recognizing the importance of regional and sub-regional collective self-reliance with respect to food security as a means of combating the adverse effect of natural and man-made calamities.

Recognizing further that the establishment of an emergency food security reserve by member countries of the South Asian Association for Regional Cooperation based on the principle of collective self-reliance would improve their food security.

Now therefore, in a spirit of solidarity and mutual cooperation, have agreed as follows:

ARTICLE I
ESTABLISHMENT OF THE SAARC FOOD SECURITY RESERVE

1. The member countries hereby agree to establish a SAARC Food Security Reserve (hereinafter referred to as "the Reserve") on the conditions and for the purpose described in this Agreement.

2. The Reserve shall be administered by the SAARC Food Security Reserve Board (hereinafter referred to as "the Board") provided for in Article VII.

ARTICLE II
THE RESERVE

1. The Reserve shall consist of wheat or rice or a combination thereof, (hereinafter referred to as "foodgrains") earmarked by member-countries exclusively for the purpose described in Article III.

The foodgrains forming part of the Reserve shall remain the property of the member-country that has earmarked them and shall be in addition to any national reserve that may be maintained by the member country.

2. Each member-country undertakes to earmark as its share of the Reserve the amount of foodgrains allocated to it in the Schedule to this Agreement. The said Schedule shall be an integral part of this Agreement.

3. The member-countries shall keep the Schedule under review and may amend it in the light of operating experience in accordance with the procedure laid down in Article XI.

4. A member-country may, at any time, voluntarily earmark for the purpose provided for in this Agreement, foodgrains exceeding the amount allocated to it in the Schedule. In such a case the member-country concerned may only withdraw the amount in excess of its allocation by giving six months' advance written notice to the Board.

5. The quality of all foodgrains earmarked by the member-countries shall be at least of "fair average quality", or comply with any other quality standards laid down by the Board.

6. The member-countries undertake to provide adequate storage facilities for the foodgrains that they have earmarked; to inspect the food grains periodically and to apply appropriate quality control measures, including turnover of the foodgrains, if necessary, with a view to ensuring that at all times the foodgrains satisfy the required quality standards; and to replace forthwith any foodgrains that do not satisfy the said standards. In addition, the member-countries agree to make every effort to comply with any guidelines on storage methods or equality measures adopted by the Board.

ARTICLE III
WITHDRAWAL OF FOODGRAINS IN AN EMERGENCY

Each member-country shall be entitled, on the conditions and in accordance with the procedures laid down in Article IV and/or Article VI, to draw a foodgrains forming part of the Reserve in the event of an emergency. An emergency shall mean a state or condition in which a member-country, having suffered a severe and unexpected natural or man-made calamity, is unable to cope with such a state or condition by using its national reserve and is unable to procure the foodgrains it requires through normal trading transactions on account of balance of payments constraints.

ARTICLE IV
PROCEDURE FOR THE RELEASE OF FOODGRAINS FROM THE RESERVE

1. The member-country in need shall directly notify the other member-country or countries of the emergency it is facing and the amount of foodgrains required.

2. The other member-country or countries on being so requested shall take immediate steps to make necessary arrangements to ensure immediate and speedy release of the required foodgrains, subject to availability in the combination requested.

3. The prices, terms and conditions of payment in kind or otherwise in respect of the foodgrains so released shall be the subject of direct negotiations between the member-countries concerned.

4. The requesting member-country shall at the same time inform the board of its request to the other member-country or countries.

ARTICLE V
REPLENISHMENT OF THE RESERVE

1. A member-country that has released all or part of the foodgrains forming its share of the Reserve shall replace such foodgrains as soon as practicable and, in any event, not later than one calendar year following the date on which the release of the foodgrains took place.

2. A member country that has released all or part of the foodgrains forming its share of the Reserve shall notify the Board of such release, of the terms and conditions on which it was effected, and the date on which the foodgrains that had been released were replaced.

ARTICLE VI
PROCEDURE FOR THE WITHDRAWAL OF FOODGRAINS BY A MEMBER COUNTRY FROM ITS OWN SHARE OF THE RESERVE

1. A member-country in need shall be entitled to withdraw foodgrains from its own share of the Reserve.

2. In doing so it shall inform the member-countries and the Board of such withdrawal.

3. It shall replace such foodgrains as soon as practicable and in any event not later than two calendar years following the date on which the release of the foodgrains took place.

ARTICLE VII
THE SAARC FOOD SECURITY BOARD

1. There shall be a Board of which each member-country shall be a member.

2. Decisions of the Board shall be taken on the basis of unanimity.

3. The Board shall elect a Chairman and Vice-Chairman based on the principle of rotation among member-countries whose terms of office shall be two years. Rules of Procedure for the meetings of the Board shall be the same as for other SAARC meetings.

4. The Board shall meet at least once a year.

5. The Board shall normally meet at the same place and time as the Standing Committee, preceding the annual Summit.

ARTICLE VIII
FUNCTIONS OF THE BOARD

The functions of the Board shall include:

1. Undertaking a periodic review and assessment of the food situation and prospects in the region including factors such as production, consumption, trade, prices, quality and stocks of foodgrains. These periodic assessment reports shall be disseminated to all the member-countries.
2. Examining immediate, short-term and long-term policy actions as may be considered necessary to ensure adequate supplies of basic commodities in the region and to submit, on the basis of such examination, recommendations for appropriate action to the Council of Ministers.
3. Reviewing implementation of the provisions of the Agreement, calling for such information from member-countries as may be necessary for the effective administration of the Reserve and issuing of guidelines of technical matters such as maintenance of stocks, storage conditions and quality control.

4. Keeping the Schedule to this Agreement under review.
5. Suggesting amendment to the Agreement, as and when considered necessary, in accordance with the procedure specified in Article XI.

ARTICLE IX
SECRETARIAT

The Board shall be assisted by the SAARC Secretariat. The Secretariat's responsibilities shall include monitoring all matters relating to the release of foodgrains from the Reserve and convening and servicing meetings of the Board.

ARTICLE X
ENTRY INTO FORCE

This Agreement shall enter into force on a date to be determined by the Council of Ministers provided that the member-countries have collectively earmarked at lease one hundred and twenty-five thousand metric tons of foodgrains on that date for the purpose of this Agreement.

ARTICLE XI
AMENDMENT

1. A member country may propose any amendment to this Agreement by submitting the proposed amendment to the Board through the SAARC Secretariat.

2. The Board may endorse the proposed amendment and submit it to the Council of Ministers for approval. Unless otherwise specified, amendments shall enter into force as from the date of their approval by the Council of Ministers.

ARTICLE XII
DEPOSITARY

1. An original of this Agreement shall be deposited in the SAARC Secretariat.

2. The Secretary-General shall be the depositary of this Agreement and amendments thereto.

IN WITNESS WHEREOF the undersigned plenipotentiaries being duly authorised thereto have singed this Agreement.

Signed at Kathmandu on the Fourth Day of November One Thousand Nine Hundred and Eighty Seven in Eight Originals in the English language.

HUMAYUN RASHEED CHOUDHURY
Minister of Foreign Affairs
People's Republic of Bangladesh

DAWA TSERING
Minister of Foreign Affairs
Kingdom of Bhutan

K. NATWAR SINGH
Minister of State for External Affairs
Republic of India

FATHULLA JAMEEL
Minister of Foreign Affairs
Republic of Maldives

SHAILENDRA KUMAR UPADHYAYA
Minister for Foreign Affairs and Land Reforms
His Majesty's Government of Nepal

ZAIN NOORANI
Minister of State for Foreign Affairs
Islamic Republic of Pakistan

A.C. SHAHUL HAMEED
Minister of Foreign Affairs
Democratic Socialist Republic of Sri Lanka

SAARC Regional Convention on Suppression of Terrorism

THE MEMBER STATES OF THE SOUTH ASIAN ASSOCIATION FOR REGIONAL COOPERATION (SAARC) MINDFUL of the principles of cooperation enshrined in the SAARC Charter.

RECALLING that at the Dhaka Summit on December 7-8, 1985, the Heads of State or Government of the member States of the SAARC recognized the seriousness of the problem of terrorism as it affects the security and stability of the region.

ALSO RECALLING the Bangalore Summit Declaration of 17 November 1986, in which the Heads of State or Government of SAARC agreed that cooperation among SAARC States was vital if terrorism was to be prevented and eliminated from the region; unequivocally condemned all acts, methods and practices of terrorism as criminal and deplored their impact of life and property, socio-economic development, political stability, regional and international peace and cooperation; and recognised the importance of the principles laid down in UN Resolution 2625 (XXV) which among others required that each state should refrain from organising, instigating, assisting or participating in acts of civil strife or terrorist acts in another state or acquiesing in organised activities with its territory directed towards the commission of such acts.

AWARE of the danger posed by the spread of terrorism and its harmful effect on peace, cooperation, friendship and good neighbourly relations and which could also jeopardise the sovereignty and territorial integrity of states.

HAVE RESOLVED to take effective measures to ensure that perpetrators of terroristic acts do not escape prosecution and punishment by providing for their extradition or prosecution, and to this end,

HAVE AGREED as follows:

ARTICLE I

Subject to the overall requirements of the law of extradition, conduct constituting any of the following offences, according to the law of the Contracting State, shall be regarded as terroristic and for the purpose of an offence connected with a political offence or as an offence inspired by political motives:

(a) An offence within the scope of the Convention for the Suppression of Unlawful Seizure of Aircraft, signed at the Hague on December 16, 1970;

(b) An offence within the scope of the Convention for the Suppression of Unlawful acts against the Safety of Civil Aviation, signed at Montreal on September 23, 1971;

(c) An offence within the scope of the Convention on the Prevention and Punishment of Crimes against Internationally Protected Persons, including Diplomatic Agents, signed at New York on December 14, 1973;

(d) An offence within the scope of any Convention to which the SAARC member States concerned are parties and which obliges the parties to prosecute or grant extradition;

(e) Murder, manslaughter, assault causing bodily harm, kidnapping, hostage-taking and offences relating to firearms, weapons, explosives and dangerous substances when used as a means to perpetrate indiscriminate violence involving death or serious bodily injury to persons or serious damage to property;

(f) An attempt or conspiracy to commit an offence described in sub-paragraphs (a) to (e), aiding, abetting or counselling the commission of such an offence or participating as an accomplice in the offences so described.

ARTICLE II

For the purpose of extradition between SAARC member States, any two or more Contracting States may, by agreement, decide to include any other serious offence involving violence, which shall not be regarded as a political offence or an offence connected with a political offence or an offence inspired by political motives.

ARTICLE III

1. The provisions of all extradition treaties and arrangements applicable between Contracting States are hereby amended as between Contracting States to the extent that they are incompatible with this Convention.

2. For the purpose of this Convention and to the extent that any offence referred to in Article I or agreed to in terms of Article II is not listed as an extraditable offence in any extradition treaty existing between Contracting States, it shall be deemed to be included as such therein.

3. Contracting States undertake to include these offences as extraditable offences in any future extradition treaty to be concluded between them.

4. If a Contracting State which makes extradition conditional on the existence of a treaty receives a request for extradition from another Contracting State with which it has no extradition treaty, the requested State may, as its option, consider this Conventions as the basis for extradition in respect of the offences set forth in Article I or agreed to in terms of Article II. Extradition shall be subject to the law of the requested state.

5. Contracting States which do not make extradition conditional on the existence of a treaty, shall recognise the offences set forth in Article I or agreed to in terms of Article II as extraditable offences between themselves, subject to the law of the requested State.

ARTICLE IV

A Contracting State in whose territory a person suspected of having committed an offence referred to in Article I or agreed to in terms of Article II is found and which has received a request for extradition from another Contracting State, shall, if it does not extradite that person, submit the case without exception and without delay, to its competent authorities shall take their decisions in the same manner as in the case of any offence of a serious nature under the law of that State.

ARTICLE V

For the purpose of Article IV, each Contracting State may take such measures as it deems appropriate, consistent with its national laws, subject to reciprocity, to exercise its jurisdiction in the case of an offence under Article I or agreed to in terms of Article II.

ARTICLE VI

A Contracting State in whose territory an alleged offender is found, shall, upon receiving a request for extradition from another Contracting State, take appropriate measures, subject to its national laws, so as to ensure his presence for purposes of extradition or prosecution. Such measures shall immediately be notified to the requesting State.

ARTICLE VII

Contracting States shall not be obliged to extradite, if it appears to the requested State that by reason of the trivial nature of the case or by reason of the request for the surrender or return of a fugitive offender not being made in good faith or in the interests of justice or for any other reason it is unjust or inexpedient to surrender or return the fugitive offender.

ARTICLE VIII

1. Contracting States shall, subject to their national laws, afford one another the greatest measure of mutual assistance in connection with proceedings brought in respect of the offences referred to in Article I or agreed to in terms of Article II, including the supply of all evidence at their disposal necessary for the proceedings.

2. Contracting States shall cooperate among themselves, to the extent permitted by their national law, through consultations between appropriate agencies, exchange of information, intelligence and expertise and such other cooperative measures as may be appropriate, with a view to prevention terroristic activities through precautionary measures.

ARTICLE IX

1. The Convention shall be open for signature by the member States of SAARC at the SAARC Secretariat in Kathmandu.

2. It shall be subject to ratification. Instruments of Ratification shall be deposited with the Secretary-General of SAARC.

ARTICLE X

The Convention shall enter into force on the fifteenth day following the date of the deposit of the seventh Instrument of Ratification with the Secretary-General of SAARC.

ARTICLE XI

The Secretary-General of SAARC shall be the depository of this Convention and shall notify member States of signatures to this Convention and all deposits of Instruments of Ratification. The Secretary-General shall transmit certified copies of such Instruments to each member State. The Secretary-General shall also inform member States of the date on which this Convention will have entered into force in accordance with Article X.

IN WITNESS WHEREOF the undersigned, being duly authorised thereto by their respective Governments, have signed this Convention.

DONE at Kathmandu on this Fourth Day of November One Thousand Nine Hundred and Eighty Seven in eight Originals in the English language all texts being equally authentic.

HUMAYUN RASHEED CHOUDHURY
Minister of Foreign Affairs
People's Republic of Bangladesh

DAWA TSERING
Minister of Foreign Affairs
Kingdom of Bhutan

K. NATWAR SINGH
Minister of State for External Affairs
Republic of India

FATHULLA JAMEEL
Minister of Foreign Affairs
Republic of Maldives

SHAILENDRA KUMAR UPADHYAYA
Minister for Foreign Affairs and Land Reforms
His Majesty's Government of Nepal

ZAIN NOORANI
Minister of State for Foreign Affairs
Islamic Republic of Pakistan

A.C SHAHUL HAMEED
Minister of Foreign Affairs
Democratic Socialist Republic of Sri Lanka

SAARC Convention on Narcotic Drugs and Psychotropic Substances

THE MEMBER-STATES OF THE SOUTH ASIAN ASSOCIATION FOR REGIONAL CO-OPERATION (SAARC)

Mindful of the principles of co-operation enshrined in the SAARC Charter;

Recalling that at the Islamabad Summit on December 29-31,1988, Heads of State or Government of the Member-States of SAARC expressed grave concern over the growing magnitude and the serious effect of drug abuse and drug trafficking and recognised the need for urgent and effective measures to eradicate this problem including the possibility of concluding a Regional Convention on Drug Control;

Recognising that a regional Convention on Narcotic Drugs and Psychotropic Substances would be a step forward in augmenting SAARC efforts to eliminate drug trafficking;

Also Recognising the need to re-inforce and supplement, at the regional level, the measures provided in the Single Convention on Narcotic Drugs, 1961, as amended by the Protocol of 1972, the Convention on Psychotropic Substances, 1971, the United Nations Convention against Illicit Traffic in Narcotic Drugs and Psychotropic Substances, 1988, taking into account concerns which are specific to the SAARC region;

Desiring to eliminate the root causes of the problem of abuse of narcotic drugs and psychotropic substances, including the illicit demand for such drugs and substances and the enormous profits derived from illicit traffic;

Taking Cognizance of the links between illicit drug trafficking and other related organised criminal activities which undermine the economies and threaten the stability, security and sovereignty of States;

Convinced of the importance of strengthening and enhancing effective legal means for regional co-operation in criminal matters for suppressing international criminal activities of illicit traffic in narcotic drugs and psychotropic substances;

Have agreed as follows:

ARTICLE I

DEFINITIONS

Except where otherwise expressly indicated or where the context otherwise requires, the following definitions shall apply throughout the Convention:

(a) "Cannabis plant" means any plant of the genus Cannabis;

(b) "Coca Bush" means the plant of any species of the genus Erythroxylon;

(c) "Confiscation" which includes forfeiture where applicable, means the permanent deprivation of property by order of a court or other competent authority;

(d) "Controlled delivery" means the technique of allowing illicit or suspect consignments of narcotic drugs, psychotropic substances, substances listed in Table I and Table II annexed to the 1988 U.N. Convention, or substances substituted for them, to pass out of, through or into the territory of one or more countries, with the knowledge and under the supervision of their competent authorities, with a view to identifying persons involved in the commission of offences established in accordance with Article 3, paragraph 1 of this Convention;

(e) "1961 Convention" means the Single Convention on Narcotic Drugs, 1961;

(f) "1961 Convention as amended" means the Single Convention on Narcotic Drugs, 1961 as amended by the 1972 Protocol amending the Single Convention on Narcotic Drugs, 1961;

(g) "1971 Convention" means the Convention on Psychotropic Substances, 1971;

(h) "1988 U.N. Convention" means the United Nations Convention against Illicit Traffic in Narcotic Drugs and Psychotropic Substances, 1988;

(i) "Freeze" or "Seize" means to temporarily prohibit the transfer, conversion, disposition or movement of property or temporarily assuming custody or control of property on the basis of an order issued by a court or a competent authority.

(j) "illicit traffic" means the offences set forth in Article 3, of this Convention;

(k) "Narcotic Drug" means any of the substances, natural or synthetic, listed in Schedules I and II of the 1961 Convention and the 1961 Convention as amended;

(l) "Opium poppy" means the plant of the species Papaver Somniferum L;

(m) "Proceeds" means any property derived from or obtained, directly or indirectly, through the commission of an offence established in accordance with Article 3, paragraph 1 of this Convention;

(n) "Property" means assets of every kind, whether corporeal or incorporeal, movable or immovable, tangible or intangible, and legal documents or instruments evidencing title to, or interest in, such assets;

(o) "Psychotropic Substance" means any substance, natural or synthetic, or any natural material listed in Schedules I, II, III and IV of the 1971 Convention;

(p) "Secretary-General" means the Secretary-General of the South Asian Association for Regional Cooperation (SAARC).

ARTICLE 2
SCOPE OF THE CONVENTION

1. The purpose of this Convention is to promote cooperation among Member-States, so that they may address more effectively the various aspects of prevention and control of drug abuse and the suppression of illicit traffic in narcotic drugs and psychotropic substances which are specific to the SAARC region.

2. Member-States in carrying out their obligations under this Convention shall take necessary measures, including legislative and administrative measures, in conformity with the fundamental provisions of their respective domestic legislative systems.

3. Member-States shall carry out their obligations under this Convention in a manner consistent with the principles of sovereign

equality and territorial integrity of States and that of non-intervention in the domestic affairs of other States.

4. A Member shall not undertake in the territory of another Member-State, the exercise of jurisdiction and performance of functions which are exclusively reserved for the authorities of that other State by its domestic law.

ARTICLE 3
OFFENCES

1. Each Member-State shall adopt such measures as may be necessary to establish as criminal offences under its domestic law, when committed intentionally:

(a) the production, manufacture, extraction, preparation, offering, offering for sale, distribution, sale, delivery on any terms whatsoever, brokerage, despatch, despatch in transit, transport, importation or exportation of any narcotic drug or any psychotropic substance contrary to the provisions of the 1961 Convention, the 1961 Convention as amended or the 1971 Convention;

(b) the cultivation of opium poppy, coca bush or cannabis plant for the production of narcotic drugs contrary to the provisions of the 1961 Convention and the 1961 Convention as amended;

(c) the possession or purchase of any narcotic drug or psychotropic substance for the purpose of any of the activities enumerated in (a) above;

(d) the manufacture, transport or distribution of equipment or materials, or of substances as listed in Table I and Table II of the 1988 U.N. Convention, knowing that they are being or are to be used in or for the illicit cultivation, production or manufacture of narcotic drugs or psychotropic substances;

(e) the organisation, management or financing of any of the offences enumerated in (a), (b), (c) or (d) above;

(f) the conversion or transfer of property, knowing that such property is derived from the proceeds from any offence or offences established in accordance with sub-paragraphs (a), (b), (c), (d) or (e) of this paragraph, or from an act of participation in such offence or offences, for the purpose of concealing or disguising the illicit origin of the property or of assisting any person who is involved in the commission of such an offence or offences to evade the legal consequences of his actions;

(g) the concealment or disguise of the true nature, source, location, disposition, movement, rights with respect to, or ownership of property, knowing that such property is derived from an offence or offences established in accordance with sub-paragraphs (a), (b), (c), (d) or (e) of this paragraph or from an act of participation in such an offence or offences;

(h) the acquisition, possession or use of property, knowing, at the time of receipt, that such property was derived from an offence or offences established in accordance with sub-paragraphs (a), (b), (c), (d) or (e) of this paragraph or from an act of participation in such offence or offences;

(i) the possession of equipment or materials, or of substances listed in Table I and Table II, of the 1988 U.N. Convention, knowing that they are being or are to be used in or for the illicit cultivation, production or manufacture of narcotic drugs or psychotropic substances;

(j) publicly inciting or inducing others, by any means, to commit any of the offences established in accordance with this Article or to use narcotic drugs or psychotropic substances illicitly;

(k) participation in, association or conspiracy to commit, attempts to commit and aiding, abetting, facilitating and counselling the commission of any of the offences established in accordance with this Article.

2. Subject to its constitutional principles and the basic concepts of its legal system, each Member-State shall adopt such measures as may be necessary to establish as a criminal offence under its domestic law, when committed intentionally, the possession, purchase or cultivation of narcotic drugs or psychotropic substances for personal

consumption contrary to the provisions of the 1961 Convention, the 1961 Convention as amended or the 1971 Convention.

ARTICLE 4
SANCTIONS

1. Each Member-State shall make the commission of the offences established in accordance with Article 3 punishable by appropriate penalties which take into account their grave nature.

2. The Member-States may provide in addition to conviction or punishment for an offence established in accordance with Article 3, paragraph 1 that the offender shall undergo measures such as treatment, education, after-care, rehabilitation or social re-integration.

3. Notwithstanding anything contained in the preceding paragraphs, in appropriate cases of a minor nature, the Member-States may provide, as alternatives to conviction or punishment, measures such as education, rehabilitation or social re-integration, as well as, when the offender is a drug abuser, treatment and after-care.

4. The Member-States shall ensure that their courts and other competent authorities having jurisdiction can take into account factual circumstances which make the commission of the offences established in accordance with Article 3, paragraph 1 particularly serious, such as:

(a) the involvement in the offence of an organised criminal group to which the offender belongs;
(b) the involvement of the offender in other international organised criminal activities;
(c) the involvement of the offender in other illegal activities facilitated by commission of the offence;
(d) the use of violence or arms by the offender;
(e) the fact that the offender holds a public office and that the offence is connected with the office in question;
(f) the victimisation or use of minors;
(g) the fact that the offence is committed in a penal institution or in an educational institution or social service facility or in their immediate vicinity or in other places to which school children and students resort for educational, sports and social activities;

(h) prior conviction, particularly for similar offences, whether foreign or domestic, to the extent permitted under the domestic law of a Member State.

5. The Member-States shall not also ensure that their courts or other competent authorities bear in mind the serious nature of the offences established in accordance with Article 3, paragraph 1 or the circumstances enumerated in paragraph 4 of this Article, when considering the eventuality of early release or parole of persons convicted for such offences.

ARTICLE 5
JURISDICTION

1. Each Member-State shall take such measures as may be necessary to establish its jurisdiction over the offences established in accordance with Article 3, paragraph 1 when:

(a) the offence is committed in its territory;

(b) the offence is committed on board a vessel flying its flag or an aircraft which is registered under its laws at the time the offence is committed;

(c) the offence is committed by one of its nationals or by a person who has his habitual residence in that territory;

(d) the offence is one of those established in accordance with Article 3, paragraph 1(k) and is committed outside its territory with a view to the commission, within its territory, of an offence established in accordance with Article 3, paragraph 1.

2. Each Member-State may likewise take such measures as may be necessary to establish its jurisdiction over the offences established in accordance with Article 3, paragraph 1, in cases where the alleged offender is present in its territory and it does not extradite him to another Member-State.

3. This Convention does not exclude the exercise of any criminal jurisdiction established by a Member State in accordance with domestic law.

ARTICLE 6
PROVISION OF INFORMATION

1. The Member-State in which any of the offences established

in accordance with Article 3, paragraph 1, has been committed shall, if it has reason to believe that, an alleged offender had fled from its territory, communicate to all other States concerned all the pertinent facts regarding the offence committed and all available information regarding the identity of the alleged offender.

2. Upon being satisfied that the circumstances so warrant, the Member State in whose territory the alleged offender is present shall take appropriate measures under its domestic law so as to ensure his presence for the purpose of prosecution or extradition. Such measures shall be notified, without delay to:

(a) the State where the offence was committed; and

(b) the State or States of which the alleged offender is a national or if he is a stateless person in whose territory he permanently resides.

ARTICLE 7
PROSECUTION

The Member-State in whose territory the alleged offender is present shall, if it does not extradite him, submit, without exception whatsoever and without undue delay, the case to its competent authorities for the purpose of prosecution through proceedings in accordance with the laws of that State.

ARTICLE 8
EXTRADITION

1. To the extent that the offences established in accordance with Article 3, paragraph 1, are not listed as extraditable offences in any Extradition Treaty existing between Member-States, they shall be deemed to be included as such therein.

2. Member-States undertake to include the offences established in accordance with Article 3, paragraph 1, as extraditable offences in every future Extradition Treaty to be concluded between them.

3. If a Member State which makes extradition conditional on the existence of a Treaty receives a request for extradition from another Member-State with which it has no Extradition Treaty, the requested State may, at its option, consider this Convention as the basis for extradition in respect of the offences established in accordance with Article 3, paragraph 1.

4. Member-States which do not make extradition conditional on the existence of a Treaty, shall recognise the offences established in accordance with Article 3, paragraph 1, as extraditable offences between themselves.

5. Extradition shall be subject to the law of the requested State.

ARTICLE 9
NON-FISCAL AND NON-POLITICAL OFFENCES

The offences established in accordance with Article 3, paragraph 1, shall not be regarded as fiscal offences or as political offences or as offences connected with a political offence or as offences inspired by political motives, without prejudice to the constitutional limitations and the fundamental domestic law of the Member-States.

ARTICLE 10
CONFISCATION

1. Each Member-State shall adopt such measures as may be necessary to enable to confiscation of:

(a) Proceeds derived from offences established in accordance with Article 3, paragraph 1, or property the value of which corresponds to that of such proceeds;

(b) Narcotic drugs and psychotropic substances, materials and equipment or other instrumentalities used in or intended for use in any manner in offences established in accordance with Article 3.

2. Each Member-State shall also adopt such measures as may be necessary to enable its competent authorities to identify, trace and freeze or seize proceeds, property, instrumentalities or any other things referred to in paragraph 1 of this Article for the purpose of eventual confiscation.

ARTICLE 11
MUTUAL LEGAL ASSISTANCE

1. The Member-States shall afford one another pursuant to this Article, the widest measure of mutual legal assistance in investigations, prosecutions and judicial proceedings in relation to criminal offences established in accordance with Article 3, paragraph 1.

2. Mutual legal assistance to be afforded in accordance with this Article may be requested for all or any of the following purposes:

(a) Taking evidence or statements from persons;
(b) Effective service of judicial documents;
(c) Executing searches and seizures;
(d) Examining objects and sites;
(e) Providing information and evidentiary items;
(f) Providing originals or certified copies of relevant documents and records, including bank, financial, corporate or business records;
(g) Identifying or tracing proceeds, property, instrumentalities or other things for evidentiary purposes.

3. The Member-States may afford one another any other forms of mutual legal assistance allowed by the domestic law of the requested State.

4. Upon request, the Member-States shall-facilitate or encourage, to the extent consistent with their domestic law and practice, the presence or availability of persons, including persons in custody, who consent to assign in investigations or participate in proceedings.

5. A Member-State shall not decline to render mutual legal assistance under this Article on the ground of bank secrecy.

6. The provisions of this Article shall not affect the obligations under any other treaty, bilateral or multilateral, which governs or will govern, in whole or in part, mutual legal assistance in criminal matters.

7. The Member States shall designate an authority, or when necessary authorities, which shall have the responsibility and power to execute requests for mutual legal assistance or to transmit them to the competent authorities for execution. The authority or the authorities designated for this purpose shall be notified directly to each Member-State and to the Secretary-General. Transmission of requests for mutual legal assistance and any communication related thereto shall be effected between the authorities designated by the States; this requirement shall be without prejudice to the right of a State to require that such requests and communications be addressed to it through diplomatic channels and, in urgent circumstances,

where the States agree, through channels of the International Criminal Police Organisation, if possible.

8. Requests for mutual legal assistance shall be made in writing. In urgent circumstances, and where agreed to by the State, requests may be made orally, which shall be confirmed in writing forthwith.

9. A request for mutual legal assistance shall contain:

(a) The identity of the authority making the request;

(b) The subject matter and nature of the investigation, prosecution or proceeding to which the request relates, and the name and the functions of the authority conducting such investigation, prosecution or proceeding;

(c) A summary of the relevant facts, except in respect of requests for the purpose of services of judicial documents;

(d) A description of the assistance sought and details of any particular procedure the requesting State wishes to be followed;

(e) Where possible, the identity, location and nationality of any person concerned;

(f) The purpose for which the evidence, information or action is sought.

10. The requested State may request additional information when it appears necessary for the execution of the request in accordance with its domestic law or when it can facilitate such execution.

11. A request shall be executed in accordance with the domestic law of the requested State and where possible, in accordance with the procedure specified in the request.

12. The requesting State shall not transmit nor use information or evidence furnished by the requested State for investigations, prosecutions or proceedings other than those stated in the request without the prior consent of the requested State.

13. The requesting State may require that the requested State keep confidential the fact and substance of the request, except to the extent necessary to execute the request. If the requested State cannot comply with the requirement of confidentiality, it shall promptly inform the requesting State.

14. Mutual legal assistance may be refused:

(a) If the request is not made in conformity with the provisions of this Article;

(b) If the requested State considers that execution of the request is likely to prejudice its sovereignty, security, public order (ordre public) or other essential interest;

(c) If the authorities of the requested State would be prohibited by its domestic law from carrying out the action requested with regard to any similar offence, had it been subject to investigation, prosecution or proceedings under their own jurisdiction;

(d) If it would be contrary to the legal system of the requested State relating to mutual legal assistance for the request to be granted.

15. Reasons shall be given for any refusal of mutual legal assistance.

16. Mutual legal assistance may be postponed by the requested State on the ground that it interferes with an ongoing investigation, prosecution or proceeding. In such a case, the requested State shall consult with the requesting State to determine if the assistance can still be given subject to such terms and conditions as the requested State deems necessary.

17. A witness, expert or other person who consents to give evidence in a proceeding or to assist in an investigation, prosecution or judicial proceeding in the territory of the requesting State, shall not be prosecuted, detained, punished or subjected to any other restriction of his personal liberty in that territory in respect of acts, omissions or convictions prior to his departure from the territory of the requested State. Such safe conduct shall cease when the witness, expert or other person having had, for a period of fifteen consecutive days, or for any period agreed upon by the States, from the date on which he has been officially informed that his presence is no longer required by the judicial authorities, an opportunity of leaving, has nevertheless remained voluntarily in the territory or, having left it, has returned of his own free will.

18. The ordinary costs of executing a request shall be borne by the requested State, unless otherwise agreed to by the States

concerned. If expenses of a substantial or extraordinary nature are or will be required to fulfil the request, the State shall consult to determine the terms and conditions under which the request will be executed as well as the manner in which the costs shall be borne.

ARTICLE 12
MEASURES TO ERADICATE ILLICIT CULTIVATION OF NARCOTIC PLANTS AND TO ELIMINATE ILLICIT DEMAND FOR NARCOTIC DRUGS AND PSYCHOTROPIC SUBSTANCES

1. Each Member-State shall take appropriate measures to prevent illicit cultivation of and to eradicate plants containing narcotic or psychotropic substances, such as opium poppy, coca bush and cannabis plants, cultivated illicitly in its territory.

2. The Member-States may co-operate to increase the effectiveness of eradication efforts. Towards this end, Member-States shall also facilitate the exchange of scientific and technical information and the conduct of research concerning eradication.

3. The Member-States shall adopt appropriate measures aimed at eliminating or reducing illicit demand for narcotic drugs and psychotropic substances, with a view to reducing human suffering and eliminating financial incentives for illicit traffic.

4. The Member-States may also take necessary measures for early destruction or lawful disposal of the narcotic drugs, psychotropic substances and substances listed in Table I and Table II of the 1988 U.N. Convention, which have been seized or confiscated.

ARTICLE 13
SUPPRESSION OF OFFENCES

1. The Member-States shall co-operate closely with one another, consistent with their respective domestic legal and administrative systems, with a view to enhancing the effectiveness of law enforcement action to suppress the commission of offences established in accordance with Article 3, paragraph 1. For this purpose they may establish and maintain channels of communication between their competent agencies to facilitate the secure and rapid exchange of information concerning all aspects of such offences.

2. The Member-States may take necessary measures to allow of the appropriate use of controlled delivery on the basis of bilateral agreements with a view to identifying persons involved in offences established in accordance with Article 3, paragraph 1, and to taking legal action against them.

ARTICLE 14
CO-OPERATION AND INFORMATION

The Member-States shall furnish information to each other and to the Secretary-General on the implementation of this Convention in their territories and in particular:

(a) The texts of laws and regulations promulgated in order to give effect to the Convention;

(b) Particulars of cases of illicit traffic within their jurisdiction which they consider important because of new trends disclosed, the quantities involved, the sources from which the substances are obtained or the method employed by person so engaged.

ARTICLE 15
APPLICATION OF STRICTER MEASURES

A Member-State may adopt more strict or severe measures than those provided by this Convention, if, in its opinion, such measures are desirable or necessary for the prevention or suppression of illicit traffic.

ARTICLE 16
SIGNATURE AND RATIFICATION

1. The Convention shall be open for signature by the Member-States of SAARC at the Fifth SAARC Summit at Male and thereafter, at the SAARC Secretariat at Kathmandu.

2. It shall be subject to ratification. Instruments of Ratification shall be deposited with the Secretary-General.

ARTICLE 17
ENTRY INTO FORCE

This Convention shall enter into force on the fifteenth day following the day of the deposit of the seventh Instrument of Ratification with the Secretary-General.

ARTICLE 18
DEPOSITORY

The Secretary-General shall be the depository of this Convention and shall notify the Member-States of signatures to this Convention and all deposits of Instruments of Ratification. The Secretary-General shall transmit certified copies of such instruments to each Member-State. The Secretary-General shall also inform Member-States of the date on which this Convention will have entered into force in accordance with Article 17.

In Witness whereof, the undersigned being duly authorised thereto by their respective Governments, have signed this Convention.

Done at Male on this Twenty-third day of November One Thousand Nine Hundred and Ninety, in Eight originals, in the English Language, all texts being equally authentic.

ANISUL ISLAM MAHMUD
Minister of Foreign Affairs
People's Republic of Bangladesh

VIDYA CHARAN SHUKLA
Minister of External Affairs
Republic of India

DEVENDRA RAJ PANDAV
Minister of Finance
His Majesty's Government of Nepal

HAROLD HERAT
Minister of Foreign Affairs
Democratic Socialist Republic of Sri Lanka

DAWA TSERING
Minister of Foreign Affairs
Kingdom of Bhutan

FATHULLA JAMEEL
Minister of Foreign Affairs
Republic of Maldives

SAHABZADA YAQUB KHAN
Minister of Foreign Affairs
Islamic Republic of Pakistan

References

Reports

Asian Clearing Union: Towards Monetary Cooperation Occasional Paper No. 11, Research Information System, New Delhi.

Foreign Aid and Development, Integrated Development System, Kathmandu, 1990.

Foreign trade barriers and export growth, Asian Development Bank, Manila, 1990.

India's Trade with some Asian countries, Federation of Indian Chamber of Commerce and Industry, New Delhi, 1985

Report of the South Commission, The Challenge to the South, Oxford University, New York, 1990.

Review of Developments in the area of Trade and Monetary and Financial Co-operation among Developing Countries, UNCTAD, March 1989.

SAARC: Study on Trade. Manufactures and Services. SAARC Secretariat, Kathmandu, 1991.

Articles

Adiseshiah, M.S., Economic Rationale of SAARC, *South Asia Journal*, Vol. 1, 1987.

Arora, V.K. SAARC: Prospects for Cooperation, *India Quarterly*, Vol.42(1), 1986.

Barac, Lok Raj, SAARC - but no SHARK: South Asian Regional Cooperation in *Perspective, Pacific Affairs*, Vol. 58, 1985.

Beg, M.A., India-SAARC Trade: A Dwindling Feature, *India Quarterly*,

Jan.-March 1990.

Chakravarthy, S., Development Experience in South Asia, *Asian Development Review*, Vol.6, 1988.

Chopra, Pran, SAARC and ASEAN: A Comparative analysis of aims, structure and progress, *SAARC Perspective*, Vol. 1 1987.

De Rosa & Dean A., Trade and Protection in the South Asian Region, Asian Development Review, Vol. 4, 1986.

Dubey, M., SAARC, Achievements and Prospects: A New impetus and Fresh Direction, Ministry of External Affairs, New Delhi, 1986.

Ghosh, P.S., Terrorism and SAARC, *India Quarterly*, Vol.43, April-June 1987.

Kazmi, Nikhat, In Search of a South Asian Indentity, *The Times of India*, October 20, 1992.

Naqvi, Syed Nawab Hyder, *Economic Integration: Meaning and Dimension*, Asian Development Bank, Manila, 1989.

Narain, Yogendra, SAARC - A Socio Economic Survey, *Financial Express*, November 18, 1990.

Morley, Mohan Lal G., SAARC: The Challenges Ahead, *Financial Express*, October 28, 1990.

Pushpa T., *Prospects of South Asian Regional Cooperation: Lessons from ASEAN, Contemporary South East Asia*, Vol.8, 1987.

Qureshi, M.L., Indian Development Strategy and South Asian Regional Cooperation, *India Quarterly*, Vol.40, 1984

Rahman, Bashgir, SAARC: Some Reflections, *SAARC Perspective*, Vol.1, 1987.

Ramachandran, K.S., SAARC: The Constraints I, *The Economic Times*, April 14, 22, 29, 1991.

Sharma, Dhirendra, Tapping SAARC Potential, *The Hindustan Times*, New Delhi, August 31, 1993.

Shroff, Manu, Liberalisation of the Economy: The Indian Experience, *South Asia*, Vol. XIII, No.,1, 1992

Singh, Tarlok, Expansion of Trade between India and SAARC Countries, *Monthly Commentary*, Vol.27 (1), Aug. 1985.

Varshney, R.L., *Economic Cooperation in South Asia, Foreign Affairs*, Indian Council of World Affairs, New Delhi, 1988.

Bibliography

Books

Agwani M.S. & Others., *South Asia: Stability and Regional Cooperation*, Centre for Research in Rural and Industrial Development, Chandigarh, 1987.

Anand R.P., *South Asia: In Search of Regional Identity*, Banyan Publishers, New Delhi, 1991.

Bela, Balassa, and Jesdijk Ardy Stont. *Economic Integration among Developing Countries*, IBRD, Washington D.C., 1974.

Bennet, Lee Roy, *International Organisations*, Prentice Hall, New Jersey, 1985.

Chopra, Pran & Others, *Future of South Asia*, Macmillan India Ltd., New Delhi, 1986.

Ghuman, Ranjit Singh, *Indo-Pakistan Trade Relations*, Deep & Deep Publications, New Delhi, 1990.

Gupta, Bhabani Sen, *Regional Cooperation and Development in South Asia*, Vikas Publishing House, New Delhi, 1987.

Hammond, Grant T., *Counter Trade: Offsets and Barter in International Political Economy*, Printer Publishers, London, 1990.

Islam, Nurul, *Pakistan in Asian Economic Development*, ed. By Cranky Onslow Ebenezer Baylis and Son Ltd., London, 1990.

Jain, P.K., *International Marketing*, Printwell Publishers, Jaipur, 1988

Johnson, Harry G., *New Trade Strategy for the World Economy*, George Allen & Urwin Ltd., London, 1988.

Kanesahingam, V. & Kemal, A.R. *Trade Liberalisation in South Asia:*

Liberalisation and Mechanisms, Macmillan India Ltd., New Delhi, 1990

Madan, B.K., *Towards Monetary Cooperation in South Asia*, Concept Publishing Co., New Delhi, 1988.

Mishra, K.P. & Others, *Southern Asia-Pacific Perceptions and Strategies*, Continental Publishing House, New Delhi, 1983.

Mishra, Promod Kumar, *South Asia in International Politics*, Udh Publishers, New Delhi, 1984.

Mukherji, Indra Nath, *Trade Liberalisation in South Asia*, School of International Studies, JNU, New Delhi, 1985.

Mukherji, I.N., *The Bangkok Agreement - An evaluation of Preferential Agreement in Escap Region*, RIS, New Delhi, 1987.

———., Economic Co. straints and Potentialities of Regional Cooperation in *South Asia: Problems and Prospects*, Vikas Publishing House, New Delhi, 1988.

Nahar, Emanuel, *SAARC: Problems and Prospects*, Sehgal Publisher's Service, New Delhi, 1991.

Naqvi, Syed Nawab Hyder, *SAARC Link: An Economic Approach*, Oxford & IBH Publishing Co., New Delhi, 1991.

Panchamukhi, V.R. and Others, *Economic Cooperation in the SAARC Region: Potential, Constraints and Policies*, Interest Publications, New Delhi, 1990.

Payer, Cheryl, *Commodity Trade of Third World*, Macmillan Press Ltd., London, 1986.

Prasad, Bimal, *Regional Economic Co-operation in South Asia*, Vikas Publishing House, New Delhi, 1989.

Qureshi M.L., *Survey of Economic Resources and Prospects of South Asia*, Marga Instritute, Colombo, 1981.

Raghavan, S.N., *Macro Economic Performance and Policy Framework in the SAARC Countries*, Interest Publications, New Delhi, 1991.

Rai, Lajipathi and Reddi, Subbi T., *India's Foreign Trade: Retrospectives and Prospectives*, Uppal Publishing House, New Delhi, 1990.

Raju, P.V. *Economic Development of Asian Countries*, Deep & Deep Publications, New Delhi, 1990.

Saeed, M., *India's Overseas Trade with her Afro-Asian Neighbours*, Agra University, Agra, 1976.

Sahoo, S.C., and Sinha, P.K. *Emerging Trends in Indian Marketing in 90's*, Academic Foundation, New Delhi, 1992.

Sen Gupta, SAARC-ASEAN: *Prospects and Problems of Inter-regional Cooperation*, South Asian Publishers, New Delhi, 1989.

Sidney, Siegel, *Non-Parametric Statistics for the Behavioural Sciences*, Mcgraw Hill International Book Co., Tokyo, 1956.

Simon,. Majaro, *International Marketing: A Strategic Approach to World Markets*, Allen & Unwin, London, 1978.

Singh, Naunihal, *Strategy of International Business*, South Asian Publishers, New Delhi, 1986.

Sood, Krishanalekha, *Trade and Economic Development: India, Pakistan, Bangladesh*, Sage Publications, New Delhi, 1989.

Talbot, Phillip, *South Asia in the World Today*, University of Chicago Press, Chicago, 1989.

Thomas, Philip, *Potential of Financial Cooperation in the SAARC Region*, R.I.S., New Delhi, 1990.

Umar, Ghulam, *SAARC: Analytical Survey*, Renaissance Publishing House, New Delhi, 1992.

Verma, S.P., *South Asia a Region: Problems and prospects*, Charanjit Channa, New Delhi, 1989

Vignaraja, Poona & Hussain, Akmal, *The Challenge in South Asia*, Sage Publications, New Delhi, 1989.

Vohra, Dewan C., *India's Trade Diplomacy in the Third World*, Vikas Publishing House, New Delhi, 1987.

Wadhwa, Charan, D., and Others, *Regional Economic Cooperation in South Asia*, Allied Publishers, New Delhi, 1988.

Wagif, Arif, *South Asian Cooperation in Industry Energy and Technology*, Sage Publications, New Delhi, 1990.

Journals

Asian Development Outlook, various issues, Asian Development Bank, Manila.

Asian Development Review, various issues, Asian Development Bank, Manila.

Contemporary South East Asia,, Vol.8, 1987.

Economic Survey, (various issues) Government of India, New Delhi.

Foreign Affairs, Indian Council of World Affairs, New Delhi.

India Quarterly, Vol.42, 1986.

Key Indicators of Developing of Asian and Pacific Countries, various issues, Asian Development Bank, Manila.

Monthly Commentary, New Delhi, Vol.27 1985.

Pacific Affairs, Vol.58, 1985

SAARC Perspectives, (various issues), SAARC Secretariat, Kathmandu.

South Asian Journal, (various issues), New Delhi.

INDEX